CW01395319

AN ADVENTUROUS LIFE

HERBERT WISDOM

authorHOUSE®

AuthorHouse™ UK Ltd.
500 Avebury Boulevard
Central Milton Keynes, MK9 2BE
www.authorhouse.co.uk
Phone: 08001974150

First published by AuthorHouse 2/23/2009

ISBN: 978-1-4389-5100-3 (sc)

Printed in the United States of America
Bloomington, Indiana

This book is printed on acid-free paper.

My story is dedicated to my wife,

IVY GRACE WISDOM
(known as wis)

for 43 years of happy married life, her dedication and loyalty and faith
in me in providing a good life together.

Acknowledgement:

to David Spicer for his technical help, for his patience and advice,
without which my story would never have seen the light of day.

Also

to Donna Vaughan of St Dunstan's Writers Forum, who has been a
great help to me.

FOREWORD BY THE AUTHOR

When my mother married Albert Arthur Wisdom in 1916, my uncle Frederick was Norman Wisdoms father. Both Norman and I had similar miserable childhoods. When Norman was 14 years old, his father told him, he could not afford to keep him and he must go out into the world to fend for himself. I recall he became a drop out, hanging around Victoria mainline station, busking and luggage carrying, to eek a living, as no jobs were available. I too was discarded into a boy's home at 8. The turning point in Normans life was when he took advise from an ex army sergeant to join the army as a boy soldier. When posted to the North West frontier he became a member of the regimental band, where he learned his skill's as a musician. He later went on to become one of England's most popular entertainers on screen, theatre and television and received a knighthood.

As my story unfold it tells of my life, and the time from the age of 8 years until I was 16 years of age that I spent in a boys home. I never saw or heard from my mother after leaving me to face the world on my own. It also tells of my formative teenage years. How I dealt with my early civilian and military life, and my post successful business life. I developed a successful domestic electrical and refrigeration business, and achieved success playing Lawn Green Bowler in both England, and Australia in my twilight years. Throughout my life, both fate and luck played a part after the poor start to my life and my determination to make a success of life.

Prolog

I made my entry into the world at precisely 4.20 in the morning on the 8th June 1916 at St. Thomas' Hospital, London. Both my mother and the nursing staff were delighted that I had a healthy pair of lungs. I was a fine, healthy baby with soft brown hair and bright blue eyes.

My mother explained to me later that, while she was lying in the hospital waiting to give birth to me, the Germans sent over their Zeppelins to bomb London at night – a new form of aerial bombardment. She also told me that, at the same time, one of the fiercest battles between the Germans and the English allies was taking place, ending a stalemate after many soldiers on both sides had been killed or injured. This was known as the Battle of the Somme.

The English also had a trick up their sleeve, for when the battle started in earnest again in the spring of the following year; they introduced a new form of land warfare by using tanks. The Germans had no immediate answer to this so, after two more years and several more battles, they were finally forced back to their own frontier when they sued for an armistice.

My mother also told me about her wartime experiences, especially about when she worked at the Woolwich Arsenal – a dreadful place to work and sometimes dangerous. As I grew older, I often felt that she really only wanted to give birth to me to get away from that employment.

My mother was aged 21 when I was born. She was known to most people as "Het", her real name being Ethel Rosita. She was 5' 9" tall, with a lovely figure. When looks were being given out, she got her fair share. She was not a cockney by birth but had a tremendous sense of the Cockney wit and humour.

I never knew my Christian name and because of my large upper front teeth, my mother nicknamed me "Bun". At school, I responded to the teaching staff's use of my surname, Wisdom, and to all my chums I was known as "Wiz" or "Wiz Bang". It was not until some years later when I applied for a copy of my birth certificate in order to apply for an apprenticeship, that I learned my real Christian names – Herbert Vincent. By that time I was called "Syd" by my best friend; a bit confusing for people who hardly knew me! Syd is the name that has stuck with me ever since. The only time I used my proper Christian names was on legal documents, business letters, and for doctors' prescriptions!

CHAPTER ONE

I hardly knew my father. My parents separated soon after the war when I was only three years old, and I stayed with my mother, a situation that created many problems. She could not afford to pay someone else to look after the baby while she was out at work, so it was decided to solve the problem by living with Het's mother. In this way, Grandma could mind me, with her own children, while Het earned some money to help out with the family's weekly budget. My grandmother had nine children in all, although only six were still living. My mother was the eldest of the children and the only girl.

My grandmother's cottage was brick-built with a tiled roof and was lit only by gas. It had a small front garden, enclosed by a picket-type fence, with a gate and a path leading up to the front door, which was very seldom used. The cottage was at the end of a row of four, with an alleyway, used mainly for refuse collection, between the side of the cottage and the rear entrances to a row of main road shops. The alley could also be used to gain access to the other three cottages. The back garden was fairly large, but as there were no men living there, it was left largely untended. There was a gate in the rear fence, leading to the back door of the cottage and the lean-to scullery as well as the attached toilet.

The kitchen was reasonably large, with two doors leading out of it, one into the scullery, the other to a passage leading to the staircase, the front room and the front door. The kitchen range was more or less in the middle of the dividing wall of the next-door cottage, set in a recess. It had two ovens, one either side of the central fire, which was used winter and summer for cooking and water heating purposes. For protection against falling ashes, there was a well black-leaded fender and a polished brass rail where the fire irons rested. As well polished as the kitchen range, was a brass companion set of tongs, poker and hearth brush. On top of the range were always two cast iron flat-irons and a fairly large cast iron pot, if not used for cooking, always with a supply of hot water. Sometimes my mother would bring home a couple of chicken carcasses – these went into the pot either for chicken broth, or if there was enough meat on them, for chicken soup, with mixed vegetables. Over the range was a mantelpiece, draped with an old-fashioned chenille cloth cover with tassels. On top of the mantelpiece was the alarm clock, a box of matches and a clay pipe, a tea caddie and some sugar and a few other odds and ends. Under the kitchen range mantelpiece, a line was fixed for airing clothes.

After wash days, which were always a tiring and lengthy chore, my grandmother loved to sit down in her easy chair by the kitchen range, fill her clay pipe with Nosegay tobacco and have a quiet puff away, waiting for the boys to come home from school. This was the only time she smoked. When they were back home, they would turn the handle of the mangle that was outside in the backyard. To keep the tobacco moist, she always put a potato peeling in her tobacco tin. She only ever bought a half ounce of baccy at a time and no one ever begrudged her this one luxury – she well deserved it.

Along the wall between the kitchen range and the corner by the door to the passage, was a full-length dresser with shelves and hooks for hanging cups. Under the shelves, used for storing crockery, was a wide worktop with cupboards underneath and two large drawers. Part of the cupboard was used for non-perishable foods. Biscuits were always a great favourite with all the family – biscuits of the day were served and weighed from seven pound tins, so there were always plenty of broken ones, which were sold off cheaper. Grandma always made sure there was a good supply in the cupboard, beside stores of flour, sugar, bread in a bin and other groceries.

The kitchen table when not in full use could be pushed into the recess of the bay window, and it was large enough to accommodate all the family at one sitting. The only covering was an oilcloth for normal use although sometimes on a Sunday, and always at Christmas, a table cloth would be brought out and used.

In the scullery there was the sink and draining board, a food safe with a fly cover and the copper for clothes washing. There was also a gas cooker, only used first thing in the morning before the kitchen range was lit. Suspended from the ceiling was an eight-foot, three-bar clothes drier, lowered and raised by a hand-operated pulley device.

Wood fuel to light the fires was acquired from a wood yard at a place called the Canal Head, at the end of a canal leading from the Rotherhithe Thames riverside docks. Timber would be brought to the yard by horse-drawn barge. My uncle Bill and I would push a carriage-type pram with a false bottom to the yard to fill it with off-cuts, giving the foreman a shilling, equivalent to three pints of ale. Another source of fuel was Queens Road in Peckham, where the road was mainly made of woodblocks, alongside the tram tracks. When these blocks became wet, they were treacherous for motorists and people boarding and alighting from the trams. When these were taken up for road repairs, Bill and I would take the trusty old pram and fill it with blocks, dropping the ganger a shilling. These blocks were perfect for lighting the fire, as they were impregnated with tar. The boys would stack them in the back yard, chop them up and store them in a dustbin to keep them dry. A small supply of wood was also kept in the hearth, for kindling in the mornings, a job for one of the boys who also had to clear the grate and light the fire. When wood was occasionally unavailable from the usual sources, it meant buying bundles of kindling from the local hardware shop. This may have resulted in them buying back their own wood as the boys sometimes chopped up surplus timber into bundles to sell to the shopkeeper for pocket-money.

The cottage where I spent so many happy years with my grandmother was eventually demolished to make way for a block of flats.

Sleeping arrangements were eventually sorted out in the small, cramped, two-up and two-down cottage. My mother and grandmother shared one bedroom, with me sleeping in a cot in the same room. Two of my uncles shared the other upstairs room and two others slept on a put-u-up bed in the downstairs front room. When I was six, I slept on a single put-u-up in the downstairs room with my uncles. These clever beds could be folded up in the day if needed, to be used as an easy-chair, especially at weekends and Christmas time.

When time allowed, I would be permitted to sit on my mother's lap in the kitchen, when she would tell him stories of some of the famous cricketers of the day, including some of the visiting Australians. I loved hearing these stories, especially about Hendren and Sutcliffe, and one day I asked my mother if there was any truth in the story that Hobbs had actually hit a ball over the local gasometer. All she could say was that she was not absolutely sure, but the ball was never found once it had been walloped out of the grounds.

My grandmother was a widow, in her late fifties, with short, greying, curly hair and remarkable blue eyes – eyes that never seemed to lose their sparkle in spite of the hard life she had to endure. She was a country girl by birth, coming to London to work in domestic service. There she met her husband-to-be, an immigrant Polish Jew, much older than she was. They set up home in Peckham, south-east London, but he died tragically soon after and left her with six children to clothe and feed.

As a means of earning money, my grandmother went out cleaning and scrubbing in the neighbourhood. She would rise at 4am to walk round to the local school in the winter to clear the ashes and lay the fires in the classrooms, for the caretaker to light, who was also responsible for bringing the fuel indoors. The teachers had to keep the fires going during the day. The only other income was from what my mother earned before she married, a small amount she had managed to save, and a modest wage earned by my eldest uncle George, a year younger than his sister, Het. He was employed by the local council as assistant superintendent at the local workhouse. He was called up when war was declared in 1914, a situation that really did not help the family fortunes. In spite of her hard and stressful life, my grandmother had a cheerful nature – a necessary characteristic to get through from one day to the next.

My youngest uncle, Bill, and I were playmates. My other two uncles, Harry and Fred, I hardly ever saw except at meal times. Because money was so very scarce and to help my grandmother, my uncle Bill and I between us pushed our old pram with the false bottom, two miles to the Old Kent Road gas works, to fill it with coke. This was the residue left when all the by-products were extracted from the coal. The coke was free to anyone providing they had their own means of carting it away. When going to the gas works, us two boys pushing the pram could hardly see over the top of it, but on the way back, all on level ground, the weight of the coke squashed the springs so much that we could see to guide the pram quite easily. Our only problem was manoeuvring the loaded pram across the wide and busy Old Kent Road traffic – in those days there were no pedestrian crossings with their 'Belisha' beacons.

Coke-fetching was a regular chore, winter and summer, to keep the kitchen range properly fuelled, for cooking and hot water. For this noble effort we were rewarded with something special for tea, if grandmother could afford it.

For their weekly bath, my mother and grandma went to the local public baths, a luxury that cost them sixpence each. Each bathroom was a separate cubicle and the attendant gave each bather exactly 5" of water from taps operated from the outside. If more water was required, a simple shout of 'more hot in number 8 please' always elicited a quick burst of more steaming water. Us boys had to make do with a tin bath in the scullery for our baths, in the summer months, with water boiled on the kitchen range in galvanised buckets. During the winter, if the weather was really cold, they lit a fire under the old copper in the scullery, to heat the water. This also helped to keep the room warm while we were bathing. When everyone had finished bathing, they put the dirty laundry in to soak, ready for the Monday wash.

Uncle George had met some Australian soldiers while on active service. After their demob, these lads persuaded him to go back with them to live in Australia. Not much was heard from him as mail was scarce – ships took many weeks to reach Australia, and as many weeks for the return journey. The family was lucky to get three letters a year, the last piece of news we heard was that he settled in Queensland, joining the fire service in Brisbane. At least there was a little more room in the crowded cottage with George far away.

When my mother was living at home, before marrying, she missed a lot of schooling, being needed to help her mother look after her younger brothers. As she was the only girl of the family, she had the task of fetching all the family food shopping. In spite of her lack of schooling, she became very good at figures and money matters. She had to be good, as a shilling made all the difference between the family eating or going to bed hungry. Sometimes indeed we did have to miss a meal, money being so short in spite of Het's very careful handling of any available cash. It was a matter of surviving as best as one could. There was no Government financial help – only the dole. To qualify for this, claimants had to have at least twenty-six employment stamps on their cards. The alternative was the dreaded 'shilling means test'. Tribunals were set up by the Government to assess people's entitlement for financial assistance. Failing this test meant the workhouse.

I settled in well with my grandmother. My mother, Het, was very lucky to find employment with a firm of caterers who supplied one of the first-class county cricket grounds in London. She also worked with the same caterers at 'over the sticks' race meetings during the October to March racing season and she was offered work waitressing at Freemasons' dinners in London. Although her work seemed to be permanent, it was actually only on a casual basis. At the time there were no Trades Unions in her area of work and employers took advantage of this, working their employees long and tiring hours, for a mere pittance.

After a couple of cricketing and racing seasons, Het became well liked with her Cockney sense of humour, being very popular with most of her customers. She was never at a loss to make them laugh with her great sense of humour. Het was always nicely turned out in her black uniform, which she had to buy herself, with clean white collars and cuffs every day. While working, her copper-coloured hair was always pinned up in a bun. She was indeed a credit to herself and her employer.

It was these summer and winter jobs, plus the Freemasons' dinners, that helped the rest of her family to survive – by taking home the untouched leftovers, she was able to keep them well fed. Her employers never objected to this, as it was considered one of the perks of the job. It was cheaper to allow this than pay overtime. The food may have been wasted anyway. In those days refrigeration was virtually unknown for the storage of food, which was usually kept in an ice-box with a large chunk of ice – not a very reliable method of storage. My grandmother was very clever with food – in times of scant resources, it was a necessity. We mostly had stews of rabbit or beef and very occasionally, a roast meal for a Sunday. What Het brought home helped a great deal, but mostly it was just basic meals. Grandma's country background had given her a sound grounding in cookery and she tried to make the meals as appetising as possible for her family.

At Het's second season at the cricket ground, she was put in charge of the members' and visiting teams' bar, with only those people allowed to use these facilities. Members of the general public were excluded. When Het asked her supervisor if this was promotion with extra pay, there was no comment, so Het supposed that with the prospects of extra tips, the management thought this would be the just reward. I firmly believed that my mother was offered this job, not for her experience, but for her looks. She was very attractive with a full figure, giving the drinkers something to talk about other than cricket and the weather.

After the bar was closed for business, the ritual of stocktaking and cashing up had to be done. Het's supervisor, Betty, and her employers knew to the penny what the bar takings should be after the stock was checked, but Het was always short, having to make up the difference herself. This worried her considerably because, where money was concerned, she was more than careful. One night as they were checking the takings while swapping jokes that they had heard during the day and having a relaxing drink, she asked Betty why it was she was always short when cashing up, seeking her advice. She told Het to keep a sharp watch on Sean, her porter. Porters were employed on a casual basis, for fetching and carrying the bar stocks as and when required. Sean's trick was to exchange two full bottles of beer and put two empties in their place when bringing stock to the bar.

It was not always possible to check the contents of the crates, before signing the docket. Because Sean knew customers were waiting to be served, he took advantage of the pressure of work and ensured his free beer at Het's expense. Somehow he managed to do this for some time without detection until one day she caught him out.

Had she reported him, without doubt he would have been instantly dismissed. Instead, Het gave him a good tongue-wagging – she was never short again. Het knew the portering was hard and thirsty work, so now and again she treated Sean to a beer out of her tips, which Sean greatly appreciated, as a result of which they became good friends.

On days when they had to travel a long distance to a race meeting, it meant an early morning start from headquarters, loading up the wines and spirits and soft drinks into the coach, transporting them with the catering staff to the racetrack. The bars had to be ready for business by twelve midday at the latest. The beer was bought locally by one of the management staff who went the day before to make sure it was ready to serve. The porters did all the hauling and lifting, making sure all was ready on time.

Het was on first name terms with most of the bookies and their runners. It was nothing to them to give her a generous tip, when they came to settle their account after racing finished. With her usual Cockney humour, she was always ready with a laugh and a joke, while the porters were putting the unsold stock back in the coach, ready for the journey back to headquarters.

All unsold stock was entered on the stock sheets to be checked when back in London. Sean would arrive for his usual reward – in fact, he was having trouble fighting off the other porters, wanting to keep Het's portering for himself. Het was only looking after her own interests, as, out of gratitude for not reporting him, Sean was like a puppet on a string – she had no trouble in having her work done swiftly and thoroughly by her friend. He was quite aware of the consequences that would have followed her reporting him for the earlier thefts – jobs were hard to come by for people like Sean.

Once back at headquarters, there was the unloading and checking of the stock to be done. After these long journeys, the stock never seem to balance – what was put on board the coach was never quite the same as what arrived back at headquarters. Somehow some of the stock mysteriously disappeared on the journey. The team was expected to work long hours for no extra pay – having a job was their reward. Obey the rules as laid down by the management, or the simple fact was that one had no job. The management turned a blind eye to the missing stock. They knew it was cheaper for them to allow this, than to pay overtime, as long as it was kept under control, and within the company's limits.

When I was about seven years of age, my mother met Tom – their first casual meetings happened in the corner paper shop. After these early, brief encounters, they decided to set up home together, leaving me to carry on living with my grandmother. I didn't mind this as I got along very well with my uncles and my grandma.

Money was extremely tight, as my mother couldn't afford to give me any pocket money. I learned at a very early age the importance of money, watching my mother struggle to make ends meet, to pay her way each week. My chance came when I was offered an evening job by the local radio shop owner, connecting up accumulators, six evenings a week from 7 to 8 o'clock, for two shillings and sixpence a week.

I was no stranger to the shopkeeper. For the sake of something to do, I would often pop into the shed at the end of his back yard, to talk to him while he was connecting up the fifty-odd accumulators that he had taken in during the day for re-charging. Rechargeable 2.5 volt acid accumulators were used in conjunction with a dry-cell HT battery, when wireless reception was first introduced to the general public. I realised this was a time-consuming job, and, as he had no other help, it was a job that had to be done after shop hours. I thought I had nothing to lose by suggesting that I could do the job for him.

After a two-evening trial, the job was mine. It was just a question of connecting up the right number of accumulators for each charging bank and for the shopkeeper to set the correct charging rate. Most of the shop's customers had two accumulators, one in use and the other for re-charging. The one in use worked together with an high tension. battery to operate the wireless set. Until radio valves came into general use, it was only possible for one person to listen at a time, with earphones.

Valves enabled wireless receivers to take over from the old 'cat's whisker' system and permitted the whole family to listen in using loudspeakers. A tuning dial gave a greater range of reception.

In helping the shop owner, I became interested in electronics and the man was very helpful in giving me a wealth of information – how to trace faults and repair them and, more exciting, how to build new wireless sets. This was a rapidly expanding market and each design was swiftly superseded by a better one. Eventually the all-electric mains were installed more universally, thereby making the messy accumulators and expensive high tension batteries obsolete. Even at this early age, I believed my future might be tied up with electronics – I thought that it was wonderful that, by putting together a few components, one could hear other people talking from a great distance. I had also heard that a man called Baird was experimenting with television, so that not only could one hear others speaking, you could also see them. The future looked exciting and very promising.

With the extra money I was earning, together with my paper round money, I felt quite independent, not now having to ask my mother for pocket money (most times with a refusal!). I recognised that my grandmother had been very good to me, often making sacrifices for me and the others, so I now thought that I could pay her back by treating her occasionally to her favourite tipple – a jug of porter. Porter, as it was called locally, was the overflow from other beers such as ale, stout, Guinness or India Pale Ale, collected in a container and sold off cheaper than other beers.

I would collect the porter from the off-licence across the road and present it proudly to my grandma. She would pour some into a glass and then plunge a red-hot poker from the kitchen range into the beer, making it sizzle and froth up. This always amused me and I asked her why she performed this ritual every time. Her explanation was that it would "increase the iron content of the beer, which was very good for one's health".

I often gave her the rest of my radio shop earnings as I was not sure whether my mother was paying anything towards my keep. The few pennies would help my grandma to buy a few special extras. With my paper round earnings, I would treat myself to a Saturday morning children's film show, deriving great enjoyment from the silent film antics of Buster Keaton and Charlie Chaplin and the other comedy film shows. On Saturday also, I could buy my favourite dinner of home-made faggots and pease pudding, from a local German butcher's shop, a few doors down from the radio shop.

On Monday nights, as was their custom, my mother would call for her mother and the pair of them would go off to a pub to have a drink together, gossip endlessly and pay some money into the Christmas club. This was the only way people could afford the extras for Christmas. The club generated money by lending to members during the year and charging interest – this allowed them to give out a bonus at pay-out time at the beginning of December.

Before they set off for the pub one Monday evening, I overheard the two of them talking about me, my grandma saying to her daughter, "I said I could look after him while you two got settled in your new home. That was a month ago. I like the boy, but his rightful place is with you. Surely you must have discussed this with Tom?"

My mother replied by saying, "Tom agreed at first then changed his mind. He made it quite clear he didn't want him living with us!"

"Looks like you have a problem", my grandma replied. My mother asked if she would have me a little longer, to give her time to try and persuade Tom to change his mind.

"What happens to the boy if he insists he cannot live with you where he belongs?", asked my grandma.

"Come, let's go round to the pub, and talk about it over a beer," was my mother's response.

The outcome of this trip to the pub and their discussions was that my grandma was talked into having me a little longer. Secretly, I was hoping to stay with my grandmother, so I was pleased at the outcome.

I had met Tom several times in the paper shop, while the newsagent was getting my morning and evening paper round together. For some reason, I took an instant dislike to him – he was a very self-opinionated man and no one was ever right but him. Tom had had a very good education at a local grammar school and was considered to be of public school standard. His parents were well-off and had planned a bright future for him, but regarded him as the 'black sheep' of the family. Tom was quite content to drift through life, lacking any ambition to better himself. What my mother saw in him puzzled me, but I decided that his 'posh' accent must have been the deciding factor.

Tom was a stocky man about 5' 8" tall, with very bushy eyebrows, a good shock of brown hair with a centre parting; he had a fresh complexion, a rounded face, slightly blue protruding eyes and he was clean-shaven. He always seemed to be smartly dressed, wearing a wing collar with a bow tie, as was the fashion in those days for men. He worked for a local builders' maintenance firm, being employed as a painter and decorator, and, on odd occasions, as a signwriter and grainer. Like most building workers of the day he found himself unemployed for the winter months. There were no unions or a guaranteed working week – this meant the dole, if one qualified for it, otherwise one had to cope the best one could. Tom had little reason to worry – he made his future secure when setting up home with my mother as she believed the very sun shone out of his eyes.

I sometimes met Tom in the newsagent's and although Tom knew exactly who I was, he showed a complete lack of recognition. The newsagent, who reminded me of Dickens' Mr.Bumble, being a big, robust man towering over his counter, was an agent for an envelope addressing company. Tom was paid so much a thousand addressed envelopes as well as completing the newsagent's monthly accounts, all in his fine copperplate handwriting. During the winter months, it certainly suited Tom to sit by a nice warm fire, while my mother was out working.

One day when I was eight years of age and still living with my grandmother, my mother came to call and ordered me to dress in my sailor suit and best patterned shoes. I thought that this was unusual for a weekday and asked my mother where we were going, in a childlike, perplexed way. I received no answer. I was puzzled because the shoes were only worn on Sundays for Sunday School. They had to be highly polished by Monday morning to be taken to 'uncle's' along with my mother's fox-fur stole, a most fashionable weekend item to be seen within the pub. The pawnbroker would exchange them each week for a few pence to be used for essential groceries and the like. With King George V being known as 'The Sailor King', it was very popular to dress young boys in sailor suits.

I stood in my finery, still perplexed about the reason for the trip and now even more puzzled by the old, battered suitcase my mother had brought with her. We caught a bus to Dulwich and then a tram to Forest Hill. I had never travelled on either form of transport before and was thoroughly enjoying the experience. At Forest Hill, we took a taxi for the last leg of the journey, pulling up outside a very imposing, detached house. There was a gravel pathway leading to the door and a long bell-pull which my mother tugged. I could hear a bell ringing inside the house. While we waited for a response and the door to open, I noticed a well-polished brass plate bearing the words 'Shaftbury House – Home for Boys'. Was this the solution to my mother's problem, I wondered.

CHAPTER TWO

The home that I had been taken to was a residential home for boys situated at Perry Rise, Forest Hill in south-east London. It was not a correction home or an institution, but a charity home funded by a prominent Victorian philanthropist of the day. I was not classed as homeless or in need of care.

In spite of the comforting given me by the matron, I cried for a long time after my mother had left, until my eyes were quite sore. For a long time, I could remember my mother leaving me there, watching her disappear out of the door, not bothering to turn round and have a last look at her son or to wave goodbye. Whether she had tears in her eyes, I never knew.

On later reflection, I suspected that this move to the home was engineered by Tom, to make sure that I did not live with them – my mother must have been talked into the scheme. I would have been in the way. Whoever had the idea, it certainly solved their problem. Eventually I unpacked the battered cardboard suitcase, wondering how, or for what reason, my mother had abandoned me, her own son. Perhaps Tom had given her an ultimatum – choose between him or me. If my mother felt any remorse she had not shown it to me.

In charge of the boys was a master, his wife the Matron and an assistant matron. The home was established in a very large Victorian house with three dormitories, one of which was quite large, with twenty beds. There was ample space for more boys if the need arose. The house stood in its own extensive grounds, of some five to six acres of flat meadow land.

Backing on to the home's far end was the sports ground of one of London's leading docks. On most Saturdays and Sundays, winter and summer, some sort of sporting activity took place, with the occasional midweek game during the summer. My favourite vantage point to watch these activities was up a big old oak tree, giving me a bird's eye view of the game in progress, sometimes lying down to stretch out on one of the broad boughs.

At the other end of the home's ground, running parallel to the main road there were advertising placards, the whole length of the home's own buildings to the gable end of a private house, some 200 yards long in all. The placards stood in the home's ground, about 10 feet in from the pavement. The hoardings served two main purposes – importantly they provided useful revenue for the home, but also acted as a boundary fence helping to stop passers-by from looking in, whether on foot or in one of the passing vehicles.

In the far right hand corner of the home's field, were wired-in chicken runs with nesting boxes. I often saw dead chickens hanging up in the stables ready for plucking. If this was done when the bird was warm, most of the stubborn feathers would come out quite easily, with little effort, and without tearing the flesh. Those chickens that were killed were replaced by hatching their own chicks, in incubators in the stables. This maintained a steady balance of laying birds. Any excess was sold off to the local butcher. Once, whilst I was in the stables, the chicks were bursting their shells, to come to life. They seem to know by instinct what to do. Once hatched, the chicks were transferred to another heated incubator, where there was food and water readily available. The chicks were sexed, and the cocks were housed in a separate run. When old enough, they were the first to be used for the kitchen table, or to be sold off. There didn't seem to be any trouble selling them, as in those days chicken was considered a luxury food. The eggs were collected twice daily, by one of the boys delegated to this task. The task of mixing the mash and feeding the chickens was given to another boy, as was the feeding of the corn. When there was an abundance of eggs, some were stored in a very large earthenware crock situated in the pantry, soaked in isinglass. Any surplus to the home's needs was sold off to local householders – when these were available, a sign was put up by the roadside.

The Matron was also the cook. She would make chicken pies with peas and diced carrots, in large trays. As a special treat, on the occasional Sunday, she would roast some chickens and potatoes. Us boys really looked forward to these meals which we enjoyed greatly. Vegetables were supplied by one of the home's governors, either from his own kitchen garden, or from a greengrocer's shop he owned in the vicinity. I was occasionally chosen to run errands to the grocers or the greengrocers. In spite of all the ground the home possessed, for some reason, the growing of vegetables was never considered, possibly because it would have been too time-consuming, or because there was a simple lack of know-how, or maybe because of the governor's own interests as most of the home's vegetable requirements were bought from his shop.

Most of the home's grounds were in regular use during the summer months. The favourite game was 'rounders', a similar game to modern baseball. Teams were chosen from the boys to add a degree of competitiveness to the game. Cricket was also a very popular sport, although both games were played with a soft ball for the sake of safety. There was no football in the winter, as most parents were unable to afford proper football boots for their lads.

Many boys preferred playing table tennis in the games room, or less energetic pastimes such as draughts or cards in the recreation room-cum-dining room, with the comfort of a welcoming warm fire. The lucky ones who received Meccano sets for Christmas would amuse themselves making structures from the instruction book, or from their own inventive ideas. During the seven years that I was at the home, my mother never came to see me once. I never received a birthday or Christmas card or any presents whatever – there was a complete lack of contact. This was something I was to suffer for in later years when I married, as I was always in trouble for forgetting birthdays and anniversaries.

We were educated at a local elementary school, about a quarter of a mile away, to and from which we were marched in an orderly fashion in the mornings and afternoons. Before sitting down to lunch on weekdays, each boy had a delegated chore to do. Mine was to hearthstone two flights of stairs, leading up to the dormitories. All the work was inspected by the Headmaster, before we could sit down to lunch, in order to make sure all the different tasks had been done properly.

During the period I was in the home, there were three masters – the first retired and the second died shortly after he was appointed. He was replaced by a very stern-looking man, who seemed to love and enjoy giving six of the best, for any slight misdemeanour. He would not give out punishment with an ordinary cane, he got more enjoyment by using a cut-down billiard cue. His favourite punishment was to try and hit the boy across the wrist part of the hand in order to make contact with the thumb. If he succeeded it would hurt for some considerable time afterwards. One of the boys' tricks was to put soap on their hands, before caning, so that, when the cue made contact, it would slide off. The Head's enjoyment was not going to be spoilt, and once he got wise to this subterfuge, he made them wash their hands before a caning. It was always a battle of wits between the Head and the boys.

I seemed to get my fair share of punishment, chiefly for talking after lights out at ten at night, winter and summer. In the summer it was always more difficult to fall asleep and I found that talking to the boy in the next bed helped, rather like counting sheep, although it was more like whispering than talking out loud. One night I was talking very softly to the boy in the next bed, when the Head came into the dormitory, billiard cue in one hand and pulling back the bedclothes with the other. As the Head went to switch the light on, I made a dash for the door. For some reason I thought that enough was enough and I scampered down the stairs, ignoring the Head calling me back. Out of the back door I ran, across the fields in my bare feet. I knew if I could climb my favourite oak tree, I would be safe, at least for the night. In the shadow of the full moon, I could see and hear the Head calling me. I decided to stay there all night and trust to luck in the morning – fortunately it was not too cold. I was expecting the worst, so it came as quite a surprise, and relief, when nothing happened as I showed up for breakfast.

The Headmaster's wife was a very pleasant lady, and very attractive, even to the boys in the home. She was about 40 years of age and very shapely.

If any of the boys was sick or ill she took good care of him. She seemed to have a loving nature, as though she was the mother of all the boys. The Head was about the same age of his wife, but a tall, thin man with cruel-looking eyes and thin lips. He seemed to grow even taller when dishing out the punishment, something he seemed to relish. I could never really understand the true purpose of the home. Maybe some parents had too many children to feed and clothe. This was the time of the General Strike, in the twenties. The home probably helped to relieve the financial burden of parents bringing up a large family.

Throughout the time that I was an inmate at the home, we boys had to go though the Saturday morning ritual after breakfast. The Head and his wife would enter the dining room, closing the only door to the room behind them, and place two containers on the nearest table. The idea of closing the door was to make sure no boy avoided taking his 'medicine'. One container was full of a foul-tasting medicine that each of us had to take. As a reward, we were each given sixpence a week pocket money. Everyone received the money, irrespective of what punishment may have been received during the week, or even if some had been given money by their parents. Some of the boys had regular visits from their parents. Boys were coming and going all the time although I and a couple of others remained a part of the fixtures.

It was after one of these Saturday morning ritual sessions that the Head told me to stay behind. While I was waiting, all sorts of thoughts were flashing through my mind – what had I done wrong? Was I due for a caning? I couldn't think of any reason why I should be but no doubt the Head could think of a reason to flex his muscles. When all the boys had taken their medicine, the Head turned to me. Instead of the worst that I had been expecting, to my surprise, the Head asked me if I would be interested in earning a little extra pocket money working on a Saturday morning.

I got over the initial relief that I was not going to be given a caning, but was still wary of the Head's intentions and suspicious of his motives. I knew there was no love lost between them, and asked what the job was that needed doing. The Head explained that the home had a fully operational laundry service in Forest Hill and asked me if I would be interested in assisting the driver on Saturday mornings, collecting the dirty laundry and delivering the clean. Now that I knew what it was all about, I readily agreed to help out.

I often wondered why a model 'T' Ford box van was always parked either outside or inside the stables. The van had a dark green body, black wings and rear mudguards. On the van's body was a boldly written sign saying 'Home Laundry' in a large semi-circle, inside which on straight lines, was written 'Dartmouth Road, Forest Hill, S.E.23'. On each side door was written 'Ask driver for details'. The side lights and rear number plate were illuminated by acetylene lamps. These were detachable so that they could be lit before use. When lit, they were firmly fixed to the lamp holders. Each lamp had a base reservoir that held a mixture of water and acetylene crystals giving off an ignitable gas. The van had two forward gears and one reverse operated by a foot pedal. When the van was stationary with the engine running there was a neutral position. If it was raining, one had to operate the windscreen wipers by hand or have the windscreen half-open and risk getting wet. The van seldom went out after dark in the winter. The engine was easy to start in the summer months even though there was no such luxury as a self-starter – it had to be cranked by hand every time. In the winter months it was a different story to start the engine. First one of the rear wheels had to be jacked up and the other firmly chocked with a brick. Then a kettle of boiling water had to be fetched from the kitchen. This was poured over the exhaust system. Once the ignition control situated under the steering wheel had been correctly set, and the low gear engaged, the starting handle to crank the engine had to be inserted. It had to be done this way, as there was no other vehicle to give a tow. The starting handle had to be held a certain way, for quick release. If the engine did back-fire, it had to be released very quickly, at the risk of a broken arm. The job of van assistant became a full-time occupation when I left school at fourteen. This meant I could stay at the home until I was sixteen, or my mother was traced, whichever was the sooner.

One evening, the Head asked me to stay behind after the other boys had gone to bed, saying by way of explanation that he wanted me to give him a hand laying the breakfast ready for the morning – a job he and his wife usually completed each evening. She had gone to bed early and it was about 10.30pm before we finished, having a cup of cocoa before going upstairs. By the time the task was finished, all the other boys should be asleep. I crept quietly to my dormitory and undressed by the landing light shining into the room, a light left on all night in case any of the boys wanted to go downstairs to the toilets during the hours of darkness.

I was just about to get into bed, when the Head entered, asking me to give him a hand with a small job in his bedroom. I followed the Head into his room, noticing as he entered that his wife was still awake, reading in bed. When she saw me, she said "Hello", putting the book down. By this time the Head had changed into his nightshirt, and was turning the bed covers down. He told me to get into bed and I realised only too late I had been tricked – I was not aware of the weaknesses or faults of men.

Wedged between the Head and his wife, I had very little choice, but to do as I was told. I could feel the warmth of her body and soon became aroused whilst the Head was calmly doing to me what he intended to do. His wife had now turned to face me and, in doing so, had put her arm around my neck, to ease me closer to herself. I could feel the soft contours of her womanly body through her thin nightdress. For a while we continued kissing and caressing, making a fuss of each other. She responded to my attentions with all her pent-up sexual desires and passion. After this astonishing experience, I couldn't understand why the Head preferred boys to his passionate and sexually starved wife. She was great to be with, giving me a night to remember. At last the Head had had his way with me, an unwilling target for his unnatural behaviour. He had in fact tried several times before but I had always managed to fob him off, much to the man's obvious displeasure. I determined to make this the first and last time the evil teacher took advantage of me – but with the teacher's wife ... who knows? I knew that I could not complain to anyone about the Head's unwelcome attentions, apart from the home's doctor and it was very doubtful that he would have done anything about it or even believed me.

The Head made two more attempts to molest me, once at a scout camp and on an occasion when I was cleaning the van in the stable block. He crept up behind me and started fondling me trying to pull my trousers down. But I was too quick for him and dashed round to the other side of the van, saying very firmly that I was not interested in that sort of thing. After a while, the Head left me to continue with my work, feeling quite uncomfortable at the man's totally unwanted intrusion. I did not know whether the Head had tried to interfere with other boys – I suspected that I would not have been the only one. It puzzled me at the time and in later years I wondered if the man had been bi-sexual, although his wife's frustration seemed to suggest otherwise.

CHAPTER THREE

When the boys were ten years old, they were encouraged to join the cubs, progressing to the scouts at fourteen. I had followed the usual pattern and was well thought of, enough to be troop leader of my section. In the August of 1930, the boys belonging to the cubs and scouts went on a summer camp to Cowes, on the Isle of Wight. It was very late when we arrived so we had to pitch our tents in the dark. Unfortunately, we could not have chosen a worse place, a well-used cow field where it was impossible to miss all the cow pats. We were all far too tired to worry about this and as soon as the tents were in place and erected, we clambered into our beds and were soon all sound asleep – even the awful smell failed to put us off going to sleep.

In the morning, after cooking our own breakfasts in our billycans, we rapidly set about changing the positions of our tents, in the best places that we could find, away from the unpleasant evidence of the cows. All the scouts and cubs were given specific tasks to do to qualify for their proficiency badges and cap stars – this was a very important aspect of scouting. The first task set was for the older scouts and, as I was troop leader, I was put in charge. The task was to walk completely around the Island and this entailed taking our sleeping bags, dry rations and our billycans, although I was given some money for refreshments. We were left to our own devices as to where to sleep so we set about finding obliging farmers who would allow us to sleep in a barn or an outhouse. A few of the farmers gave us something to eat in the morning, also allowing us to have a good wash down in the farmyard.

The walk took three days to complete. It was not a timed task. We all thoroughly enjoyed the experience and the challenge, except one poor scout who developed blisters on his feet. Another task given to all the boys involved us being taken to the middle of Parkhurst Forest, and being left to make our own way back to camp. This was more of a compass-reading exercise. On our way through the forest, we came across the grounds of Parkhurst Prison. Stopping to have a rest and a breather, we noticed that there was a cricket match going on, so stayed and watched for a while. As all the players were dressed in white, we could not tell whether any inmates were playing or not.

Most of the boys seemed to rely on me to get them back to camp safely and under my guidance, we arrived back before dark, all being completely exhausted after such an exercise. We were all delighted to have a hot meal and a warming drink even if there was no enthusiasm or energy for camp fire songs or stories that night. As one, we all headed off to bed for an early night.

The Headmaster of the home was the senior scout, so he was also at camp. One night he came into my tent, making it quite clear what his intentions were by becoming quite familiar with me. He had tried this before, when I was younger, in the stables at the home. In no uncertain terms I said that I was not going to have anything to do with that sort of behaviour and the Head apologised to me and left.

It was agreed by all that we had had a very good time, while we were at the summer camp. It was a wonderful experience for us all, and one we would not have had, if it had not been paid for by the home.

I left school in July 1930 having lived at the home for six years. During this entire time I still hadn't seen or heard from my mother. It wasn't as though she was miles away from the home, as the place where she lived was just a few miles away and easily accessible by public transport. I could not write to her as I did not know her address. She was supposed to notify the home if she moved, but she had not done so – whether this was an oversight, or quite deliberate, I had no way of knowing. I thought about her often and would have dearly loved to see her, wondering constantly how she was.

I was now working at the laundry job for four days a week and this helped to take my mind off my concern about my mother. I had other females to worry about – the women at the laundry were certainly a rum lot and I kept out of their way as much as I could. One woman, whenever she saw me, suggested that I should be initiated into the laundry service, whatever that meant. I had a shrewd idea, but after the van was unloaded or loaded as the case may be, I wasn't going to hang around to find out for sure. While the driver was attending to the paperwork, or any complaints or shortages, I disappeared into the public swimming baths next door. The driver was a cheerful, caring sort, giving me a fixed time to be back. With my first week's wages, I bought myself a five-shilling illuminated dial wristwatch, a very proud possession, being my first ever watch, even if I had bought it myself.

The driver and I got on very well together. Being out and about, away from the home, I did at least have the opportunity to meet a wide variety of people. There was far less risk of getting into trouble and also less chance of a possible caning. This may have been the reason why the Head offered me the laundry job – he either became tired of caning me, or perhaps could not make me cry or wince, like many of the other boys. I realised that the Head derived some feelings of power when beating the boys.

Most of the householders the laundry van called on, lived in the 'posh' districts of Forest Hill or Sydenham, with live-in maids and butlers. Some of the housemaids were really saucy when they saw me, especially Maisie. She was always around when the driver and I called, usually about 11am on Mondays, to collect the dirty laundry. There was always a cup of tea waiting with a piece of delicious apple pie. On Fridays at about the same time, we would deliver the clean laundry hamper. As it was so heavy, it was always a two-handed delivery. On Fridays, we were offered the usual cup of tea but usually with a piece of chocolate sponge cake. Maisie would be there as usual as if she was waiting for me, who thought that the cook had a crush on the driver, the way she seemed to be flirting with him. Whether they met after work, I had no idea, but I suspected that they did, the relationship seemed so familiar.

Maisie had a baby-doll face, very much like Clara Bow, the film actress. Her blonde hair seemed to be constantly pinned up under her dust-cap. She had the most distinctive large blue eyes and was well proportioned for her sixteen years, although the uniform was rather plain and unflattering, much to my disappointment. Maisie made it quite clear, not so much by what she said, but by her actions, that she was available if I was interested. And well I may have been, except that none of the boys was allowed outside the home after 5pm, at any time of the year. Of course, my mind was working overtime to see how I could get round this inconvenient problem – I had thought of making a secret tryst with Maisie. If I had been found out, I knew it would put my laundry job at risk. I did not want to lose my freedom of movement – I loved being out and about. The temptation was great but sadly I considered there was too much at stake at that time.

So with much regret, I decided not to get involved, much to Maisie's annoyance and frustration. I tried to smooth her feelings by explaining my great disappointment with the 5pm curfew. Maisie just adopted a petulant attitude, pursing her lovely cupid shaped lips, saying that if I was really interested, I'd find a way. I could see a tear forming in her beautiful eyes, showing how upset she was. It wasn't a question that love alone would find a way, but more a matter of finding a practical way around the problem.

On my next visit, while the cook and the driver were looking in each other's eyes completely oblivious to what was going on around them, I took Maisie by the hand and led her into the next room, the scullery – not the most romantic place. When we were inside the damp little room, and out of other people's earshot, I told her that I thought I could find a way round our problem. "As you know, Wednesday is my day off – I will try and arrange a series of dental appointments. If you can organise your afternoon off to coincide, we can go out either to the cinema or walk through the park".

Hearing me say this was like music to Maisie's ears. Her eyes sparkled like two large blue sunlit lagoons. She moved up very close to me, showing her delighted agreement to the suggestion, saying in a very excited voice, "I am sure I can arrange my time off to suit", giving me a loving kiss to seal the suggestion. Just at that point the driver called for me – frustrating, but just as well that he did, for after that kiss, I could have become really carried away, more than interested now in what might follow with Maisie.

By careful scheming, it only took me a couple of weeks to manage the meetings with my dentist. Maisie and I arranged a time and place to meet to fit in with my alleged appointment. On our first date, when I caught my first sight of Maisie, with her lovely blonde hair arranged in a page-boy style, now released from being hidden by her dust-cap, and dressed in her finery, I hardly recognised her. There was only one word to describe her appearance – ravishing. She had clearly taken a great deal of trouble to look so lovely and desirable. Her hair was her crowning glory and she wore a close-fitting black hat, setting off her blonde shoulder-length tresses – a hat more for adornment than weather protection.

Most times we went to the cinema where Maisie always made sure that we sat in the back row of the stalls, in the darkest possible location. To my absolute delight, she seemed more interested in me than the movie. If there was a romantic scene on the screen, she would snuggle up really close to me. When it was time to leave, she was always reluctant. I saw her back to her work place where we lingered for as long as possible kissing and cuddling. On parting, Maisie would say, "See you on Friday as usual, love". One final kiss, then I would make my way back to the home – such a contrast from the last few hours. It was only a ten-minute walk from Maisie's, but my steps were heavy after the delight of being with my girl.

Sometimes, instead of going to the cinema, if the weather was bright and warm, we would go to a secluded part of the local park, spending the afternoon there. Occasionally we would travel to Horniman's Museum and Gardens where we could admire the marvellous view over southern London. Wherever we went on our afternoon excursions, Maisie was the clinging type, not letting me go until the last possible minute. Because of this, I made arrangements with one of the other boys at the home to cover for me if I happened to be late returning – this cost me a precious shilling. As long as I managed to be back by 6pm for the evening meal I was not missed.

When the dental appointments were finished, I had to think up some other reason to continue seeing Maisie on Wednesday afternoons. I hit on a sound idea and asked the Head, as I had to leave the home at sixteen, whether I could have Wednesday afternoons off for job-hunting. The Head readily agreed with the idea and gave his permission to the suggestion. When I next saw Maisie, I told her of this new arrangement, when she became very excited at the prospect of continuing our outings. The whole idea brought tears of joy to her lovely blue eyes.

Maisie was getting much fonder and more serious towards me, eventually suggesting that we should become engaged, hinting that if we did, we could enjoy the 'fruits' of our loving relationship. Maisie was a very passionate type of girl and, with our kissing and caressing, it was often very difficult to restrain ourselves. Although I was very fond of Maisie, I felt that she was trying to spin a web around me, trapping me like a fly, where there was no escape.

I did not want to commit myself at this stage and told her that I thought we should wait until my future was more secure. I added sensibly that I had no real home, no guaranteed job, and more importantly, that I had no money. This, I stated, was not the best way to start a serious relationship. Maisie was determined not to be deterred that easily, and suggested that we could go into service together, thus solving many of our problems. Being together was what really mattered to her. I replied by saying that such an idea would be all right in the short term – I wanted more out of life than waiting on people, and cleaning their shoes, although I meant no disrespect to those in service. I had my own clear ideas what I wanted to do. I reluctantly decided to ask Maisie to wait until my future was more secure, at the same time confessing to Maisie that I really did love her.

Maisie replied by saying that she was not prepared to wait indefinitely, giving me six months at the most. I knew I could not achieve what I had in mind in such a short time, so it was mutually agreed to end our relationship. It was a sad decision that we both deeply regretted – it took a great deal of willpower and not a few tears to come to terms with our separation.

I was now approaching my sixteenth birthday and was one of the most senior boys at the home. I was well established in the home's routines and found a considerable sense of security in them. Friday nights were bath nights. The young boys were bathed first, one at a time with the assistant matron being responsible for supervising the operation. One of her more serious duties was to inspect the boys' hair for lice. She had not been at the home very long, so very little was known about her by the boys. She was about 30 years of age, slender and somewhat manly in her appearance because of her close-cropped brunette hair and the fact that she wore no make-up. Her bluish, faded uniform with white collars and cuffs did nothing to enhance her femininity, giving her an austere appearance. Whether she took any delight in watching the bigger boys bathe was difficult to say – she never touched anyone, so the boys had to wash each other's backs.

I was late getting back on one of these Friday nights due to my laundry work, so consequently I was the last to bathe. As I was undressing, I said to her that there was no need for her to stay, but she swiftly reminded me that it was her job to supervise. While I sat and washed myself, she perched on the edge of the bath, both chatting away lightly. Somehow I sensed that she was taking more than a mere supervisory interest in me. I was now a well-built sixteen-year-old, in good health and playing plenty of sport. The laundry job with all the lifting of bundles and hampers had quickly developed my muscles and physique.

In my dormitory there were only eight beds, because the assistant matron's room took up a third of the floor space. Hers was a private room, more like a bed-sit than just a bedroom. A few nights later, after bathing and once all the other boys were asleep, she woke me up quietly, and led me by the hand to her room. I had been woken from a deep sleep, so really did not know quite what was happening. However, I was soon fully awake, and aroused, as she started to fondle and kiss me very passionately. I soon became excited as she slipped off her nightdress, letting it slide to the floor. By the dimmed light of the bedside light, I was more than surprised to see the well-shaped body that the uninspiring uniform had been hiding. She helped me to take off my nightshirt too, which also just fell to the floor. There was no mistaking what she wanted, taking me by the hand and leading me naked over to her bed. We both climbed in not bothering to cover ourselves. She wasted no time, starting to kiss me very passionately. This was another amazing experience for me, allowing her to make all the sexual moves, at which she seemed quite experienced. I did not manage to sleep much that night – in fact, I was rather surprised when I saw daylight through the bedroom window. Eventually, I slipped out of the warm and now rather crumpled bed, reluctant to return to my dormitory, picking up my nightshirt on the way. I quickly collected my other clothes and went down to the ablutions for a good wash down.

Spending the night in her room became a frequent occurrence, with me becoming more experienced in the art of lovemaking. She was an excellent teacher, and I was an able and willing pupil, enjoying the experience while it lasted.

On Wednesdays the van did not go out, so, for the sake of something to do, I often washed and polished it. The driver went over to the laundry to help prepare the deliveries for Thursday and Friday, or attended to maintenance work on the van. While I was lathering and polishing, I decided to help myself take my mind off my uncertain future, and get over losing Maisie, by renewing my interest in building radios and operating them.

Having made this positive decision, I made a start. The various components required were easily available, and not too expensive. My tips and Christmas boxes from the laundry customers helped a lot. Early radios were simple in design, not needing many components. I made a list of all the necessary items and when time allowed I acquired exactly what I wanted. In those days, most radios had three four-pin valves, a tuner to select a transmitter wavelength, and a few resistors and condensers. To receive a strong signal, the radio also needed an aerial. I managed this by stringing a temporary aerial across the dining room. With all the components to hand, I set about building my first radio receiver.

All radios of the day were operated by a dry cell, high-tension battery, incorporating a nine volt grid bias battery. I managed to borrow one of the Head's accumulators, the man needing no persuasion when he knew what I wanted it for. The accumulator, which was the unspillable type, was necessary to heat the valve filaments. When heated, the filaments sent a stream of electrons to the anode of the valve. The grid bias controlled the flow of these electrons according to the voltage tapping. The main trouble when the voltage became low was that reception became distorted. A short-term remedy was to put the battery in an oven, making sure the bitumen pitch on top did not melt. When radio valves first came into use, they were made of plain glass, which caused the valve to oscillate on high volume. To overcome this, the manufacturers ensured that the glass was oxidised, or they enclosed the valve with a metal screen, which helped to cut down this sort of interference.

Necessity being the mother of invention, it was not long before voltage converters came into use, as many houses were being converted to electricity, both in town and city. This made the messy accumulator redundant as more houses were changed over from gas lighting. In the last few years since my first involvement with radio, reception had made great strides. My interest never wavered – on odd occasions, I would buy a weekly publication to keep in touch with modern developments. The old wooden cabinet was discarded in favour of bakelite, the forerunner of plastic. Many cabinets had an inbuilt aerial, so instead of the radio being a fixture, it could be used in any room of the house, with little or no trouble. With the introduction of improved and different types of valve, reception was much clearer, not 'tinny' as with the earlier radios. All the improvements taking place in the early thirties helped a great deal to relieve the unemployment problem. At the same time, John Logie Baird was making great strides with television transmission and reception.

People were saying that as radio reception was vastly improving and becoming a household necessity, it would put the cinemas out of business. This was not so however, as people still had their Saturday night treat to the cinema, judging by the massive queues that still formed outside the picture palaces.

All radio transmissions were controlled by the Government, who introduced a licence fee for all householders who had a radio. As radio transmissions developed with long and short waves, it opened up new dimensions to radio reception. On odd occasions, one could even tune in to American broadcasts.

So I built my first radio receiver, following the instructions carefully and choosing and acquiring only the best of components. I became extremely good at this, giving myself many hours of pleasure and satisfaction both in building the sets and in listening to the broadcasts. At the same time I was giving many of the other boys an interest and great pleasure as well. These were the very early days of wireless transmissions from Marconi House, where the call sign was 2LO. The boys listened to some of the comics of the day, Tommy Trinder ('You lucky people!'), Max Miller, the Cheeky Chappie, Old Mother Riley, George Robey, Marie Lloyd and her old cock linnet, Nellie Wallace and many others. Sometimes there were plays broadcast and on many occasions, there were extracts from music halls and theatres. Once the BBC moved to their purpose-built studios and headquarters in 1932, wireless listening really took off in a big way.

Chapter Four

Some way before my sixteenth birthday, the day came when I had to appear before the Board of Governors, one of whom was the home's appointed doctor. The home had tried several times to contact my mother but had failed. I had no job to go to and the rules of the home stated very clearly that no boy could stay on after his sixteenth birthday.

The doctor, who was a kindly man, offered me a job as residential caretaker to his private practice. As it was the only option open to me at the time, I had no choice but to accept it. The doctor took me by car to his surgery to show me round. It was a part of a big Victorian house in Brockley, south-east London.

The doctor even made a suggestion that when I was eighteen, he would, if I was interested, put me through medical school, but in the meantime he would teach me about medicines and their uses. I left the home just before Christmas 1931, not knowing what uncertain future lay ahead of me. I had feelings of considerable trepidation. In spite of my mother's indifference to me, I felt the years in the home had been in my best interest. They had made me self-reliant and independent and I had a strong belief that I was going to make a success of my life, with or without my mother's help. Like her, I had a powerful inbuilt survival instinct.

I took my few possessions with me in my old battered suitcase. The radio-building kits I passed on to another boy who had showed a particular interest in this fascinating hobby.

The doctor explained to me what my duties were, and showed me where my bedroom was. The room had only the bare essentials – bed, water jug and basin on a small table, and a wardrobe, just large enough for my few possessions. The room was at the back of the house, overlooking a very untidy garden. After the morning surgery hours the doctor would disappear, only coming back for his evening surgery, and then promptly disappear again. He did not seem to live there, so once he had left in the evening, that would be all that I would see of him until his next morning surgery. He always gave me clear instructions what to do and equally made sure that there was enough food in the house. I had to do all my own cooking but I did not mind this at all. My scout training came in handy when I needed a meal. On the few occasions when the doctor forgot to bring in the usual supplies, I went to the café a few doors along the road and had my meal there, paid for it and later gave the bill to the doctor who never complained when I did this. I thought that perhaps it would teach him a lesson not to forget the shopping in future.

Before I took the job on, the doctor explained to me that he would receive free board and lodging, laundry for household goods, and ten shillings a week pocket money. My principal task was to keep the house, surgery and the waiting room clean and tidy although it was not expected that I would have to stay in all the time. There were times when I had to give the doctor a little prompting regarding my pocket money, but the man always apologised for the oversight. The doctor was more than pleased with the way I kept the house clean and tidy, saying it was the best he had ever seen it.

Shortly after starting at the surgery, I decided that I would use some of my spare time to try and find my mother, although I had very little information to work on. I knew that my grandmother and my mother were very close, and that my Uncle Bill was my mother's favourite brother. I had a hunch where to start looking for her – I knew that my mother and grandmother liked going out for a drink together, when paying the Christmas Club money. I remembered the hours on end I had to wait for them, as a seven-year-old, while they were drinking inside. I also knew which was their favourite pub, assuming that they were still living in Peckham, which seemed fairly certain.

So the Peckham pub was the first place to start looking for her. My mother had been a member of the pub's Christmas Club for years, and it was very unlikely she would give it up. It was the only way the working class could afford the little luxuries for Christmas, and it also gave her the opportunity to have a drink, and a quiet chat with her mother on Monday nights. I chose a suitable Monday evening and made my way to Peckham. It was only a short journey by bus to reach the pub. When I arrived, I quickly discovered they were both inside. I knew I had a long wait, as it was very unlikely they would come out before closing time at ten thirty. Just in case they did, I thought it best to stay and wait having decided not to go into the pub myself. While I was waiting, I wondered what sort of reception I was going to get, and what my mother's reaction would be, not having seen her son for the last eight years. As far as she was concerned I could have been dead – she had no way of knowing what had happened to me, by not keeping in touch with the home.

When my mother at last came out of the pub, and saw me standing there, quite calmly without any emotion in her voice, or any physical expression, she greeted me as though the last eight years had never existed. My grandmother showed more emotion, giving me a kiss and asking how I was. My mother just said, "How are you Bun?", using her old nickname for me. There was no hug or kiss or even an I'm-pleased-to-see-you gesture. I thought that one of her pub cronies would have received a better greeting.

I persuaded my mother that we had to talk as soon as possible and asked if we could arrange a meeting shortly after Christmas. We agreed a day and time to meet at one of Lyons' Corner Houses. Before parting, I said, "If you don't turn up I will come knocking at your door – I know where you live!" To prove my point, I told her, having gleaned the information from my grandmother, who just could not understand her daughter's attitude towards her son.

There was no suggestion that I should go to my mother's house for Christmas so I spent the festival alone in the doctor's spacious house. I set out to amuse myself as best I could and managed to find an air pistol with some dart pellets. I began by taking pot-shots at the coloured balls on the Christmas tree – why it was there, I had no idea. The doctor did not show up until after Christmas was over although he did supply me with a Christmas hamper, so there was plenty of food in the house. The air pistol did help to pass the time away. After a little practice I became a good shot. When all the balls had been broken, I fixed up a target for further practice using a dartboard I found in a cupboard.

At one stage while I was working at the surgery as resident caretaker, I decided to use some of my spare time to make my grandmother a wireless set – she would never be able to buy one for herself. I acquired all the components and a rather nice cabinet for a pound and set about putting it all together. After a week, I had it finished and on test. I then delivered it, and showed her how to use it to the best advantage, telling her to use it sparingly as the cottage was only gaslit, with little chance of the electric mains being laid on – I would replace the HT battery when need be. She was overjoyed with her new device, although I felt it was a poor gift in return for all that she had done for me, when I was living with her as a youngster.

At the second meeting with my mother, we had a much more productive talk – my mother begged me to forgive her for not keeping in touch while I was in the home. Apparently Tom had forbidden her to keep in touch, telling her in no uncertain terms that it was a simple choice between him or me.

I made it clear that I was not going to ask whose idea it was to put me in a home – that was all in the past – but that I was more concerned with the future. My mother was still my legal guardian and responsible for my welfare. There was no way I wanted to stay much longer in the large, rambling house on my own. I stated quite clearly that I would have to return to my mother's house, whether Tom liked it or not. I knew what a schemer my mother was and how she would be thinking of the money I could be earning when I found a job. The response was that she would have to have a word with Tom, to which I replied that I would give them just two days to decide. I finished with a threat that, if I heard nothing after two days, I would come knocking on their door.

Begrudgingly, Tom agreed to let me live with them, but I knew from the moment I saw Tom, that there was no love lost between them. I instinctively knew it was going to be a hateful relationship. This was the man who supposedly forbade my mother from seeing her son. Tom clearly had no intention of allowing me to upset his cosy existence – for some reason he was obsessed with jealousy.

For most of the winter months, Tom was out of work, a situation that suited him well, having a dislike for work. My mother kept him in beer, forty cigarettes a day, plus an ounce of pipe tobacco. It was a regular occurrence when my mother came home from waitressing at a Freemasons' dinner, that she would bring home cigars at all stages of smoking. Tom would then spend a good deal of time chopping them up for his pipe. His smoking used to stink the rooms out. He would keep any whole cigars for the weekend to show off, smoking them in the pub.

My mother worked extremely hard to keep Tom through the winter months. When spring came, he had become so used to doing nothing and being kept that she really had to badger him to make him stir from his cosy winter way of life. His regular boss always took him on again, when business picked up in the spring as, to be fair, he was a good tradesman. Tom was just bone lazy, and didn't see why he should work, when he was getting all the comforts of home doing nothing. His attitude made me extremely angry, but wisely I kept a low profile, and said nothing. I decided that I would just wait and see what developed, not risking upsetting my mother. What my mother saw in Tom really baffled me – any other woman would not have given him a second look, he was no catch. In spite of the fact that he contributed very little to the household finances, he had the audacity, not to ask, but tell her, what he wanted for his meals, usually a fillet steak or some other expensive food. Being too compliant, she, like a fool, did as she was told. She thought the sun shone out of his eyes.

I soon found myself a local factory job assembling radios. The company made radios for a national cigarette manufacturer who issued coupons in their packets of twenty. Their logo was a butler serving cigarettes from a silver platter. It was a surprise to me how many people were smoking themselves to death just to accumulate sufficient coupons to receive a free radio. There were no health warnings about the hazards of smoking, and rarely anyone commented on the dangers. It was just as normal as eating and drinking. My company were hard pressed to keep up with demand, having to work quite a lot of over time to fulfil the order book. I did not really want to stay there. Although the money was good I knew my prospects were virtually nil, and I felt that it was a dead-end job – I wanted something more rewarding for my labour. With this in mind, I studied the national papers to see if I could find a way to better myself.

I applied for an electrical apprenticeship in the West End of London, not far from Oxford Circus, near Portland Place and the BBC. After fierce competition for the job, I was offered it on a three-month trial. I was told if I was successful, the three months would count as service towards the seven-year apprenticeship. New ambitions were visible on the horizon and I was highly delighted that my future prospects were looking a lot brighter and more assured. As a bonus, my new boss also repaired cars in the same building. It was explained to me, if I wasn't busy doing electrical work, I would be expected to help out in the garage. This suited me greatly as I felt I would be learning two trades at the same time. All this happened just after my sixteenth birthday.

As my future was much more assured, I thought he would approach my mother to try and persuade her to leave Tom. She was not married to him, they were just living together. There was no home atmosphere for me, living with Tom. I tried my hardest to convince her it would be for the best. This man seemed to have some strange, Rasputin-like hold over her. Even after Tom had spent a term in prison, for embezzling the pub's dart fund, she took him back. I had inherited my mother's strong work ethic and sooner or later there was bound to be trouble between the two of us over the way Tom was scrounging off my mother. Tom and I often had battles of words with my poor mother having to act as a referee. I called him to his face, amongst other things, a lazy sponger, saying that if my mother wanted to keep him, the more fool she was. I had no intention of encouraging him in his laziness. My mother usually finished up crying, while these verbal battles were progressing. Tom dare not hit me – he was too much of a coward. I was a big, strong lad for my age and I secretly thought that Tom was afraid of me. All of my offers of setting up a new structure home were wasted.

CHAPTER FIVE

On most evenings, winter and summer, I went out. One of my favourite cinemas was the Capitol in Forest Hill, bringing back fond memories of Maisie and myself necking in the back row of the stalls. Before I had left the boys' home, I had heard she had taken up with the butcher's delivery boy. I was never one for pub drinking, preferring to spend my leisure time visiting the cinema – I was an ardent film fan. Most cinemas of the day had a change of programme each Thursday, and a special film for one night on Sundays. Sometimes before or after the programme, I would call into the café a few doors away from the cinema.

On most occasions when I visited the café, the same four fellows, aged between 19–21 would be sitting together talking. Their main topic of conversation was world politics, particularly speculating on Hitler's motives. I was always interested in what they were discussing, although I had no political persuasions myself. Their banter was always friendly and lively – no one was trying to score points off the others. I was 17 when I became the youngest member of the gang.

One of the gang was called Mac – he was without question the life and soul of the group. He was thickset for his 21 years, with a shock of unruly black hair, heavy jowls, bushy eyebrows, and keen alert hazel eyes. Apart from having a terrific sense of humour, he had a wonderful command of the English language, very useful as a freelance writer. He had a guttural laugh that seemed to come from the pit of his stomach. He was never without his Sherlock Holmes-type pipe – when trying to make a point, he would take his pipe out of his mouth and point it assertively at the person he was talking to. He was a real Max Miller type, his repertoire of jokes and quick one-liners was endless, and he managed to keep the rest of the gang in fits of laughter.

He wrote regular monthly articles but, because of their suggestive, sexual content, it was in an 'under-the-counter' publication called 'Razzle' where they were published. His articles were very saucy and near the bone – the gang always thought his stories were good for a laugh with their double meanings and innuendoes when they were read in the cafe amongst themselves. Chris, the café owner had a matching sense of humour just like Mac's and always added to the fun. Why Mac chose not to take up writing professionally, I could never understand – he had all the attributes.

Mac always wore a black shirt with a white tie. He was a loyal supporter of Oswald Mosley, who at the time was the leader of the English Blackshirts – a Fascist organisation. Just for something to do when Mosley had a local meeting, the gang would troop along to listen to what he had to say. Afterwards they would return to the café and have an in-depth discussion on what they had understood about his theories. With Mac being a loyal supporter of Mosley and Gillingham, the intellectual one, being anti-Mosley, some lively discussions took place, always in a friendly manner, in spite of their difference of political opinion. Gillingham, a regular member of the gang, was of average build and height, clean shaven, with a thin but pleasant face and keen, steel grey eyes that seemed to penetrate into other people's minds. He was clearly an intellect and very clever with words. He never seemed to say anything without giving it a great deal of thought – hence his nickname, 'the intellectual'.

When he and Mac were discussing anything, no matter what, the rest of the gang just listened without interruption. They both had a marvellous command of the English language, and knew how to use words to their best advantage. Both would have been good novelists or, at the worst, politicians! On an occasional evening while the gang were all in the café, Gillingham would teach the others Esperanto. A great deal of fun was had during these learning sessions. Mac learnt it very quickly, I found it more difficult. Once when Gillingham and I were in the café waiting for the others to arrive, I was to receive some of the best advice from Gillingham that I could be given, and that proved invaluable over the years. He told me that he sensed at times that I was overcome with his use of words, and saying that he thought me to be a little credulous. He finished by advising me never to develop an inferiority complex, advice that I was to be thankful for in the years to come.

I went to the café on most evenings, except Sundays. One evening when I arrived at the café, the others were there as usual but with a new face in addition. Mac introduced him to me as Dennis. Apparently, Mac and Dennis were old friends, from the time before Dennis joined the International Brigade in Spain, during the Spanish Civil War, where he had volunteered as an ambulance driver. While there he met and married an Austrian nurse, coming back to England to set up home together.

The Spanish Civil War was essentially a political struggle about who was going to rule the country, the Fascists or the Communists. Dennis's presence in the group opened up a new dimension to our political discussions. Although the debate was sometimes heated, the gang members always remained friendly. Dennis had seen the war at close quarters and some of his stories were not all that pleasant to listen to.

Dennis and his wife were going to set up home in the Forest Hill area, renting a double-bay, three-bedroom house not far away. One evening Dennis's wife came along to the café, and was introduced to the gang as Veda, adding the feminine touch to our meeting and. bringing a touch of brightness to the gang. She blended in well and the whole group interacted famously together. She was an extremely attractive woman, about the same age as Dennis, around the early twenties, about 5' 7", of medium build, with perfect, carefully styled shining brown hair, and hazel eyes that seemed to light up every time she used her beautiful smile. She had a fair complexion, that did not require make-up other than just a touch of lipstick, and she obviously had a keen dress sense. All this and a good sense of humour, made her a welcome addition to the gang, particularly as her English was very good. When she read some of Mac's risqué stories that he submitted each month to what was then the foremost sexy magazine in England, she laughed out loud and thought them extremely funny. Veda once asked Mac how he thought the stories up, and with his usual bellowing laugh, he confessed that that would be giving trade secrets away – not quite the answer she was expecting.

One evening in casual conversation with Dennis, I mentioned my problems at home, describing the friction between myself and Tom and the lack of any real home environment. Without any hesitation Dennis invited me to come and live with Veda and himself, saying that they had plenty of space, and impressing me that I would be more than welcome. I was extremely grateful and asked Dennis if I could have a couple of days to think about it, really giving myself time to allow my mother another chance to reconsider my previous offer of setting up home together, but without the troublesome Tom. When I arrived home later that night, my mother was busy in the kitchen. Having been told that Tom was in the pub, no doubt spending my mother's money, as I commented sarcastically, I again had an opportunity to make an approach about setting up home together. I pointed out that my mother would be far better off money-wise, not having to keep that lazy layabout of hers. I tried every angle and argument to convince her that it would be for the better, but nothing would change her mind.

"Okay, if that's your final word", I said, emotion clearly showing in my voice, "I will be leaving this weekend, on Saturday. I made this arrangement with friends at Forest Hill in case you turned my offer down. There's no life for me here. I only sleep here. You made your choice some years ago, now I am making mine, but unlike you I will keep in touch".

My passionate speech really shattered my mother – it was her turn now to plead, with the same negative results. I would not be moved. I confirmed with Dennis and Veda that I would be moving in on the next Saturday afternoon.

While packing my new suitcase ready to take to Dennis's, my mother again pleaded with me to stay. Again I made a speech that told her exactly what I felt:

"Sorry mother, but I have made up my mind to start a new life for myself. I was never really welcome here. Your only interest was the money I was bringing into the house, to help keep that layabout Tom of yours. I cannot stay here and watch him treat you like a dishrag. Either you don't want to see it, or you must be blind. You are welcome to him, listening to the pair of you constantly arguing over money. Mother, if you insist on staying here, I am going to lose you again. I lost you for seven years, but the difference is this time is it's me leaving you. If you ever change your mind, my offer remains open. In my opinion you are wasting your life with Tom. You deserve someone a lot better than him."

I gave my mother my new address, kissed her, then left. In spite of the way she had treated me, I still had respect for her. In many ways she had some good virtues, mostly towards other people, never towards her me. Maybe, I felt, it was my fault for not accepting Tom. It was her bad luck she got mixed up with the wrong man. There was no way I could condone Tom's laziness, and work-shy attitude. It wasn't as though he suffered any disability.

I settled in at Dennis and Veda's and quickly became one of the family. I had my own room, although it would not have mattered if I had had to share – it would not have been the first time. Veda had furnished my room comfortably – it looked as though it had been newly decorated, in a pleasant pastel shade. The floor was carpeted, and the room had just sufficient furniture for my needs – a much better room than I had at home or at the doctor's. Barry, another of the gang, also lived there. For the first time in my life I felt I was needed, and I now had the opportunity to enjoy a family life. Both Dennis and Veda made me feel really at home, sharing many happy evenings and times together.

My apprenticeship was progressing satisfactorily, now in my third year. I firmly believed that, whatever happened in the future, electricians would always be required.

By helping out in the garage as well, I was learning two trades, both to come in handy in later years. The money was reasonably good – I was receiving tips when working in some people's homes, besides free cups of tea and sometime something tasty to eat. I felt I had made the right decision. My boss had eight lock-up garages which he rented out to the most prosperous of the medical consultants that lived in the area. I saw an opportunity for earning extra money – my boss was only interested in keeping the cars in good repair, not keeping them clean. I asked my boss if he would have any objection if I offered to wash and polish the consultants' cars. He agreed readily provided that I did it in my own time – he had been very satisfied with the way I had cleaned his own car.

The consultants' cars never seemed to have a regular clean and I felt that, being in the medical profession, these eminent doctors should ride around in clean cars. In those days there were no drive-in car-washes – it all had to be done by hand. As many of the cars of the day had spoke wheels, these too had to be cleaned manually.

One day, soon after the idea had come to me, the chance happened for me to offer my services. On several occasions, I had seen the daughter of one of the consultants, a very pretty girl in her early twenties, washing her car, although I had never spoken to her beyond a polite greeting according to the time of day. It was this that gave me the idea, feeling I had nothing to lose, only gain. When I next saw her washing her car, I went up to her and jokingly suggested that, surely, she had better things to do than wash cars, adding that I would do it for her for five shillings. She thoughtfully pondered for a short while then said yes, please. I promised that I would make a really good job doing it, but could only do it in my free time. The car was a Wolseley Hornet semi-sports saloon.

Nearly every weekend, she would go off to Anglesey. Whether she had a boyfriend there, she would never divulge, but I, out of curiosity, made a note of the speedometer readings and proved to myself that she certainly had done a lot of mileage over the weekend. The car more often than not came back filthy dirty, usually covered in mud. I could drive the car to where I could work the best – I had no trouble with car keys, as there was always a spare set hanging up in the workshops. So I set about cleaning the girl's car for the first time of many. The wheels took me longer to do because they were wire spoke wheels and had never been cleaned properly before. To make a good job of them, I had to jack up each wheel in turn to clean the inside of the hub and spokes and then rotate it as I worked my way all round. All subsequent cleaning would be a lot easier and quicker, once I had finished the initial clean, so it was certainly worth the effort.

She was always pleased with the finished result – so much so that she thought it was worth a little more, giving me ten shillings. I in return would give the car an extra special wax polish once a month. I also cleaned her father's car, a big Sunbeam saloon which was only a town car so did not become quite so dirty, and thus being much easier to keep clean and polished. After a while, I took on all the other consultants' cars to clean and polish and very satisfied were my clients with the finished results. In fact, I had to turn away custom as word spread round, from potential clients from the BBC and from guests staying at the Langham Hotel, both very close to my place of work. On average I was earning about four pounds a week, including my wages. The weekly wage at the time for an unskilled worker was about three pounds a week, so I thought I was doing really rather well.

I taught myself to drive whilst shunting these cars around the mews . There was one particular car I loved to drive – it was a five-seater, open tourer Humber Snipe – a real beauty. The car belonged to a consultant, not long back from India, and was a rich maroon in colour. For my good works in keeping it clean, I always received a pound from him – he was a really generous gentleman. Because I was earning this extra money, I felt that, even if there was a depression on, I wasn't feeling the effects of it, although many thousands were.

Having a few spare pennies in my pocket, about one Saturday afternoon a month, I would travel to Peckham to see my grandmother. She had been very good to me as a youngster, and I felt I could now pay her back for the love and care she gave me, when she could hardly afford to do so. I asked her not to mention these visits to my mother.

The years of the Great Depression in the thirties were desperate times for most people, especially those living in the north of England and south Wales. You had to live through those days to experience the poverty and financial hardships the working classes were suffering. Those who were without a job had only their unemployment pay to meet their everyday needs – a huge challenge to their survival. At the time, England had a

National Coalition Government and, in spite of being the richest country in the world, in true British tradition, very little was done to relieve the people's sufferings. The only help the Government gave was to set up soup kitchens and assistance boards in the worst affected areas. To qualify for financial help from a tribunal, applicants had to bare their souls, and humble themselves to appear before them. The tribunals became known as the 'Shilling Means Test' and as very few people qualified, they then faced the sobering alternative of the workhouse. The unemployed of the north-east of England, mainly from Jarrow, organised a peaceful demonstration, marching from Jarrow to London, a little more than 200 miles away, with the hope of making the Government aware of their plight. On the way, they received massive support from the people, and a rousing reception when they reached London. There was little response or enthusiasm from the Government, just a few vague promises.

England was not the only country suffering from the Depression – all Western countries were facing the same problem. In the USA ('Buddy can you spare a dime' era) they adopted a realistic approach to the people's needs by creating jobs. Roosevelt managed to acquire federal money to finance the construction of a network of highways right across the USA from coast to coast, 3,000 or so miles in all, as well as the construction of the Hoover Dam and the Empire State Building. These major projects became known as 'The New Deal'.

The French decided to build a series of fortifications, the Maginot Line, along their land frontier bordering their arch enemy Germany, which history proved to be a waste of time and money, much to France's shame. In Germany, under Hitler, they decided to create the autobahns across Germany, for quick movement of troops and materials should war come.

In England, true to tradition, nothing was done. It took the Second World War to change the system, and the election of a Labour government after the war. (There was no way the victorious returning servicemen and women were going to be hood-winked, like their fathers were after the First World War.)

Earning the extra money gave me a feeling of security and I decided he would open a Post Office account with the surplus as a safeguard against a rainy day. Just after my eighteenth birthday in October 1934, I applied for my driver's Licence. I felt very confident about my driving. I cheerfully set off for Westminster County Hall to fill in the appropriate application form, handing it over with the five shilling licence fee. In return, I was handed my 'All Groups' driver's licence – there was no suggestion of a driving test as this was not instituted until the following year.

Considering the money I was earning, paying my weekly expenses and putting some cash into savings, I decided to save to buy a car. It took a while, but once I had enough money saved, I went along to a Peckham car dealer, selecting a 1926 Citroen four-seater tourer. It was already taxed, so the only other expense was for it to be insured for Third Party, Fire and Theft. I gave the dealer my nine pounds for the car, plus the insurance money, and then drove off, full of proud ownership, to Forest Hill to show Dennis and Veda my new possession. The very next Sunday, I took them both out for a spin, more pleased with myself than I had been for a very long time.

Although I had acquired my driver's licence for all groups in October 1934, I was quite surprised when I received notice the following February to attend the driving test centre at Norbury in south-west London the following month. I showed the notice to my boss, asking him what I should do. My boss read the notice and confirmed that, as it was an official notification, I would have to attend, promising to help me with the arrangements. Calling over his chief mechanic, he told him about me having to attend the test centre at Norbury, and arranged for him to take the company's van home the night before the test. Then he could accompany me to the test and bring the van back in the event that I failed. My car could be picked up later. The van was used as a general run-about for collecting electrical gear and spare parts from their suppliers, delivering them to where they were needed, or taking them back to the workshop. I had been driving the van around London's West End since holding my licence so I was very familiar with the vehicle and its peculiarities. There was no proper passenger seat in the front, just an old, grubby box used for small components, occasionally used as a passenger seat when turned upside-down.

On the morning of the test, I met the chief mechanic as arranged and together we travelled to the test centre. On arriving there, I reported in at the stipulated time, then returned to the van to sit and wait for the examiner. When he came out to the van, he opened the passenger door expecting to find a nice comfortable seat, but instead saw the grubby old box. The examiner took a closer look and I noticed the perplexed expression on his face, making me give a wry smile, hoping the examiner didn't notice. Thankfully, he did not seem to be too upset and quietly closed the door. Standing on the pavement, he put his head through the window opening, and pointed out a left hand turning about 100 yards away. He then instructed me to drive there, reverse into the turning and then return to where he was waiting. I managed this with little difficulty, in spite of a number of cars being parked there. I managed it at the first attempt very much in the style of a three-point turn. Back I drove to the examiner, stopping on the right side of the road and giving the correct hand signals to show that I was stopping. The examiner crossed the road to where I was still sitting in the van, telling me that I had passed the test. There were no questions on the Highway Code as these were not introduced until later on the same year. It seemed to be just a very simple driving test and I had no way of knowing if this was normal procedure or if the examiner was lenient because it was my living at stake, driving the van.

When the examiner had told me I had passed, he did not give me a pass certificate or papers confirming my pass – I assumed the test centre just notified County Hall. Very pleased with myself, I returned to the café where I had left the mechanic while I was taking the test. When he saw me so soon after leaving him, he expressed his amazement at the quickness of it all. I agreed that it was almost a farce, telling the mechanic about the expression on the examiner's face when he saw the grubby box. We celebrated my famous victory with a cup of tea and made our way back to the workshops laughing. I explained to my boss that, although I had passed, I had not been given anything to confirm it. My boss was happy that I had passed as he relied greatly on me driving the van. My driving licence was subsequently renewed each year, even after my war service, when a licence was not necessary, as long as one could show competence to drive.

The Citroen car was a bit scary to drive, especially on wet roads – it seemed to have a will of its own, giving me a few anxious moments. One of its main troubles was that it would go into a skid, with the driver not knowing where it was going to finish up. The main reason for the skidding tendency was that there were no front brakes. The foot brake operated a brake on the drive shaft, behind the gearbox, consequently locking the drive shaft, which in turn locked the rear wheels.

Some evenings I had to work late, doing electrical work after normal working hours on customers' business premises. On one such occasion, it had been raining earlier in the day and I was in my car making my way home. As I was proceeding round Trafalgar Square at about 11pm, making my way into Whitehall, I changed into top gear when, for some unknown reason, the car went into a front wheel skid. The car would not respond to corrective action but just careered diagonally to the other side of Whitehall, coming to a standstill when hitting the kerb. This could have proved fatally serious had a bus or another vehicle been coming in the opposite direction. After inspecting the car very carefully, I was relieved that there was no noticeable damage to the car.

Fortunately, the theatre-goers had left, otherwise there could well have been cars parked where my car finished up. If I hadn't stayed to have a drink with my electrician, after we had finished work, the consequences might have been much more serious. A small crowd was beginning to form around the car wondering how it finished up there, on the wrong side of the road. As it clearly could not stay there all night, I decided after further inspection, to drive it home, going slowly.

On reflection when back home, I put the cause down to a greasy road, plus the smooth tarmac road surface. One thing I decided for sure was that I was going to change the car – this one had given me too many scares, and I felt if I wanted to live longer, it would be the best thing to do. I saw the car I wanted in a nearby showroom, but before buying it I asked my chief mechanic to give it a critical inspection. He was quite happy to do this for me and after his inspection he gave it the all clear, but said to the dealer that it needed a new clutch before his friend would buy it. The dealer was quite prepared to do this, so I was advised to buy it. I made arrangements when I could collect the car, leaving a deposit, agreeing to trade the Citroen in part exchange. The car was a 1932 Fiat three-seater with a 'dicky seat', with a fold-down windscreen and four-wheel brakes. With the hood down, it looked a very smart car and, over the years, it proved to be a gem, easy to drive, and with no braking problems at any time.

I contributed a good deal of effort to the household, helping around the house and making myself generally useful in the garden. Dennis loathed any form of gardening, and would not even cut the grass. I made sure that I kept my own room clean and tidy – Veda remarked how domesticated I was. My years in the home and the scouts were good training.

One day, looking out of Dennis's sitting room window, I saw a beautiful, red four-seater Singer Le Mans standing outside the house parked by the kerb. These cars were produced in competition to the very popular MG Sports car. Standing there with its hood down, its long slender bonnet and silver wire, easy-change wheels, it was certainly a car to pull the girls, I thought. The car had been recently acquired by Dennis so the idea of attracting girls with it was out of order as far as Veda was concerned. It certainly put my car to shame. One Friday evening when all the gang, including Veda, were in the café, the question of car performance came up in conversation between Mac and Dennis. Mac had a small six horsepower Fiat, known at the time as a Doodle Bug. Because they could not agree which was the faster car, Mac challenged Dennis that he could beat him to Brighton and back. The challenge was accepted, and agreed to take place in the morning at 7.30am, for a small wager. I had ridden in Mac's car and knew it could 'go'. Mac thought he had an advantage, having the smaller car to negotiate through traffic and towns on the way and back. There was only one stipulated rule – each must bring back a photograph of Brighton Pier with the appropriate car in the foreground. It was a close finish. Dennis won by twenty minutes.

Occasionally on a Saturday night, Mac and Joe would go in Mac's car to a local club that had an open-air swimming pool, dancing, tennis and other social amenities, situated not far from Forest Hill. Mac was a down-to-earth sort of person – he could not stand people who tried to make out that they were better than they really were. He called the place 'the Snobs' Club'.

CHAPTER SIX

I had just over a year to do before completing my apprenticeship. One day a beautiful, new black and blue 14 horsepower Morris car was driven into the mews. I noticed that it had a sunshine roof and plenty of chrome to clean and polish. As the driver brought the car to a standstill, he asked me if my boss, Mr. Harrison, was in. I told him politely that he was indeed in, upstairs in the office. The man was in his middle fifties, smartly dressed in a brown business suit. He gave no name, but asked me if I would ask Mr. Harrison if he could spare a minute of his time. I climbed to the office and dutifully knocked on the door, before being told to enter. I explained to my boss that there was a man downstairs who would like to have a word but had to say I did not know who it was – he did not give a name – and that he did not look like a rep. Mr. Harrrison moved to the window that overlooked the mews, to see if he recognised the man, now standing by the side of his car. I was sent back down to invite the man up to the office and while I was talking to him, I noticed a younger man sitting in the back of the car, making no effort to get out. The man followed me upstairs, knocked on the door and was asked to come into the boss's office. I returned to my duties downstairs. After a while, both men came downstairs, my boss calling for me, telling me to wash my hands, and take off my overalls. When I returned, my boss instructed me to go with Mr. Tenenbaum to help to get his son out of the car. He had an appointment in a short while with one of their consultant customers. I was instructed to bring the car back to the mews and give it a thorough wash and polish. Mr. Tenenbaum would telephone the office when he wanted the car returned.

The younger man in the car, Mr. Tenenbaum's son, was severely physically handicapped, a wheelchair invalid. With the help of the nurse-receptionist, I managed to assist him out of the car and into the consultant's room. I returned to the car and drove it back for its wash and polish, delighting in the experience of handling such a beautiful car, one of the new range of Morris cars that Morris (later Lord Nuffield) had designed, a complete contrast to the 'sit up and beg', high-off-the-ground models. There were four new models of this type, 8, 10, 12, and 14 horsepower, either in a standard or deluxe finish. Only the 8 horsepower could be bought as an open tourer, or as a two-door, four-seater saloon. These proved to very popular, as were the other models. All models indicated their horsepower by a bonnet mascot fixed to the radiator protective cowling. The horsepower indicator on all cars of this period was introduced as cars were road taxed at £1 5s 0d per annum (£1.25) per unit of horse-power, thus resulting for instance, in an 8 horsepower car being taxed at £10 for the year.

The main difference in manufacture of this new breed of cars was a prefabricated under-slung chassis of pressed steel, as opposed to the heavy, 'U' shaped steel chassis that ran from the front to the back of older cars. This new type of chassis allowed the car to sit low to the road, giving it better road-holding in bad weather. Another improvement introduced was a new type of hydraulic, four-wheel braking system and shock absorbers (dampers) instead of the old friction type. The old cable- or rod-operated brakes always required a great deal of attention to make them effective. Another new feature was the electrically operated and illuminated traffic indicators showing which way the driver intended to turn. These were solenoid-operated by a switch on the central boss of the steering wheel. When not in use, the indicators rested within a slot in the middle door pillar. This ingenious device saved motorists from giving hand signals, which by law the driver had to give, whatever the weather.

The deluxe models were fitted with plenty of chrome to clean, leather seats, walnut dashboard, thick interior carpeting, and many other refinements, making the car a joy to own and drive. I noticed its smooth six-cylinder engine, easy handling and when cleaned and polished with its easy clean wheels, the whole vehicle looked beautiful, and as seductive as any film star of the day. The new body styling gave width to the car, easily seating three average adults in comfort on the back seat. I really thought that Morris had a winner with this car – at the time there were thirty-four other car manufacturers in England, not to mention the competing French and American cars. The best known British marques were all well established by this time, such as Morris, Austin, Bentley, Ford, Vauxhall, Rover and Hillman – amongst other marques, which eventually disappeared such as Alvis, Jowett, Lea Francis, Lancaster, Crossley, Talbot and A.C.

I drove the amazing new Morris back to the workshops for its wash and polish, feeling very superior. I took great pains over cleaning the outside, vacuuming the inside and giving an extra shine to the windows. Anyone would feel more than proud to own such a car. I took the car back to the consultant's and rang the doorbell, to let the receptionist know that the car was outside. After a few moments, I helped the handicapped young man back into the car and handed the car cleaning bill to Mr. Tenenbaum, who paid me immediately, together with a five shilling tip, saying what a good job I had made of the valeting.

Mr. Tenenbaum drew me out of hearing of his son and asked me if I did anything special on Sunday evenings. I admitted that I had no specific plans and asked, out of curiosity, why the question. The man explained that he needed a driver from 6pm to 11pm on Sunday evenings, as it was the only time he and his wife could go out together due to their son requiring constant attention. He was able to arrange for a friend to help out by minding the son, and particularly wished to take his wife to a West End cinema and then out for a meal. As it was an evening out for his wife, he did not want the hassle of parking the car – a chauffeur would be much more convenient. He also proposed the occasional trip down to Brighton, on a nice Sunday afternoon, for a change of scenery and a breath of sea air, followed by their usual cinema visit. He was sure that the change would do her good as she had a very tiring task looking after their son day by day. He surprised me by adding that he had one extra request, not his, he hastened to say, but that his wife would like the driver to wear a chauffeur's cap while she is being driven. This remark made me smile wryly but I foresaw no problem provided that Mr. Tenenbaum supplied the hat. Laughingly, Mr. Tenenbaum agreed, admitting that his wife was a bit of a snob. I said jokingly that she must feel like a Queen being driven around in such a beautiful car and could not blame her for that.

When Mr. Tenenbaum asked me where I lived and found out that it was in nearby Forest Hill, he was delighted, telling me that he lived in Canadian Avenue, Catford, only a short distance away. I knew the location well as it was just opposite Catford Town Hall, a route that most motorists used as a short cut on their way to Bellingham or Bromley. I must have passed their house many times but was puzzled as to where he kept the car, as there were no garages attached to the houses. It was explained that he had a private lock-up, not too far from the house, with light and water laid on. Mr. Tenenbaum gave me his business card, telling me to give him a ring any evening after seven if he should be interested. With no hesitation, I said that I could give him an answer immediately and very swiftly a time was agreed when I could start, all sealed by the two of them shaking hands. There was a further surprise for me when Mr. Tenenbaum asked me if I would like a Sunday morning job, driving over to clean the car on a regular basis, he was so pleased with the good job of it I had made that day. I was delighted and agreed to talk about that when we met on the next Sunday. I politely declined an offer to be taken back to the workshop – it was only a short walk away – and set off full of ideas about these new jobs I seemed to be collecting so readily.

On the Sundays while I was living with my mother, to keep out of Tom's way and prevent any arguments with him, I would often go to Peckham Rye Gardens, to smell the wonderful array of flowers, watch the peacocks strutting around and sometimes feed them, then wander through the rose-perfumed trellis gardens. I would sit there for a while, then walk down to Queens Road, Peckham, to enjoy a pint of Taylor-Walker's Mainline beer. After a while, I became friendly with some other young men who used the pub at Sunday lunchtimes. Although I had my weekday friends (the gang) who were intellects, always discussing art, literature and world affairs, these were working class lads who enjoyed a drink and watching a game of football on Saturday afternoons. They usually met again in a pub in the evening to have a drink, and would then go on to a local Palais for a dance, and to try their luck with the girls, finishing off the evening at a stall for a coffee and a bite to eat. On

Sunday evenings they would meet in one of their houses, to play cards, and listen to the latest gramophone records of Guy Lombardo, Roy Fox, Harry Roy, Eddie Calvert on his trumpet, Nat Gonnella, Fats Waller, and many others who were popular at the time. On odd occasions, depending on the weather, they used to go to a cinema. I often wondered why God created Sundays – was it just a day to torment people as to how best to enjoy it, and pass the time away? With me doing this new Sunday job for Mr. Tenenbaum, at least it gave Tom and my mother the chance to enjoy Sunday without the constant rows and aggravation.

The next Sunday, I travelled over to Mr. Tenenbaum's house at 5.30pm as arranged, from where we both set off to the lock-up to see where the car was garaged. When we reached the garage he gave me a bunch of keys, saying that he had a spare set for the garage and the car. He instructed me to keep them to save me having to go each time to the house, continuing by pointing out that there were a couple of hats in the boot for me to try on. The Tenenbaums wished to leave at 6pm, so I could leave my car in the garage until the Morris was brought back after the outing.

The hat business really tickled me, who had never worn a hat before and I wondered what I would look like as a chauffeur. The hat was certainly no match for the suit I was wearing, and I was concerned that, when Mrs. Tenenbaum saw me, she would make her husband buy a matching suit to go with the cap. I sat in the car outside the Tenenbaums' house, waiting for them to come out. Mrs. Tenenbaum came out first, walking down the pathway to the front gate. I smartly leapt out of the car to open the rear door for her saying, "Good evening, Ma'am", at the same time touching the peak of my cap – I thought I would give her the full treatment. As her husband climbed into the car, he thanked me in a quiet voice.

Mrs. Tenenbaum was very smartly dressed, obviously intending to make the most of the evening. She was good-looking, wearing a multicoloured, calf-length dress, a close fitting hat with no brim, partly covering her short, curly greying hair, and an expensive fur stole, fully fashioned silk stockings, and brown suede brogue shoes. She also had a necklace of cultured pearls and several gemstones on her fingers.

I closed the door when they were seated, and then walked round to get into the driver's seat, asking where I should take them – the reply, Leicester Square. During the ten-mile journey, they did not say a word to each other. I was watching Mrs. Tenenbaum's facial expressions in my internal driving mirror – I supposed she was mentally taking note of my driving skills as I negotiated the busy London traffic. Arriving at Leicester Square, I pulled up outside the cinema but, before I could get out of the car to open the door for them, the cinema commissionaire beat me to it. I just stood by the driver's door, not wanting to stop any tip the commissionaire might be given. When they alighted, Mr. Tenenbaum approached me and pressed some money into my hand at the same time telling me that he could use the car for whatever I wanted. He also suggested that I should find myself something to eat, but that I had to be back outside the cinema at 11pm sharp. I was well pleased with the evening so far and drove the car away to find a suitable parking place. After this first chauffeuring trip, to pass the waiting hours away, I would sometimes go back to Dennis and Veda's, having bought her a box of chocolates with Dennis's permission. Once in a while, I would go to see my grandmother, treat her to her favourite tipple, a jug of porter, talk with her about past times and slyly slip her a ten-shilling note. She had had a very hard life, always struggling to make ends meet. Now that I was earning good money, it was one small way I could pay her something back. I often wondered what would have happened to me if she had not taken care of me. On one occasion I asked about my favourite uncle Bill, to be told that he had joined the army as work was very hard to find and that he was presently fighting the Afghans on the north-west Frontier, one of the worst possible theatres of war – he was eventually invalided out after suffering malaria.

When I was not involved with the Tenenbaums, I would meet my Sunday drinking friends and make arrangements to see them in the evening for a game of cards, and listen to the latest gramophone records. In this way my Sunday leisure time was evenly spent. I never bothered to spend time with my mother, but not because I did not want to. On most Sunday evenings, she and Tom would go to the pub so that she could show off her fox fur and Tom with his cigars, and I had no intention of spending my hard-earned money on Tom.

I would travel to Catford and meet the Tenenbaums as arranged, take them out for the evening, return them home, put the car away, and then drive my own car back home, leaving the cap under the seat for the next time. It was a clear and simple routine. One Sunday soon after the system started, while I was cleaning the car, Mr. Tenenbaum arrived at the garage and described to me how delighted his wife was with the arrangement. He then asked me if I was doing any thing special that afternoon, but I only expected to see my usual lunchtime friends. Mr. Tenenbaum explained that as it was going to be a nice day, he thought a trip down to Brighton would do both himself and his wife good, to take in the sea air. I said that I would be available, so we agreed a departure time of 2pm and I was pleased that Mr. Tenenbaum agreed to pay me extra for my time. I was enjoying driving this car, its smooth acceleration and road-holding being a real driver's delight. The prospect of trying it out on the open road appealed to me.

I decided that I ought to check with Mr. Tenenbaum that I was not likely to upset his wife by travelling too fast. I recognised that the car could make very good speed and, if she was of a nervous disposition, then she could be upset. Mr. Tenenbaum was impressed by my consideration and agreed that a top speed of between 50 and 60mph would be completely acceptable. I thought that this would be good enough to satisfy my wish to try the car out on the open road. The car was a dream to drive, covering the 50-odd miles in just over the hour – Morris must be onto a real winner with this car, I thought as I drove the lanes of Sussex with my eyes sharp and my chauffeur's cap at a jaunty angle – I was in my element.

On reaching the outskirts of Brighton, I was instructed to make my way to The Grand Hotel on the seafront. As soon as I had pulled up outside the hotel, the hotel's doorman rushed forward and opened the door for the passengers to alight. Mr. Tenenbaum asked me what my estimation of the time was for the return journey, in order to arrive at London in time for their usual cinema visit. At least an hour was my calculated guess so we agreed that I should return to the hotel in order to leave at five sharp. I drove off along the scenic coastal road to Black Rock, with the most spectacular views across the English Channel, from at least 100 feet above sea level, staying there until it was time to go back to the hotel.

During the summer months that year, I made several trips to Brighton, not only being paid to do so, but enjoying the benefits of a day out at the seaside myself.

I had been doing the Sunday driving job for just on a year – it was filling in my spare time wonderfully, plus paying me for a job I really liked, driving the Tenenbaums around in such a splendid car. He was a good man to work for, generous when paying me, and never appearing as a demanding sort of man. Mrs. Tenenbaum had confided to her husband that she felt quite at ease and comfortable with me driving her around. On the occasional Saturday afternoon, I would take her shopping, then go over to Woolwich to pick up her husband at his place of business.

I had noticed from Mr. Tenenbaum's business card that he was a credit draper, known in the trade as a 'tallyman'. A tallyman has a business that supplies goods on credit, such as women's and men's personal clothing, suits and dresses, and household goods such as sheets, towels and blankets. These goods are supplied on the understanding that the customer paid a shilling in the pound for goods supplied. The credit limit was ten pounds, but could be topped up as the account was being paid off. Very many people were finding this way to clothe themselves and the family, and to renew household items when required, a wonderful and convenient way of shopping. Customers could only go over the credit limit if authorised by Mr. Tenenbaum himself.

One Sunday morning while I was cleaning the car, Mr. Tenenbaum arrived and after a casual chat, he asked me if I would be interested in earning some extra money. I was somewhat surprised by the question and was interested to find out what sort of work it would entail. Mr. Tenenbaum explained that in his line of business it was impossible not to have some bad debts. It was necessary to trust people to honour their debts but sometimes he needed to be more forceful. He described how he operated with three collector salesmen, working on a salary and commission basis, to sell goods and collect the money. He explained further that, if the customer did not pay for four weeks, he would be automatically put on the bad debt list. The majority of his customers had been with him for years, with little or no trouble, but there were bound to be a few bad apples amongst the good ones.

I was intrigued to know how I would fit into this pattern. Mr. Tenenbaum continued with his explanation by describing how the bad debt people knew the salesmen and himself, and what was needed was a new face, someone they did not know or recognise. This new face could be where I came onto the scene. At the moment they did not bother to come to the door, but they might do for me – Mr. Tenenbaum was prepared to pay five shillings in the pound for debts cleared. I could not resist this challenge but had to say that I could not do it during the day. This was not a problem as the best time to call on the people was Friday evening, on pay day. I would be able to use either Tenenbaums' car or my own, but would be paid extra if I used my less well-known vehicle. I thoughtfully pondered for a moment, then said that I would give it a trial for a month, agreeing that it would be best if I used my own car, as they might recognise the Morris.

That seemed sensible to Mr. Tenenbaum, so we arranged that I would travel to Woolwich the next evening to talk about it. In the meantime he would make out a bad debt list. When I arrived at the Woolwich offices as agreed, I was given a list of names and addresses, the amounts owing and for how long. I started this new challenge the following Friday evening working from five to eight, with most of my calls being at North Woolwich, travelling there by the free ferry. While I was on the ferry, I spent some time studying the A-Z street guide, at the same time wondering what sort of reception I would get, if any, when I started knocking on doors.

The doors I started to knock on were in a long street of terraced houses, with the main front door level with the pavement. I knocked on my first 'client's' door. A little girl answered the knock.

"Is your mummy in?", I asked, in a kindly tone. "No", was the quick response, with a look of childish innocence. While I was talking, I noticed the curtains move at the downstairs window.

"Is your father in?", I asked, slightly more severely. The girl was hesitant, not knowing what to say, and turned round and ran down the indoor passage. After a moment, a woman came to the door, closing it behind her as she clearly did not want anyone to overhear what was being said.

I had been primed by Mr. Tenenbaum as to what to say and do – always make sure you are talking to the right person, and above all always be polite, irrespective of what they say to you, was his good advice. I looked meaningfully at the clipboard, and asked her if she was Mrs. Forester. Having received her agreement that I was talking to the right person, I told her that it was more what she could do for herself than what he could do for her, explaining that I was there to collect money either from her or her husband, on goods supplied to them by Mr. Tenenbaum, and I informed her what the balance outstanding was. The mere word husband seem to unsettle the woman – many husbands were completely ignorant and unaware how their wives drifted into debt.

The woman was quite frightened and told me that she could not pay off the debt in full, timidly asking if she could give me a pound to start the repayments. In a very businesslike way, being as polite as possible, I made it very clear to her what my instructions were. I had to have the debt cleared as soon as possible, so I would accept the pound now and a pound a week until the debt was cleared. If I did not get payment, Mr. Tenenbaum would have the right to pass the matter over to the police as a case of acquiring goods under false pretences, as he had their signature for goods supplied. I added firmly that he wanted to avoid unpleasantness, and would be prepared to renew their credit, once the payments were made and the debt cleared. The woman opened her purse and offered me a pound, for which I gave her a receipt from the receipt book I had been given.

When I handed the woman the receipt, I repeated sternly what I had said about not letting me down. I would call the same time next Friday and expected to take another pound – the consequences would be entirely hers, if she failed to do so.

This was the pattern of most of the calls I made. Each time a young child answered the door, I supposed it was because it was so easy for mothers to train their children to tell fibs with childish innocence. I wondered if they would do the same, when they grew up and had children of their own. I certainly hoped not.

I stuck with the debt-collecting job for a month. In many ways, I felt sorry for these women who had dug themselves a financial hole, from which there seemed to be no escape. They were trying to make the best of a bad job, trying to feed and clothe themselves and their families, in the days of the depression. It was too easy to drift into debt.

Most of the men living in North Woolwich and the surrounding area worked in the London Docks – the majority were casual dockers or stevedores, receiving on average two days' pay a week. On the other days, they had to sign on the dole, receiving just sufficient money to keep body and soul together. Not many married women worked before the Second World War, relying solely on the husband's earnings to feed and clothe the family. To claim the dole, they had to have at least twenty-six consecutive weeks' stamps on their cards, to be eligible. The only other option was an appearance before the 'means test' tribunal. I knew how these people were suffering, so told Mr. Tenenbaum that I did not want to carry on doing this work for him.

It was sometime later that Mr. Tenenbaum told me that most of the people I had called on had cleared their debts. He gave me the money he owed me, commenting that whatever I had said to them had done the trick. I had certainly seen the raw side of life, and hoped I never found myself in the same situation, as I put the money in my Post Office account, watching it grow steadily.

On another occasion, Mr. Tenenbaum asked me how much longer I had to do before finishing my apprenticeship. When he was told that it was only a couple of months, he asked me how I would like to work for him as his office manager. Although I liked working for the man very much, I really did not want to spend the rest of my days in a 'dog eat dog' situation, apart from the fact that the idea of being shut up in an office all day did not appeal to me one iota. I asked Mr. Tenenbaum if I could have time to think about it, letting him know later on, just to keep my options open.

CHAPTER SEVEN

It was now 1938. I had finished my apprenticeship, and was promptly sacked, as was the custom. Very few apprentices, if any, carried on working for their former bosses – that was the common practice. While I was serving my apprenticeship, I was cushioned from the harsh realities of life, unlike so many millions of others during the days of the 1930s depression years. I was now a fully-fledged tradesman, and I had absolutely no intention of staying out of work for long. I had Mr. Tenenbaum's offer to fall back on if everything else failed.

When my boss called me up to his office for the last time to hand me my cards and my certificate of apprenticeship, it was a sad occasion for both of us, clearly showing in our conversation. Mr. Harrison was almost apologetic for having to sack me and told me quite clearly that I had been a bright pupil and a quick learner who really should not find it difficult to secure suitable employment in the near future. He actually expressed a wish that he would like to, but could not keep me on. I understood the situation, with a hint of sadness. When we shook hands on my departure, my boss assured me that, if any future employer wanted a reference, I could be sure it would be one of the best. I was most grateful for this generous offer. With the parting formalities over, I left the office for the last time to say my goodbyes to my workmates – a sad occasion after years of good relationships. "Please keep in touch", was the chief mechanic's request – I promised that I would. With that, I got into my car and drove off for the last time.

I had now joined the ranks of the unemployed, like so many millions of others. Faced with the prospect of finding a job, I signed on the dole to be told by the clerk that the first three days did not count towards claiming benefit. For my first full week, I was paid nineteen shillings – not enough to pay Veda for my keep. I carried on doing the Sunday job for Mr. Tenenbaum, although I did not tell him that I was out of work. I thought if I was still out of work after a month, I would approach him, but I did not want to rush into making the wrong decision.

As I was not offered any electrician's jobs by the Labour Exchange, I went to the local library to study the local and national newspapers. While scanning the national papers looking for my own type of work I noticed an advertisement for aircraft fitters at Fairy Aviation in Hayes, Middlesex, on the other side of London. I decided to go there to make further enquiries, and was very pleased to find that I had no trouble getting an interview. The interviewer, with pen and paper at the ready, asked me many technical questions, writing my answers down on the pad in front of him. After the questions were finished, the interviewer excused himself, coming back after a short while with a micrometer and a vernier gauge, giving them to me to read the settings, which I managed to do very easily, giving the correct answers. I was then asked if I could start on the following Monday, at 7.30am. I was able straightaway to give the man a reassuring answer. In spite of the fact that I had taken my certificate of apprenticeship with me in case it was needed, it was not even asked for, my answers and the technical demonstration had spoken for themselves. When leaving to go back home, I was feeling well pleased with myself. The rate of pay offered, being the top rate for skilled tradesmen, was one shilling and a penny an hour, plus war bonus of three pence an hour and a production bonus based on time and motion studies – all based on a 42-hour week.

I rushed back to Dennis's and told him the good news – both he and Veda were delighted and offered me their warm congratulations at finding work so quickly. For two years since coming back from Spain, Dennis had not been able to find a job and his absence abroad for those two years made him ineligible for unemployment pay. Veda had found a job as a nurse at a local hospital and at about the same time as my good fortune, at last Dennis had some good news of his own. He had been offered a job by his old boss as site foreman, building militia huts down at Fleet, not far from Aldershot, to commence in the spring in a few months time. In the meantime, he could work at Head Office, in London, in preparation for this Government contract. Dennis explained that he may have to give up the house, when starting his new job. With the threat of war looming, it meant the splitting up of the gang. It had been the most enjoyable years of my life – I had learnt a lot, and each member of the group had contributed in their own way in shaping my outlook on life. I felt very sad at the prospect of the gang dispersing, although I managed to keep in constant touch with one of the gang, Bert Greaves, who lived at Dulwich in south-east London.

When I reported for work at 7.30am sharp on the first day of my new employment, I was taken along to the wing-making section. Here I was introduced to the foreman and the chargehand. When I shook hands with the foreman, Mr. Pilgrim, I received a firm grip of welcome, but with the chargehand his handshake was limp and showed little enthusiasm of welcome. Mr. Pilgrim was in charge of the wing-making section and had an office situated against a wall with its entrance up a few steps from the workshop floor. When inside this neat office, he had a good clear view of the whole shop floor. He was in his middle fifties and seemed to have a pleasant personality. He had a full head of greying hair, a rounded but pleasant face, blue eyes, and a clipped military-type moustache. He wore no protective clothing, but dressed in a dark suit. The chargehand was an entirely different character and wore a khaki-coloured working coat. He had shifty eyes, never looking me in the face while talking to me. He was about thirty-five years of age – I thought he was not the type one could trust at all, and I had a strange feeling of not being at ease while talking to him.

I was shown to my workplace by the chargehand. He did not seem very helpful in showing me what I had to do – it seemed to me that he had taken an instant dislike towards me. At the morning break, I had a word with one of the other workers, to introduce myself, and to find out what tools I had to supply myself. I asked the chargehand for a chit for tools that the company supplied from their stores, quite surprising him that I had asked for these without any help from him. During my one hour lunchtime, I visited the local hardware shop to buy the tools I had to supply myself. Fortunately they were not too expensive and I even had time for a quick cup of tea and a sandwich before starting work again.

After lunch I was issued with a job card and settled down to some serious work. When the wing ribs emerged from of the press shop, they were all distorted and out of shape – they had to be straightened and fitted into a standard jig. To make it easier, the ribs were annealed in a special vat to soften them and make them pliable, to help the operator put them in their proper shape before hardening off again. While I was doing my apprenticeship, working in the garage, cars would come into the workshops with their panel work staved in. After stripping out the upholstery, and with the right amount of pressure in the right place, the dent would come out quite easily, with little trouble. I had been shown many tricks of the trade by the panel beater of their small workforce. This knowledge came in handy for the new type of work, and after I had completed two or three, I soon got into the rhythm of working – it was like shelling peas. I finished the first batch of fifty well within the set time, earning myself some immediate bonus. When I reported back to the chargehand, the man could not believe that the wing ribs could have been done properly. He crossed to my workplace and tried each one in the jig. As much as he wanted to find fault he just could not – everyone was exactly finished to the required standard.

As a result of this first encounter, the chargehand gave me more difficult jobs – ones that were not bonus-earning. I asked for and got the time and motion man to re-set the time, following discussion between the operator and the expert – the chargehand was not consulted. These men were very seldom on the operators' side. As long as the worker had a convincing argument they would listen, and on most occasions re-set the time. When I took my unilateral action, I seemed to rile the chargehand and as much as he tried to curb my bonus earnings, he could not. It was important to keep the bonus time within reason, so as not to spoil it for future earnings. The system could work the other way. If the time and motion study people thought that the operator was earning too much bonus, the time could be cut, so it was best to keep to the happy medium. This would, for instance, allow those that smoked to nip off to the toilet for a quick cigarette, without losing any time to their bonus earnings.

I decided to ignore the chargehand's attitude – I could feel the strong undercurrent of dislike towards me.

With the chargehand being staff, he was on a fixed salary and he rapidly became jealous of anyone earning more than him. It was easy for him to see what the operators earned, as in those days details of all the wages were written on the outside of the pay envelopes. It was always possible to recognise a tradesman by the way he went about his job – this chargehand was no tradesman. I thought that Pilgrim probably got his son-in-law the job, to keep him from being called up for military service and I sensed that there would be trouble between myself and the fellow at some time in the future.

By this time, the Government had introduced laws that prevented workers from changing their jobs without the permission of the Ministry of Labour, the idea being that they could move the workforce where they were most needed – this particularly applying to single men. I had thought of asking for a transfer within the factory. I got on well with my workmates – it was only the attitude of the chargehand that rankled, with his trying to make my life a misery during working hours. In a way I was finding some amusement in the verbal tussles between myself and the chargehand – it helped to relieve the monotony of factory life – so I decided to stay, and be a thorn in the side of my chargehand. Pilgrim, the foreman, did not seem to mix with his workforce, only seeming to be interested in keeping up production schedules, and leaving the day-to-day running of his section to his chargehand.

For three winter months, I had travelled from Forest Hill to Hayes, a journey of one and half hours, there and back. The workers had to clock on at the factory by 7.32am. If anyone was late, they had to clock in by 8am the very latest, after which time the doors were locked until lunchtime. These times were strictly adhered to. By the time I arrived back at Forest Hill at around 8pm in the evening, there was not a great deal of time for a social life. Saturday working until 4pm was introduced soon after I started working there and this cut into my leisure time even more. An employee had to work these hours, or be reported as an absentee to the Ministry of Labour. If it happened too often, the worker had to appear before a tribunal who had the authority to punish the offender as they thought best although there was an appeal procedure.

As Dennis was giving up the house in Forest Hill to move down to Fleet in Hampshire to start his new job, it meant that I would have to find new digs. This was a blessing in disguise, primarily because I was not looking forward to travelling to and from Forest Hill to Hayes during the next winter – one winter had been enough, making my working day too long and exhausting. I was visiting the Forest Hill Club on my own much more frequently, usually on a Saturday or Sunday evening. I had previously met a girl there, and I wanted to find out more about her. Up to this time my contact had been little more than a casual chat, a drink and a dance. She seemed to have many admirers, but was obviously unattached to any one male in particular, I had noticed. She always left the club with a girlfriend and I really wanted to get to know her better.

While having the last waltz, I cheekily asked her if I could see her and her friend home and, much to my surprise, she agreed. I escorted the friend home first to give myself a moment alone with the girl I really wanted to be with and, before saying goodnight, I made a date to see her during the week to go to the cinema. With such a promising start to my new friendship, I took time off to make sure I was able to keep the date.

The girl's name was Grace. She was slightly older than me, of slim build, and with dark brown hair in the popular pageboy style of the day, and lovely brown eyes. Her beautiful slender fingers were well cared for and she had a dark complexion – I thought she was Greek or Italian when I first saw her but, in fact, it was a result of a holiday with her cousin at Eastbourne where they enjoyed the sun that shone most of the week.

I had told Grace that I was in lodgings at Forest Hill, but would have to find somewhere new in the near future. Discussing this with her, I said that if I found digs at Chiswick in West London, it would be about half way between my work and Peckham where she lived, thereby asking her if she wanted to continue seeing me and what she thought of the idea. To my great delight, she said that she thought it was a splendid idea. Although I was not too sure of her response yet, I tentatively said that this would mean that we could carry on seeing each other on a regular basis. Grace was positive that she would like this too and I cheekily asked her if we could seal the suggestion with a kiss. We embraced and kissed for the first time, not passionately or lingeringly but just long enough to convince me that this was the girl I was going to marry.

It was arranged we should both go over to Chiswick on the following Sunday afternoon to have a look around. Then, if time allowed, we could go on to Kew Gardens, where there was a display of all the exotic flowers of the world kept under glass. I bought a local paper at Chiswick and looked at shop window advertisements. There was one that interested me, merely giving the address, but no phone number. Before going to take a closer look at the premises, we decided to have a cup of tea and a sandwich and checked with the café proprietor where Burlington Road was, the location of the possible digs. On the way there, we found that the underground station was within easy walking distance of the address.

I found the number I was looking for and parked the car a short distance away. Burlington Road seemed to be a very nice district, the houses well kept, and with a few cars parked in the road as there were no garages attached to the three-storey Victorian houses. The street doors were at pavement level, only a few paces from the front gate. Grace had decided to stay in the car and do a crossword – she was a crossword fanatic, solving the most difficult ones. I knocked on the door and was answered by an elderly lady. I asked her if the advertised accommodation was still available and she invited me in, leading me down a short passageway to the kitchen-cum-dining room, offering me a seat. The landlady still had the room available and asked me if I would like to see it, then taking me up to the first floor. At the top of the stairs she opened a door into a room at the front of the house, spacious and nicely furnished, with a double bed, a wardrobe, a tallboy, a bedside cabinet with a shaded light standing on it, and carpeted floor. I was shown where the toilet and bathroom were, just a short distance away on the same floor. I liked it immediately as the house reminded me very much of the doctor's house at Brockley. The room faced east so I knew I would have the benefit of the sun in the mornings.

Returning downstairs the kindly landlady offered me a cup of tea which I willingly accepted. She struck me as a very likeable person – tall and slender, about 60 years of age, her greying hair kept in a style that reminded me of a Chelsea bun, and neatly pinned up in position at the nape of her neck. She had sensitive features with no trace of make-up. Her eyes were bright blue, and her fingers, he noticed, were long and slender and well cared for. She appeared to me to lack any dress sense. I thought that she must be a widow as she was wearing a wedding ring, the only jewellery that adorned her well-manicured fingers. I mentioned to her I was now travelling from Forest Bill to Hayes for my work, and wanted to cut down the travelling time allowing me more of a social life. Having already decided that I really liked the room, I asked if I could move in, in which case I said, I could furnish good references if required. I was assured that they would not be necessary.

The rent was negotiated, including breakfast and an evening meal if required. It was agreed that I would let her know about needing an evening meal before leaving in the morning. I told her that I would have to leave by 6.30 in the morning, so there would be no need for her to fix me a breakfast as I usually only had grapefruit and toast with a cup of tea. She said that they would wait and see about this. I also mentioned I had a car and asked if I could leave it outside during the day, as I preferred to travel to work by public transport. That proved to be no problem either. A date was set for when I could move in, paying her two weeks rental in advance. She offered me a key straightaway, but I said I would pick it up when I moved in.

As I walked back to the car, feeling pleased with the day's transaction, I was thinking how well everything had worked out. Grace was still patiently waiting and eagerly asked me how the investigation had progressed. I responded with a smile that I was sorry to have kept her waiting so long but that it had been worth it as everything was now arranged and I would be moving in shortly. Grace was very pleased for me. Unbeknown to me, the landlady had followed me to the front gate and, when she saw Grace sitting in the car, she admonished me for not bringing the girl into the house with me. I thanked her but said that I did not want to trouble her and in any case, Grace was very keen to finish her crossword puzzle. As we drove away, we gave the landlady a wave as we passed – she seemed a really pleasant person. In fact, I had not been all that long, possibly no more than twenty minutes and it was still early afternoon, so I suggested to Grace that we should go on to Kew as planned as it was a such a nice afternoon. Grace very cheerfully replied that she would love to do that, but reminded me that she had promised her friend Valerie, a vivacious redhead, that she would see her at the club at 8pm that evening. So, after having a meal out, Grace and I made our way over to the club, so that the girls could have their usual Sunday get-together and chit chat. Valerie was Grace's best friend – a very likeable girl but the snob of snobs. One thing that I had noticed about Grace was that she had no snobbish airs – she just acted normally and naturally.

The club had an outside heated swimming pool so I decided to have a swim, while the two girls had their usual weekend chance to catch-up with the latest gossip, or other things girls talk about when together. No doubt I would be included in their conversation now that Grace and I were on the same wavelength.

I had already told Bert Greaves, my best friend, that I would not be seeing him on Sunday, as usual, because of having to find new digs. I hoped that the change of plan would not upset him and I was quite surprised to be told that it would give Bert a chance to catch up with some of the work that had been piling up indoors. Bert undertook a lot of French polishing for a local radio shop, on radio sets either repossessed or which had been out on hire. All the internal workings were taken out of the cabinets, before being delivered to Bert, to make it easier for him to handle and re-polish. Apparently the proprietor of the shop was getting a little concerned at the delay in the return of the finished cabinets, which was making his work overdue. Bert wanted to keep this work, as it was something he could do at home in his spare time, each cabinet taking only a short while to restore, once the scratches and other marks of misuse had been eradicated. One of the reasons why Bert particularly wanted to keep this work was because the shopkeeper always paid him promptly when he collected them – it was a useful bit of extra pocket money for him.

Up to the time I started courting Grace on a more permanent basis, the two girls met at the club on most Saturday and Sunday evenings. It was now arranged that Grace and I would see each other on Wednesday and Saturday evenings, then go on to the club so that I could take Valerie and Grace home afterwards. The two girls could thus have their usual get-together on a Sunday, while I spent some time with Bert Greaves. I also went out with Bert on Thursday evenings.

When I next saw Dennis and Veda, I told them about my new digs and thanked them most sincerely for all the good times we had together and what they had done for me. I gave them my new address, hoping that they would keep in touch. As yet they had no new address themselves, but said they would write as soon as they had found a suitable place in Hampshire.

I settled in to my new digs, finding them very much to my liking. The landlady made me feel comfortable and at home. I called it my half way house – travelling to and from work was much easier and better, not having to get up so early in the mornings, and usually being back indoors by 6.30pm. If I was in a hurry to get somewhere quickly after work I would take the car – usually on Wednesdays to see Grace, so we could have as much time together as possible.

The night before Dennis and Veda were setting off to live at Fleet, they decided to throw a party for the gang to celebrate Dennis's new job – it would be their last get-together. It was not the jolliest or the happiest of occasions, and not even Mac with his great fund of stories, could raise our spirits. What was intended to be a happy time turned out to be an anti-climax. It was suggested and agreed that each of us would keep in touch with Chris, the café proprietor, one way or another. We all wished Dennis and Veda good luck with his new job. It was now a real parting of the ways, all disappearing in our different directions. One way or another, we all decided, each would be involved if war should come to the country.

Chapter Eight

Spring 1939 was just around the corner and the evenings were becoming lighter day by day. I would travel over to Peckham and Dulwich by car three evenings a week. On Wednesdays and Saturdays my plan was to see Grace, my girlfriend, and on Thursday evenings and Sunday afternoons I would spend time with my best friend, Bert Greaves.

I had decided to smarten up the car so I had bought a new folding hood, as the original one leaked dreadfully whenever it rained. Most cars of the day were sprayed all-over black or blue, or a two-tone black and blue. I was ever the individualist, so when I had finished all the preparations, I painted the car white. When the new hood was fitted, it looked very smart indeed and was well worth the time, trouble and money spent doing it.

The car was not used regularly for travelling to and from work as I found it was more relaxing to use public transport, fortunately running almost door to door. If I did use the car for work, it meant driving along the Great West Road – with the traffic of the workers travelling to and from the factories along this road, and with traffic lights on virtually every road crossing, it took a great deal of time and patience to travel to Hayes. I did not think it was really worth the hassle, as there was no time gained taking my own vehicle. The only advantage in doing so was on the days I planned to leave work and journey directly to see Grace.

Bert Greaves, the friend with whom I spent Thursday evenings and Sundays, was six feet tall, in his early twenties, with hazel eyes and brown receding hair. He was lithe and willowy in his movements, especially on the dance floor, and always seemed to be in a happy frame of mind, never at a loss in conversation. He could turn on the charm when it suited him, even more so if there was a girl involved. He had no regular girlfriend but preferred to be footloose and fancy free, making the most of any opportunity that came his way. He expressed himself like a continental, gesticulating with his hands, showing off his long and slender fingers.

Bert was a self-employed French-polisher, and extremely good at it. I occasionally saw some of his work when I picked him up at Maples, the famous London furniture emporium, before going out together. For them, he mainly re-polished repossessed grand pianos, or those that had been out on loan, bringing them back to a brilliant finish – so good, I thought, that one could safely use the surface as a mirror for shaving.

On most Thursday evenings, Bert and I would go to one of London's main ballrooms. Bert was a magnificent dancer – being tall and lithe, he moved like Fred Astaire. No matter what the tempo or rhythm was, he had no trouble finding partners. I thought he had missed his vocation, really believing that he should have been a professional dancer on the London Stage – his dancing was sheer poetry in motion. For some reason unknown to me, Bert had a positive attraction towards Jewish girls – he could never understand why. By the time that the dancing had come to a close, Bert had always linked up with two girls, one for himself the other for me. He must have done his persuasive homework on the dance floor, before asking to see her and her friend home. On most occasions this involved a trip over to Whitechapel in east London.

As soon as we were in the car, Bert wasted no time asking for a kiss and a cuddle and I could never remember any girl refusing him. He was a great charmer and all the young ladies seemed to melt when in his company. As the driver, I had to concentrate on driving, keeping my eyes and mind on the road in spite of the activities of my friend and the girl in the back seat. My car had a bench-type front seat, so if the girl Bert had found for me was the snuggle-up type, this was a little awkward and I really needed to focus on the driving rather than the alluring charms of my passenger. The truth was, I regarded myself as semi-engaged, and did not want to cheat on Grace – I would just settle for a goodnight kiss. I went along with Bert's liking for girls, as he was such fun to be with. Of all the girls we saw home, not once did he make any further arrangements to see them again. It was hail and farewell, see you on the dance floor.

Bert never boasted about his exploits with any of the girls we had seen home. His simple philosophy was that girls were to be enjoyed, and how far this enjoyment went was up to the girl. He was a born philanderer. On several occasions, I tried to coax it out of him but each encounter was a closed chapter. Not even with his best friend would he share his exploits – it was as though he had made a secret pact with each girl, hugging the secret only to himself.

I very seldom went out with Grace on Sundays, not even for a trip down to the coast. Grace wanted to spend time with Valerie, her best friend, to try different hairstyles and talk girl-talk. They had been friends for a long time, long before I came on the scene and I did not want to spoil their relationship. So, winter and summer, I went out with Bert instead. On one such occasion, Bert thought we should try our luck at the Ritz in London's Piccadilly. He had found out that Tea Dances were held there on Sunday afternoons in the hotel's lavish ballroom and that they were open to the general public for a mere three shillings and sixpence entry fee. Refreshments were available for an extra charge. For some reason, although Bert enjoyed his dancing, he did not fancy any of the girls, or any of the rich widows that frequented the Ritz, or possibly even lived there. With no girls to spend the rest of the day with, we set off for Hyde Park, for a drive around in the fine weather. We stopped for a while to listen to the orators at Speakers Corner, putting the world to rights and haranguing the crowds with their own particular opinions and remedies. This proved to be our only visit to the Ritz and although we agreed that it was a reasonably good day, we decided that we preferred our usual patterns for having a good time on Sundays.

More often than not, on summer Sundays after having lunch at Bert's home, the two of us would set off for a spin around the local park. The speed limit was 5mph so I could not be 'had up' for loitering. This speed limit suited Bert, as he was always on the lookout for pretty girls to pass the time away with – if he spotted some likely prey, he would ask me to pull up. Without any hesitation at all, he would approach them, even complete strangers, and after talking to them for a short while with his charming line of patter, the girls would be in the car. We would all sit in the car for a while talking and then go to the park's café for a cup of tea or an ice cream, and maybe afterwards a boat ride on the boating lake.

Bert seemed to have some inbuilt sense of picking the right girls. Not many people owned cars before the war, so car rides were always an added attraction to relieve the Sunday boredom and we two lads with our splendid white car were a real lure to the young ladies of the day. I would often drive to our favourite Sunday place which had a beautiful view over most of London, a spot mainly visited by courting couples. Naturally Bert would be trying his luck with the girls we had picked up, frequently staying to see London in silhouette against some wonderful sunsets. Afterwards, we would take the girls home or to wherever they wanted to go. Some of these girls may have thought I was a bit slow, and although I was tempted to follow Bert's uninhibited example on many occasions, it did not seem right with Grace in my life. For certain, I knew all about the birds and the bees from my earlier involvements, so it was not a matter of not knowing what to do. As far as Bert was concerned, variety was the spice of life and he had no inhibitions about girls – it was just a pleasant way of spending a Sunday. Although Bert and Grace never met, I used to tell her about his antics, and also about taking the girls home. I had nothing to hide – as far as I was concerned, it was just a harmless bit of fun. Grace never showed any dissent about me doing this or asked me not to continue my escapades with Bert – in fact on many occasions she had a good laugh at the tales. She seemed not to be jealous about the dancing either, although she was an extremely good dancer, having been encouraged by her mother to take up ballet and ballroom dancing as a youngster.

During 1939, England was gearing up for the threat of war. At the Fairy Aviation factory, they were keeping a steady flow of Swordfish torpedo-carrying planes in production. These were sea-based planes operating from an aircraft carrier – very few were land-based. When these planes were first designed by the Air Ministry, no one at the time thought they were going to be the 'sitting ducks' they turned out to be, against the Germans' powerful and accurate Bofor rapid-fire guns.

Because I was so busy at the factory assisting with the build-up of arms and armaments, holidays and weekends off were very precious times for relaxation. The official list of reserved occupations was published in the National Press – mine was on it, but Bert's was not. The Government's idea behind this was to segregate the non-essential workers from the essential, in relation to the war effort. The non-essential classifications of people were to be called up for military service first. More women were being trained to take over many of the skilled jobs in factories that men were presently doing, thus releasing men for call-up or for more important and essential war work elsewhere.

Because of Bert's classification in non-essential work, I suggested to him that we should have a holiday together sometime late July or early August. Bert chose early August as Grace had a long-standing holiday arrangement with Valerie – most people only had one week's holiday a year:

When the chosen time came round, Bert and I gathered some clothes and other items together, packed the car and set off for our holiday. We had nothing special planned, deciding to take each day as it came. We travelled westwards, with me heading in the direction of Cheddar Gorge in Somerset in the West Country, hoping to make it our first overnight stop. Arriving there around 5.30pm, we were fortunate enough to find some excellent digs at three shillings and sixpence each, for bed and breakfast. After a swift wash and brush up after the long car journey, we decided to find a local pub where we could have a beer and a sandwich each.

The nearby pub was friendly and we found the beer first-class. For the sake of something to do, we started playing darts – I was reasonably good but Bert was not so skilful. Not far away in the bar were some young fellows watching, possibly weighing up the opposition before suggesting a match. The visitors eventually accepted a challenge from the local lads and won the first game – but that was the only one – the locals won every game throughout the rest of the evening, with all of them having a very good time at Bert's and my expense. At closing time the pair of us could not remember where our digs were – it was daylight when we had left for the pub. We knew the general direction to go but by now it was pitch dark and the whole village looked altogether different even though we knew it was no more than five minutes walk away. We had both had a fair amount of fine Somerset beer to drink, so our vision was slightly impaired. Walking back and forth, stumbling somewhat in the dark, we eventually found our lodgings. It was by good fortune that the landlady had switched on the outside light. The fact that the cottage had a very long front garden made it much more difficult to find the right place and, if it had not been for the light, we would probably not have found our digs at all that night.

There were no street lights in that part of Cheddar, just an almost total darkness. Because of this, when we arrived to book in, the landlady suggested leaving the car off the road, at the back of the cottage, for safe parking. In those days, any vehicle parked on a public road during the hours of darkness had to have parking lights left on, risking a flat battery in the morning. It was well past 11pm when we found our digs and the poor landlady had had to stay up, because we had not been given a key. We both apologised profusely, realising that we had caused the good soul some inconvenience. She saw the amusing side to the situation – 'townies' coming down to the countryside and being routed at darts by the locals and plied with strong ale. She offered us a welcome cup of cocoa after which we trundled off for a much needed sleep. In the morning, after a good English breakfast, we thanked the landlady warmly, giving her a box of chocolates as a mark of our appreciation.

After seeing directions to the Cheddar Gorge, we swiftly found our way to the spectacular gorge itself and took a trip down the caves, taking a number of souvenir photographs, staying there for several hours to make sure that we saw all the sights. From there we headed further west towards Weston-super-Mare, the Somerset seaside resort, arriving at about 5pm. Bert and I found more good digs, for two shillings and sixpence each for bed and breakfast. Being early evening when we arrived, the landlady offered us a cup of tea and a sandwich each, at an extra charge, which we both gratefully accepted. While eating, Bert asked the landlady if there were any dances or entertainments on anywhere locally. She replied by saying that she wasn't too sure, but pointed out that on most evenings, there was dancing at the Pier Hall. I suspected that Bert had itchy feet or was girl lonely.

After spending a few minutes tidying ourselves up for an evening out, we directed our steps towards the Pier but not before asking the landlady for an address card and telephone number. This time they were able to leave the car outside the digs as there was a parking place off the road, in front of the boarding house.

We were in luck – there was dancing was going on in the Pier. Bert wasted no time, either with his dancing or finding a girl. Having been very quickly onto his feet and having greatly enjoyed the dance, as was the custom in those days, he escorted the girl back to her table where her friend was sitting. Bert stayed talking to both girls, then beckoned to me, who had been sitting some few tables away. Bert introduced his partner as Anne and her friend as Mary. Anne appeared to be in her early twenties, very good-looking, a brunette with long, wavy hair resting on her shoulders, brown eyes and generous lips and mouth. She was fashionably dressed in a flared, floral calf-length skirt with a white satin blouse, making her look very attractive. Mary was not to be outdone. She was in her late teens, a very attractive blonde with a coiffure hairstyle, a trim petite figure and perfect blue eyes. She was wearing a red and white patterned summer dress with a halter neckline, not only revealing her figure but also a gold cross and chain around her neck. Both girls lived in Plymouth and were on a week's holiday at Weston.

As usual, Bert was not slow in coming forward, and was quick to make the proper introductions, asking if we could stay and join them at their table. The girls looked at one another and said in unison that they would love us to. Very contentedly, we spent the rest of the evening together, drinking, dancing and enjoying pleasant conversation, finding it a very enjoyable evening in such attractive company.

After the dancing, at closing time, it was suggested by one of us that, as it was such a lovely summer evening, we should take a walk along the beach. The girls readily agreed to the suggestion. They did not seem to be in any hurry to return to their digs, no more than Bert and I were, making the evening stretch out as long as possible. In jovial mood, we set off for a stroll along the beach. The tide was in and the sea was just lapping along the wide, flat sand so we decided to have a paddle along the way – quite a welcome relief after dancing for most of the evening. We strolled along now in separate pairs, with Mary and I leading the way, me with my arm around Mary's waist, checking now and again to make sure that Bert was not lagging too far behind with Anne.

All the dancing, talking and the sea air had created a thirst, so we stopped at a beach café for a coffee, when Bert offered to see the girls back to their digs. On the way there, Bert suggested to Anne that she and her friend would be welcome to join him and me, touring Devon and Cornwall for the rest of the week. He added that, although we greatly enjoyed their company, we would not be able to see them again as we were planning to leave in the morning to continue our touring. We arranged for Anne to telephone Bert by 9am the next morning if they wished to accept the invitation to finish the week together – then I could call round to their lodgings to collect the baggage.

Once we arrived at the girls' lodgings, Bert made sure that he received his goodnight kiss as usual. There was no phone call in the morning, me thinking it was just as well – our budget would not stretch to the luxury of treating girls to a free holiday. I had taken my Post Office savings book in case of car emergencies, or in need of extra cash but even so, there were only limited funds available. As on many previous occasions, Bert managed to get carried away when he saw a pretty face.

I was secretly pleased that Bert's persuasive charm had not worked this time and, to my relief, Bert did not seem too upset at the prospect of having only my company. I supposed it was worth having a try as there was everything to gain, nothing to lose.

After a marvellous breakfast, we loaded our gear into the car to make our way along the north Devon coast to Minehead, staying there only a short while for a coffee. Then on to Porlock where we could admire the most stunning view across the Bristol Channel. From there, I drove to the most picturesque twin seaside coastal villages of Lynton and Lynmouth, staying for lunch. We continued our exploratory journey to Ilfracombe, another of north Devon's beautiful coastal towns and thence to Clovelly which I thought was the quaintest of all so far. If we had had more time, we would have taken a donkey ride up and down the steep main road of this charming and unique village. Talking it through, Bert and I agreed that it was a pity that we could not stay longer in any of the places we had so far visited – each one deserved a longer stay, but I wanted to arrive at Tintagel in time to find digs for the night.

Eventually we made it to Tintagel, arriving rather late and choosing to have a meal before seeking digs. Unfortunately we had left it rather too late and there were no rooms available in the town. I really did not want to double-back to Boscombe and the nearest town of any size was Newquay, farther down the coast. As we both particularly wanted to see King Arthur's Castle, we reluctantly decided to sleep in the car that night. Of all nights, there had to be a thunderstorm – fortunately there was no wind, with the rain coming straight down, otherwise we might have received a soaking as there were no side screens on the car to keep the rain out.

In the morning, after a very uncomfortable and damp night, we took a quick look around the ruins of the castle, taking a few photographs, and then continued to Newquay to find somewhere for a very necessary wash and a warming breakfast. Newquay is one of the few seaside towns in England where one can go surfing, with people coming from far away to enjoy the sport. I drove on down the north Cornwall coast, passing through some very delightful and wonderful scenery before reaching St. Ives, where we stayed for lunch, taking in the charm and scenery of the town. It was decided over lunch that our next overnight stop would be at Land's End, the extreme tip of mainland England, but that we would be sure to find suitable digs first. The idea of sleeping in the car for two consecutive nights did not appeal to either of us.

Our luck was in again and it was not difficult to find a very pleasant bed and breakfast establishment quite quickly. Whilst talking over a meal later, it seemed that Bert was not interested in dancing or girls that evening. I wondered if he was thinking that there was more to life, after travelling through some of the most spectacular and beautiful scenery that that part of England had to offer. Many times while travelling down the north coast of Devon and Cornwall, he had remarked that he did not think such scenery existed, saying that it was a pity we could not have stayed longer in some of the places we passed or visited if we wanted to complete the tour we had planned.

Leaving Penzance, after a visit to St. Michael's Mount, we made our way along the south coast of Cornwall to Mevagissey, a picturesque Cornish coastal fishing village, arriving at around 5pm, in time to find lodgings and a good meal. The place we eventually found overlooked the picturesque harbour. We spent some time after supper, wandering round the town and harbour, taking in all the new sights and sounds. In the morning, having enjoyed a cooked English breakfast, we took a last look around before leaving and noticed, down by the harbour, an 8-foot shark hanging up on a jib. I took a photograph of this monster which had caused quite a stir with the locals and the visitors.

The next stop was Polperro, travelling there by way of Lostwithiel. We arrived in the early evening at this, our last overnight stop before heading home, and secured accommodation at a cyclists' hostel boarding house. No visit to Polperro would be complete without visiting The Three Pilchards pub, where Bert and I had a very enjoyable evening, laughing and joking with the local fishermen. I decided that fishing must be a thirsty business as the two fishermen we were sitting with each drank at least six pints of rough cider. Polperro itself was a quaint and delightful place to visit and stay – the pub was within a stone's throw of the quayside. We found a long, high cliff walk where we could rest and enjoy looking over the English Channel. In the morning before setting off on our 200-odd mile journey home, we were given breakfast of boiled mackerel, finding it tasteless and not at all appetising, and bread and jam with our cup of tea.

The money had only just worked out, without me having to 'dib' down my Post Office savings account. I wondered what would have happened if the girls had accepted Bert's invitation to join us. I was not sure whether Bert had a Post office account book – he never mentioned it. In those days, for most people, it was the only way one could carry spare cash around – one could draw up to ten pounds on demand at any Post Office.

Before leaving Polperro, I serviced the car for petrol, filling the tank up, topped up the engine oil, and checked the water level in the radiator. Finally I checked the tyre pressures, ready for the long drive back home. Up to then, the car had been behaving perfectly and apart from the one night's thunderstorm, the weather had been perfect, allowing me to drive most of the time with the windscreen folded down. Over the journey, the car averaged forty miles to the gallon. The journey home was uneventful, taking six hours driving time to reach Chiswick, where the car suffered a puncture.

While in Chiswick, I thought I would show Bert my digs, with the idea in mind of a cup of tea, and maybe something to eat. We were unlucky for once as the landlady was, out so I pushed a note through the letterbox, to let her know I was back safely, and would see her later. Feeling peckish, we returned to the car to take Bert home, staying there for a while to have a very welcome cup of tea. I left Bert to tell his mother all about our trip and, as it was still early afternoon, I decided to call on Grace, hoping that she would be in. Before leaving for my trip, I had made no firm plans to see her, as I was uncertain what time I would be back. Luckily Grace was in and we immediately fell into a warm embrace and a welcome kiss, enjoying the pleasure of each other's company after a few days apart. Grace remarked on my bronzed appearance. I explained that I had been driving most of the time with the windscreen down as the weather had been gorgeous all week, and I supposed that that was the result. Grace knew what it was like as she preferred to travel with it down, depending on where she was going.

I had said good evening to Grace's mother when I first arrived and she invited me to stay for a meal at teatime after which it was suggested that we go up to the club. While Grace was making herself presentable, I chatted to her mother, telling her how my trip went, and the wonderful scenery and interesting places I had passed through. When Grace was ready, we set off for the club, hoping that Valerie would be there – as a rule she would be. As I expected, she was there, still husband-hunting. She had set her sights very high – there would be no factory worker for her. As soon as I saw her, I pulled her leg by asking whether she had had any luck yet in the search for a suitable man. We stayed chattering, dancing and enjoying a few drinks until it was almost midnight. I offered to take Valerie home – she lived on the other side of Peckham, not far from the Old Kent Road – but she was not without admirers and had already fixed herself up with a lift home. Before leaving the club, Grace asked Valerie if she would mind skipping their Sunday meeting. It was not a problem for her, and she nodded understandingly. I thanked her, giving her a gentle peck on the cheek, for being so considerate, telling her that she was an angel.

When we returned to Grace's mother's house, her mother was in bed, but still awake. Until her flock came in she always left her bedroom door ajar – the last one to say goodnight to her closed it. Grace was the last in and quietly went to ask whether, as it was so late, could I stay overnight. She agreed but added quite sternly that it would only be provided I slept in the brother's room. Grace replied swiftly that, of course, that would be the way.

Grace said goodnight to her mother, closed the door and returned to the sitting room where I was waiting, saying with a bright smile that her mother agreed to my staying over. I was well pleased with the idea and happily accepted Grace's offer of a quick nightcap. As we stood in the kitchen waiting for the kettle to boil, she and I kissed tenderly, and held each other very close. I could feel her enticing body as I embraced her tightly and longed to continue our intimacy through the night. It was now nearly 1am, and it took a great deal of restraint on both sides to part, to go to our respective bedrooms, after several more lingering and loving kisses.

In the morning before I was really awake, I was greeted by Grace with a kiss and a steaming cup of tea. It was customary for one of the family to get up first on Sunday mornings to allow her mother to have a welcome lie in. After she had done this, she then returned to me, sitting on the end of the bed. I pleaded with her not to sit so far away but to snuggle up closer. As Grace moved up towards me, I threw the covers off inviting the girl to join me in bed. Instead Grace replaced the covers and lay down beside me on top of the bed, allowing me a kiss and a cuddle whilst preserving her modesty. I had to accept the situation, and would have to be patient as far as the lovely Grace was concerned.

Grace wanted to know what plans had been made for the day, and I acknowledged that I did not anticipate seeing Bert that day, but as the weather forecast sounded fine, I thought that a trip out in the country somewhere after lunch would be acceptable. Grace welcomed the idea and the two of us spent a cheerful morning together, helping with lunch and offering to do the washing-up afterwards. While Grace was getting ready, I thanked her mother for allowing me to stay overnight.

We had no particular place in mind for our trip but it was a pleasant, warm and sunny day with very little cloud or wind. I installed Grace in the car and we motored along at a steady speed until we came to a local beauty spot known as Box Hill, not far from Dorking, spending the rest of the day there. We walked hand-in-hand, talking about our various plans for the future, and taking in the splendour of the panoramic view from the top of Box Hill, enjoying each other's company for every minute of our day's outing. To end our visit, we sat at the open-air café for a refreshing cup of tea and a sandwich, then drove back to Grace's home. I had to be at work in the morning, the first day back after my splendid break, and I did not want to be late back to my digs.

When we arrived back at Grace's home, we were greeted by Grace's mother asking if we had had a good day, and curious to know more about this young man who had started to take such an interest in her daughter. Grace's mother had experienced a hard life, bringing up seven children single-handed from their early teens, when her husband had deserted her. There were now only three at home, Grace, her younger sister Margaret, and her elder brother. Despite all the hardship, she always had a bright and cheerful disposition. She was in her early sixties, short and stocky, a country girl born and bred. Her short, curly, greying hair needed little effort to keep neat and tidy. Because of her rosy cheeks, she always reminded me of a cherub with her cheerful face. Her married name was Mrs. Chapman, but she was known to her friends and family as 'Mrs. Chap'. It had been quite a long time before Grace introduced me to her mother, as we always met at the club or some other place. When I eventually did meet her, we got on famously, maybe due to the fact she had six daughters, and only one son, so another man around the house was welcome.

I had no trouble having time off for a holiday, as the factory operated staggered holidays to help keep production going. A worker could only take one week at a time. After one year's service, a second week could be taken but only as odd days off. Grace and I had made no plans to have a holiday together as it really was not practicable at that time.

The next couple of months seemed to pass fairly normally, although the threat of war was increasing and hostilities looked inevitable. One did not know what to expect next. Gas masks were being issued to the general public, with instructions on how to use them, as a precaution against sudden attack. Local Councils were delivering Anderson outside air raid shelters to every household, with instructions on how they should be installed. These shelters were named after Sir John Anderson (later Lord Waverley), the Home Secretary of the day. If people were too old to do this themselves, the Council would send workers to complete the work for them. Local Councils were building community air raid shelters and all men over military age or who were medically unfit, had to register for air raid precautions, known as the ARP. At certain locations, huge water tanks were built to provide water for fighting fires from incendiary bombs. When Winston Churchill took over and formed his own Government, the new Home Secretary was Herbert Morrison – many homes were issued with indoor shelters, named after him. The Morrison indoor shelter was six foot long and five foot wide, with a quarter-inch steel plate on top, heavy-gauge steel corner supports and heavy wire mesh around the sides to prevent debris coming in. These had to be erected in a downstairs room where there was sufficient space. Only a direct hit would shatter either shelter.

When I next met Bert, it was decided that we would call in at the café to see if any of the other gang members had shown up, and to catch up with the latest news. In between serving his other customers, Chris, the owner, was able to report that Dennis was doing well down at Fleet, Mac was on the reserve list and had been called up and Barry was Dennis's office manager. Gillingham, he believed had been threatened by his father, an old soldier, who had promised to kick him out of the house if he failed to join up. No news had come from him for some time, so they did not know exactly what had happened to him. It seemed clear that the gang were not to meet again, much to my dismay. Bert and I were still meeting as usual on most Thursdays and Sundays. We were able to travel around quite a bit as petrol had not yet been rationed, although it was expected to be at any time.

Bert had confided to me on several occasions that he would not answer his call-up papers when they came. He explained that he was the family's breadwinner – his mother was an epileptic and could not work, he also had a younger brother and an 11-year-old sister to support. I was very sympathetic, realising that Bert was in a very difficult situation, with many responsibilities.

Chapter Nine

War was declared on Sunday 3rd September 1939, at precisely 11am, the ending of the time limit given by Chamberlain to Hitler. For a few months, it was known as the 'phoney war'. No land forces were engaged in battle – the only activity was at sea, between the British Navy and German U-boats.

Life seemed to go on very much as usual, as far as the people were concerned. The Government introduced petrol rationing, along with rationing for food and some other commodities. Ration books were issued to all civilians – everyone was treated the same, except for farmworkers, who were entitled to an extra two ounces of cheese per week. Because of petrol rationing, I had to cut down on my journeys to Peckham and Dulwich. I could only see Grace once a week, on a Saturday evening for a few hours, and, if time allowed, I was able to meet occasionally with Bert just to keep in touch.

In addition to the Saturday shifts at Fairy Aviation, Sunday working was introduced, so for me it was mostly bed and work. Neither my landlady nor Grace was on the phone so there was no way we could keep in touch, other than my Saturday evening visits to Grace. For this reason, I asked my landlady if I could invite Grace over for the weekends, from Friday to Sunday evening. This was the only way as far as I could see that we could spend more time together. I offered to pay the landlady extra money if she agreed to my suggestion. Much to my surprise, the landlady readily agreed to this arrangement without any reservations at all – she seemed to treat me more like a son than a lodger.

When I next saw Grace, I told her of the arrangement I had just negotiated with my landlady. Just as I was, Grace was feeling very unhappy that we could not see each other as often as we used to, or wished to. She was delighted at my news, and reacted full of elation – she called me a genius, a wonderful man and sealed her approval with a passionate kiss, much to my delight. As might be expected, her mother was not all that pleased but she had to accept it. Grace and I then sat down together to work out how best to put this exciting plan into action, starting the following weekend. There was no problem in Grace taking the time off, as she only worked a five-day week, for a company in Kingsway in west central London.

The landlady and Grace were well disposed to each other, especially as Grace helped around the house, making herself useful. The landlady would not accept any extra money when Grace stayed – she was pleased to have the company while I was at work. The only time Grace and I went out was for an occasional visit to the cinema, either on Saturday evening or Sunday afternoon. As a special treat and a thank-you gesture for the landlady, the three of us would sometimes visit a restaurant for a meal out before going on to the Chiswick Empire, where they had live stage shows.

Much to our relief, the landlady did not raise any objection to Grace and I sharing the same bedroom. In fact, it was Grace's suggestion, during discussions about this, before she started going over to Chiswick for the weekends, providing the landlady raised no objection. On Sunday evenings after a quiet meal, Grace and I would take the underground to Victoria in south-west London. From there, it was quite easy to ride by either a bus or tram back to Peckham. As Grace was not a nervous type of girl, she did not mind travelling on her own during the blackout. We would kiss goodnight at the bus station in Victoria, then wave when she was on her way – I would make my own way back to Chiswick.

In April 1940, Grace and I became officially engaged, but not without some hassle with her mother – she was not against the engagement as such, but she was thinking in terms of the money she would lose when Grace married. So far this had not been mentioned or considered.

At about the same time, the war started in earnest – the Germans releasing all the war power at their disposal against the Low Countries and France. They released a new form of warfare called the 'Blitzkrieg' – 'lightening war' in German. First they would send their bombers in against strategic targets, then send their fearful 'Stuka' dive bombers. The noise alone frightened people and made them nervous. This was followed up with tanks and ground troops. At the time, there was no answer to this type of warfare, and consequently the whole of northern Europe was in German hands within weeks, including the whole of Norway. The British generals must have had the surprise of their lives at the swiftness of the German advance – they were possibly thinking of fighting the war in 1914 style, from the trenches. The French Maginot gun fortifications were facing the wrong way – the Germans just skirted around them. Likewise, the British guns at Singapore were facing out to sea, useless against the Japanese when they invaded overland by way of Malaya, as it was known then.

For one year, Grace travelled regularly each weekend to Chiswick. On one occasion, she was lucky to get in touch with me through the lady next door who was on the phone, asking her if she would kindly pass a message from her to me. They were not strangers as they would sometimes have a conversation over the garden fence. The message was to say that she would not be over on this particular weekend as her mother was not feeling too well. She asked me if I would visit her instead, and stay for the weekend with them if this would be possible. When I received the message, I made arrangements to have one of the days owing to me at work. I telephoned Grace at her workplace to tell her to expect me at around 5pm on Saturday, as I would be coming straight from work.

As events turned out, it was for the best. On that Saturday early in September, almost a year after war was declared on Germany, at about 5pm as I was crossing Peckham Rye on my way to see Grace, I heard the ominous droning of aeroplane engines. I knew from the sound they were not British so I stopped the car and climbed out to have a look. What I saw at quite low altitude, was a formation of German bombers, making their way towards the east side of London and the London Docks. They seemed to have the reign of the skies – there were no puffs of smoke in the sky to indicate ack-ack fire – there were no British fighter planes. The only defence were the blimps (barrage balloons), tethered above the city to prevent low-flying attacks. These enemy planes were making their way in broad daylight, with little cloud cover, giving the pilots perfect vision to pick out their targets, a job they did quite successfully, setting that part of London well and truly ablaze.

I found it hard to believe my eyes – was this the beginning of the German offensive against London and England? After dark, the German bombers came back in strength, to stoke up the fires they had started during the daylight hours. This offensive continued for most of the night, well until daybreak. The fires must have been like beacons, visible for miles. I thought that if the Germans, after the defeat of France, had followed up immediately with an attack against England, there may have been a different outcome. Instead they gave Churchill the luxury of preparing for what was to be expected. It allowed Britain to expand its production of fighter aircraft, especially the Spitfire, which in the end destroyed the German Air Force. Of course, neither I nor anyone else knew this in 1940 – England was suffering all sorts of defeats at the time.

Climbing back into my car after the amazing sights in the London sky, I continued my journey to see Grace, wondering with some sorrow what was going the happen next. Both Grace and her mother were outside as I drove into their street, watching what was going on. Once I had parked, all three of us went inside the house, wondering if England was going to suffer the same fate as other areas of Europe. Part of London was well and truly ablaze, only a few miles away.

After we had assured Grace's mother that we would only be away for a short while and making sure that she was comfortable, Grace and I decided to go to the club to see if Valerie was there. On the way, I thought I would take a look at what was going on farther across the capital. I headed for the place where Bert and I took the girls to watch one of the miracles of nature, viewing the golden sunsets over London. The distant skyline was a glow of a different kind, not of nature's doing, but of man's. It was a grandstand view, a sight not to be forgotten, an unbelievable sight. We could see, quite clearly, St. Paul's Cathedral standing out in defiant silhouette against the glowing sky, as the bombers were dropping their weapons of destruction, stoking up the fires. Huge clouds of smoke and dust reached for the sky, at times obscuring the view of St. Paul's and the glow of the raging fires. I supposed it was impossible to bomb the docks without civilian casualties and I wondered how the people of north Woolwich were suffering, the people from whom I had the unenviable task of bad debt collecting when I worked for Mr. Tenenbaum. Their houses were just across the road from the docks.

When we arrived at the club, Valerie was not there. We stayed for a while to have a drink, hoping that she might turn up. Grace was anxious to return home to keep her mother company although her younger sister was at home. On the way to the car, I suggested that we might travel over to see Valerie after lunch the next day – we were both particularly concerned about her, as she lived near the docks and must have been quite near where the terrible barrage had fallen. In those days, very few people had a telephone at home, mainly due to the lack of available lines. It either meant visiting or sending a postcard.

From later reports, it appeared that a German bomb did enter St. Paul's through the dome. By a stroke of providence it failed to explode – God was certainly on the side of the British that night.

When Grace and I arrived at Valerie's home the next day, we were very relieved to see she had not suffered any damage. As the crow flies, her house was less than a mile from Tower Bridge and the timber docks at Rotherhithe. I guessed that both girls, since they had not seen each other for some time, would have plenty to talk about, so I would leave them to chat whilst I returned to keep Grace's mother company. I established from Grace the best time to call back for her. I had arranged to stay over, and make an early start in the morning, this being a much more sensible idea than travelling in the blackout. Both girls were in full agreement with me and welcomed the opportunity to have a little time together for girl-to-girl matters.

Having left Grace at Valerie's, I had a good deal of thinking to do on the journey back to keep her mother company. I came to the conclusion that, if Grace was willing, we should get married. No one knew how long the war was going to last, or what the eventual outcome would be. At the time, British morale was at its lowest ebb. At the appointed time, I returned to pick up Grace and, when we were alone together later that evening at Grace's home, I popped the question. After her initial surprise Grace excitedly said yes, but was keen to know when I had in mind. I promised her that it would be as soon as possible, taking her in my arms for a loving kiss. We agreed that there was no objection to a Registry Office wedding and the two of us embraced again to kiss and seal the proposal.

In the morning, we told her mother of our plans. She was somewhat taken aback at the sudden decision and Grace was quick to sense what her mother may have been thinking, stepping in swiftly to reassure her that it was not for the reason she might have assumed when she was told. We both telephoned our respective bosses to say we would be somewhat late arriving for work, and I explained to my foreman that I would give him the full details as soon as I had clocked in. I then visited the Registry Office to book a time and date for our wedding, the clerk there finding a suitable time at 10.30am on the 12th of October, a mere four weeks away. From there I set off to hire a saloon car for two days, for the wedding and to carry our personal possessions. My own car was not suitable for this important event, being an open tourer and, in any case, there was a petrol allowance with a rented car. I paid the required deposit and finalised the arrangements for collecting the car on the day.

The German air raid onslaught against England and the southern counties had now started in earnest. At the beginning, most of raids were during daylight and in the first few weeks, the German losses in aircraft were several hundred, so the general public were told. They must have been extremely heavy because the Germans, not wanting to risk further heavy losses of aircraft, started after-dark, night bombing. At the time, and throughout the war years, England was on 'double summer time', so it did not get dark until late. The bombing continued for several months, throughout the winter. There was no massive concentration of heavy bombing, just nuisance raids to prevent Londoners from enjoying a good night's sleep. The German Luftwaffe were also concentrating on large provincial cities such as Coventry, Plymouth, Liverpool and several others. If there was a particularly heavy raid the previous night, the King and Queen would personally visit the devastated area, talking to the people, trying to bolster their spirits and morale. These visits would be shown on cinema newsreels, or the front pages of the national press. Churchill would also sometimes visit these areas, giving his defiant and famous 'V' sign with his fingers.

With the continuing night bombing, I thought it best for Grace to stay at home at weekends for safety's sake. I would go over to Peckham after work on Saturdays for a few hours. The following weekend we made arrangements with Bert and Valerie to act as witnesses at the ceremony. Both our good friends readily agreed to do this and Bert happily accepted the role of Best man. Grace decided to make good use of this time at home, to make herself a wedding suit from material given to her as a wedding present.

When I saw my landlady after returning home from work on Monday evening, I told her of our plans to marry. It was a mixture of pleasure and regret for both of us. The landlady wished both of us all the best for the future, adding that she would miss Grace at the weekends. She really took pleasure in our company. I assured her that she would have a chance to see Grace when I called in later to collect my belongings

By this time, many central Londoners were using the Underground platforms for sleeping purposes. People brought their bedding, a thermos of hot drink, and something to eat. Most seemed to make themselves quite at home – at least they were certain to get a good night's sleep, hoping that they had a home to go back to in the morning.

The day before the wedding, I went along to collect the hired car and then travelled to Bert's, staying for a while talking to Bert's mother, who gave me a small present from the family. I was very touched by their kindness and thanked them warmly. When Bert was ready, we went to the local pub for a celebration drink. Neither of us was a big drinker and we spent the evening reminiscing about all the good times we had had together, the amazing antics we got up to, and all the wonderful girls we had met. I took time to explain to Bert why I had decided to marry – the war was going to upset people's lives, we had already lost touch with the gang, and

I thought I might not be called up, as my job was a 'reserved occupation' but I had no guarantee. Bert could still be called up and I wondered if he was still in the same frame of mind about not answering his call-up papers. Bert assured me that he had not changed his mind. Whatever he decided, I said, I would like to remain friends, promising to keep in touch either with Bert or his mother. After a cheerful but thoughtful evening, I took Bert home, spending a little time with his family, before driving back to Chiswick.

Although Bert had said that he would make his own way to the Registry Office, before leaving, I took the precaution of having a quiet word with Bert's mother, asking her to jog Bert's memory to be at there prompt at 10.30 in the morning – he was inclined to be a little absent-minded.

My car was not really suitable for the wedding. It held two people comfortably on the front seat, three with a squeeze, but I could not imagine Valerie, with all her finery, climbing into the dicky seat – it was all right for casual use, but offered no protection should it rain. On the morning of the wedding, I made my way over to Grace's home on a perfect, sunny morning with a clear blue sky. I wondered if there might be an air raid, almost expecting the sirens to go off at any minute. Thankfully they stayed quiet. London at the time was taking a real hammering, mostly with after-dark air raids although there were the occasional sneak daytime raids too. On one occasion, Buckingham Palace suffered a direct hit, but fortunately there were no casualties.

I arrived at Grace's home promptly at 9am. Grace was putting the finishing touches to her wedding suit which she had been making from the material she had been given. Clothing could only be purchased by surrendering coupons, so this was a welcome gift indeed. All the while Grace was making the suit, she was very secretive about what she was doing, hoping to surprise me with her needlework skills – at no time could I get even a glimpse of the wedding suit. When Grace emerged dressed in her suit she looked positively stunning. It was a cherry red worsted material, that suited her dark complexion. Grace had made a single-breasted, calf-length, two-piece suit, with a matching coloured pillbox hat, worn on the crown of the head with a short white veil. She had a white blouse with a cravat-style neckline and the whole ensemble was complemented by white high-heel court shoes and matching coloured handbag and gloves. When I saw her I was very pleased and proud of her – she was perfection indeed.

After a quick cup of tea and a piece of toast, we said cheerio to Grace's mother and set off in high spirits for the Registry Office. When the wedding plans were being discussed, it was agreed that only the four of us would attend the ceremony – Grace and I, the bride and groom, Valerie as matron of honour, and Bert as best man. We drove swiftly to Valerie's home and I knocked on her door. When she emerged, she also was a sight for sore eyes – she was dressed in a powder blue, two-piece suit with a matching, close-fitting hat. With her natural red hair she looked really lovely – in fact, it would have been difficult for a stranger to pick or even guess which of these two ladies was the bride, both of them looking extremely attractive.

Much to my relief, Bert was there waiting outside the Registry Office. After greeting each other warmly, we went inside to meet the registrar who was ready to perform the official duties. It was a simple but pleasant ceremony, with just the four of us there with the official. Bert and Valerie signed the witness book and Mr. and Mrs. Wisdom were presented with our copy of the Marriage Certificate. After much hugging and many congratulatory kisses, we all returned to Grace's mother's house for the wedding breakfast, a really good spread which had been laid on with the help of the neighbours, generously supplying rationed foods. Everyone drank the health and happiness of the bride and groom, really meaning what they were saying in the middle of the troubled times of a country at war.

Once the celebrations had come to an end, I took Bert home first, thanking him for his sterling work as best man. I then dropped Valerie at her place of work, giving her a kiss of appreciation, promising that we would keep in touch one way or another. Finally I returned for Grace, taking her to her twin sister's house where we had planned to spend our wedding night as Grace had promised her.

CHAPTER TEN

When the date for the wedding was set, it had been mutually agreed between Grace and I that we would live at Hayes. Married women were virtually given a free hand about where they worked – labour controls did not affect them but they were expected to find work to help the war effort. I started to look around for a suitable place to live and was fortunate to find a very reasonable flat to rent, quite quickly. It was a fully furnished, two-bedroom, self-contained upstairs maisonette within a few minutes walk of my workplace. The flat belonged to a young married couple – the husband had been called up for military service. His wife, Elsie, was going to live with her mother and unmarried sister in the neighbourhood. As Elsie had a small son, this suited her, as her mother would look after him while she was at work.

During the morning after our wedding, we left Grace's twin sister's house, and made our way to her mother's to collect her personal belongings. Her mother wished us well for the future and both Grace and I thanked her very warmly for making our big day such a success. There were a few tears, mostly of happiness, and we promised faithfully to keep in touch, either by the occasional visit or by post. After saying our farewells, we set off to make another call, this time at my digs to collect my belongings.

The landlady, when she saw us both, said with a tear in her eyes how sorry she was to lose me as a lodger, for she had become quite fond of me. She greeted Grace with a kiss, and said how wonderful she looked, adding that she would miss us both. She gave Grace a parcel explaining that it was her wedding present to us both. I thanked her with real feeling, giving her a gentle kiss on the cheek. We stayed for a while talking about the wedding, apologising for the lack of a piece of wedding cake as the ingredients for making one were virtually non-existent. It would have been possible to order one from a specialist baker, by ordering well in advance, but Grace did not have the time to allow this. As we were leaving, I assured the landlady that we would keep in touch and try to see her on odd occasions as time allowed. She agreed that that would be very pleasant and charged Grace with firm instructions to look after me well, an idea which Grace readily agreed to. It was kisses all round and we set off at last to our new home in Hayes, to the flat which Grace had not yet seen.

On our way to Hayes, Grace asked me what was in the parcel the landlady had given to her but I did not want to spoil the surprise, as I already knew what it was in the carefully wrapped box. It contained a beautiful Damask embroidered tablecloth – I had watched the landlady working on it, truly a work of art requiring extreme patience. I told a little white lie, saying to Grace that I had no idea and urging her to be patient and wait until we arrived at the flat before she opened it.

When we arrived at the flat, it was late afternoon, so Grace and I unloaded the car swiftly to make best use of the daylight and then allowed ourselves a well-deserved cup of tea, made with the materials that Elsie had kindly supplied. Then I showed Grace around the flat – she did not know what to expect but everything was there as Elsie had promised. All we had to supply themselves were sheets and towels. She was delighted with our new home and remarked how nice the flat was, especially considering what a reasonable rent it was.

The hired car had to be returned and my own picked up – with the hired car I had been given more than enough petrol coupons for the wedding and the short journeys that we had made, so I had some left over for my own car. I settled the car hire account, picked up my own car and drove straight back to Hayes. I was pleased to find that Grace had already put everything away, and also had time to go down to the nearby shops to buy a few necessities. Wearily we sat down for a very enjoyable meal, our first as a married couple. While living at home before marrying, she learned very little about cookery as her mother would not allow anyone in the kitchen while she was cooking, and consequently, Grace's knowledge of preparing a meal was virtually nil. It was her visits to Chiswick and the chance to help the landlady, who showed her how to cook worthy of presentation, that gave her the knowledge and confidence she needed. War-time cooking was a work of art, making the best from whatever one could get that was not rationed.

The flat had not long been built, and consisted of two bedrooms, a sitting room, bathroom and kitchen. The main bedroom faced over a pleasant back garden – it was furnished with a dressing table, a free standing large double-door wardrobe, a double bed and a bedside cabinet and light. The floor had a large central carpet, with a lino surround. The sitting room faced the side street that led into the main road – from the window, one could see Hayes railway station. There was a glazed tile fireplace with a back boiler, and the room was comfortably furnished with a tapestry-covered three-piece suite, an occasional table, and a radiogram, although Elsie had taken all her records. The floor was carpeted in similar style to the bedroom.

The smaller bedroom also faced the front of the house, overlooking the street, but this room was not furnished at all. In front of the door to this room was a short passage leading to the kitchen On the immediate left was a modern bathroom and toilet, next to which was a large airing cupboard with a hot water tank for supplying the bathroom and kitchen. At the end of the passage, were a few steps leading to the front door. The kitchen was a little on the small side, with built-in cupboards and pantry, and of course, a gas stove and sink. It was a well-planned flat, nicely arranged for easy cleaning. Facing east and being a corner site property, it had the benefit of the early morning sun, and the evening sun in the kitchen and main bedroom. In spite of the absence of central heating (not known in those days), the flat never appeared to be cold, not even in the middle of winter.

Grace soon found herself a job, working in an office for a large national sweet and chocolate manufacturer. This suited her very well as sweets were on ration and she was allowed a coupon-free issue of sweets each week from the rejects and seconds – Grace had a very sweet tooth. She wrote to all her relations and friends saying she was now married, at the same time apologising for not sending out invitations, as it had all been done in a hurry.

For about a year our life moved along smoothly although, naturally, there were a few minor hiccups during our settling-in period. We both agreed that we considered it a wise decision to marry.

As our first wedding anniversary approached, I decided that I wanted to surprise Grace by arranging a romantic weekend at one of our favourite Thames riverside towns. Not telling her of my true intentions, I suggested that we should spend a weekend at Maidenhead the next time I had an official weekend off, one as near as possible to the actual anniversary. She thought it was a wonderful idea. When the weekend arrived, before I left for my obligatory Saturday morning shift, I asked Grace to pack a suitcase for the weekend, so that we could set off immediately after lunch – I added that she should pack her favourite red off-the-shoulder evening dress.

We arrived at the hotel that I had previously booked at around 4 o'clock and were shown up to a pleasant, spacious room with a delightful outlook over the river. I excused myself and set off to put my plan into action by seeking out the manager, explaining that as it was our wedding anniversary, could the manager arrange a candlelit dinner with a bottle of champagne and a dozen red roses on the table. The man saw no reason why this could not be set up and cheerily agreed. The hotel dining room included a small dance floor and there was a three-piece band in attendance at weekends, giving the place a very pleasant atmosphere where people could really enjoy themselves.

On my way back to the room, I was feeling pleased with myself that everything had been arranged, hoping that the evening would work out exactly as I had planned. As it was still quite early, Grace suggested a walk around the town and if time allowed, a stroll along the riverbank.

When we returned, we dressed for dinner, and I checked that the 18 carat gold wristwatch that I had bought earlier in Hayes was with me, in its presentation box. Grace looked wonderful in her stunning red dress and wearing her favourite silver ballerina brooch. She had also used her special perfume, 'Evening in Paris'. The manager himself showed us to our table, with the lighted candles and the roses setting off the finery. It all looked beautiful, as I had hoped, set in a secluded corner of the restaurant. The evening passed even better than I had expected, and Grace was very happy to wear her new watch. We kissed while we were dancing and she thanked me for the surprise and the wonderful evening.

We were both in a very happy state of mind as we left the restaurant for our room, anticipating a warm and sensual night together. At the exit from the restaurant were heavy, mahogany swing doors and I held them open for Grace to pass through. We were so preoccupied with each other that I did not notice the door was gradually trapping my middle finger tight. I did not realise this immediately because of the numbness, but by the time we reached the room, it was throbbing and aching painfully. I held my hand under the cold tap to seek relief and although Grace showed concern, there was nothing that she could really do for me. What I had planned to be the climax of our evening turned out to be a real anti-climax, sitting up in bed most of the night nursing an extremely sore and painful finger. How different it could have been if I had taken more notice of the heavy doors.

Air raids had now ceased, the RAF had won the 'Battle of Britain' and losses were heavy on both sides although more so for the Germans. The fortune of war was gradually turning in Britain's favour. The elite Afrika Korps were routed from North Africa, bringing the war back to the mainland of Europe. The Italians, who had very little stomach for the war in the first place, were driven out of Albania, Somalia and Abyssinia, back to Italy. The Americans were now in the war, forced in by the cowardly Japanese surprise attack on Pearl Harbour.

I took one of my days off to visit Grace's mother and my one-time landlady. When we arrived at my old lodgings, the landlady was delighted to see us, and we her. Grace had already thanked her by letter saying how pleased she was with her present, but she wanted to thank her personally to tell her how pleased she was to receive such a treasured possession. We stayed there for an hour, reminiscing about old times over a cup of tea and learning about her two new but elderly lodgers. Reluctantly we had to leave, saying our farewells but promising to keep in touch as frequently as possible.

Our next call was to Grace's mother to see how she had been keeping and coping. Once we had made our greetings and I was sure that the old lady was in good spirits, I asked if I might go and call on Bert, whilst Grace and her mother had some private time together. This was perfectly acceptable, so I travelled over some familiar ground to my old friend's house.

Bert's mother answered the door to my knock and warmly invited me in. Bert himself was not there and she explained that he had received his call-up papers but had gone on the run. Mrs. Greaves was most upset that her son had done this, although I admitted that Bert had told me he would disappear when his call-up papers arrived. In the event, his mother did hear from him from time to time and he was sending her some money, although he never told her where he was or what his address might be. I tried to comfort her by explaining that it was just as well that she did not know his whereabouts, as the military and civil police would take a very hard line on her, if they thought she was withholding information. They had a reputation for not taking too kindly to absentees trying to avoid military call-up. We both thought he was foolish, and would have to live with his decision. In an odd way, I admired him for sticking to his principles. There wasn't much I could do or say to cheer her up – all I could urge her to do was to try not to worry too much. I added that what really worried Bert was how she would have coped if he had answered his call-up papers – that, I believed, was the main reason why he decided to go on the run.

I left Mrs. Greaves still worrying about her errant son and returned to Grace's mother, who suprisingly enough, had been coping quite well. Her younger daughter was now married, just before her husband was due for overseas service with the RAF. Grace's younger sister worked for a bank in the City of London and when the air raids started, she and the rest of the staff were evacuated to Derby. This left her mother living on her own, but within easy reach of another daughter and granddaughter living near by.

One evening, I was on my way home from collecting some necessary spares for my car, making my way over Hammersmith Bridge in West London, when the car hit a pothole, loosening the exhaust pipe, causing the car to develop a deep roar. As it was dark, there was nothing I could do, only hope it would hold together until I arrived home. As I was proceeding gently down Chiswick High Road, I was stopped by a motorcycle patrolman. The car had been recently washed and polished and looked really smart – the policeman made a thorough inspection all round the vehicle with his torch. When he arrived next to me, still sitting patiently in the driver's seat, he shone his torch inside the car.

I started the conversation by explaining that, even if the officer did not believe it, the car had struck a pothole loosening the exhaust, only a few minutes previously. I was saying that I would fix it first thing in the morning, but realised that the patrolman seemed to be ignoring what I was saying. The man interrupted my explanation by asking me if I wanted to sell the car, much to my surprise. I had not thought about this as an idea and believed that the policeman was joking. "Make me an offer and I will consider it", I quipped, but the policeman must have been serious, as he immediately offered me £35 cash. It did not take me long to consider this good offer and I immediately accepted the price, to include the spare parts I had just bought. Arrangements were made for the car to be delivered at an agreed time and place the following day and the two of us shook hands on the deal. None of this was quite what I had expected when the patrolman first pulled me over, but I continued my journey to Hayes, without any further attention from the police.

When indoors, I explained to Grace why I was late, saying that, although I did not really want to sell the car, acquiring petrol was becoming a problem and it was a particularly good offer. I believed that I would do better selling it now while it was still in good condition. To reassure Grace, I said that I could always rent a car, for the occasions when we wished to travel to Peckham to see her mother – at least that way we would be sure of having sufficient petrol.

I fixed the exhaust – the manifold exhaust pipe connection had come adrift when I hit the pothole and only needed tightening back in place, ready to take over to Chiswick. The policeman was even more delighted when he saw the car in daylight. I handed over the log book and spare petrol coupons and, in exchange, the policeman handed over the cash. The proud new owner asked me if it was the same car that used to stand outside a house in Burlington Road, obviously having seen it before. I told him that I had lived there before I was married, but that I now lived in Hayes as the log book would show him.

While the car was in my possession, I had travelled 7,500 miles, without any serious troubles at all. I really did not want to part with it – it had served me well and had been a good and faithful friend. However, I considered it was for the best, thinking nevertheless that in other cars I had more girls than in this one, bringing back many sweet memories. I thought perhaps my motoring days were over.

It was sometime early in 1941 when Grace received a letter from her cousin Rose. She had married in 1939, before I had come on the scene, so they had never met although no doubt, Rose had heard of me. Rose wrote to say she was expecting a baby. Grace had gone to her wedding, acting as Matron of Honour. The letter explained that her husband, Alf, had received his call-up papers and was expecting to report for service in the RAF in the near future. When they were married, they lived in Lewisham in south-east London and, when the bombing first started, Alf thought it would be safer to move outside London. He knew he would be called up sooner or later. He did not want the stress of worrying about Rose, and possibly his family, while he was away on service. He rented a semi-detached house on a newly built, private estate twenty miles outside London. The house backed on to a mainline railway to London. Alf worked three nights a week for a popular national newspaper as a casual printer and on Saturday nights for a Sunday newspaper. As there were no early Sunday morning trains back home, he had to use his car.

In the letter, Grace and I were invited for the weekend and I managed to take the time off from the days owing to me from my annual entitlement. The bombing had now eased off, in fact there had been quite a lull. The RAF were now in complete control of the skies over southern England and the Battle of Britain (1940–41) was over. With the aid of a sketch Rose enclosed in the letter, we had no trouble finding the house and we arrived for the visit just about at lunchtime. Rose and Alf were both in when we arrived – after formal introductions, we were shown into the sitting room. I had not seen either of them before, but had heard about them from Grace. The four of us settled down comfortably with a welcome cup of tea and a sandwich. Conversation flowed until Alf had to leave for work in his car. Before leaving, he gave his wife a kiss, gave Grace a peck on the cheek, and shook hands with me, saying that he would see us all in the morning. The two girls talked about their lives in general – Grace remarking on what a lovely house they had and how it was nicely situated.

The house had two large bedrooms and a box room, which would be used as a baby's room, a bathroom and a fair-sized airing cupboard. Downstairs there was a hall that led into two pleasant, large rooms, the lounge and the sitting room-cum-dining room, with French doors leading out to a very long, untidy garden stretching down to the railway lines. The garden badly needed tidying up, being strewn with builders' rubble. Rose explained that they had promised to come and clear it away, but had not got round to it yet. The only fault I could see was that the kitchen was too small. The fuel hot water boiler seemed to take up a good deal of floor space. Outside there was a reasonable-sized garage, just a short distance away from the rear kitchen door. There was a drive in from the road and a small front garden overlooking open countryside. What surprised both Grace and I was the twenty-five shillings a week rent, plus the rates. They had been paying a little more than that for their flat in Lewisham. Here they had the quiet solitude of the country, instead of the noisy traffic of London.

Alf arrived home at 6am after a busy night shift and straight away made a pot of tea, taking a cup up to Rose. He put his head round the door to ask Grace if she would like a cup of tea, which she accepted – I was still too sleepy and declined. Alf went straight to bed until lunch time, but at least he was off work until Wednesday night. When he eventually roused himself, he washed and shaved, then arrived downstairs much refreshed, dressed in his casual clothes. He was a short, stocky man, with a full rounded face, blue eyes, neat tidy brown hair, and a clipped moustache. He was blessed with a pleasant personality. Rose was a jovial, motherly type, also short and stocky, very likeable and easy to get on with. She had the knack of making people feel at ease – nothing seemed to be too much trouble for her. As a married couple, they were ideally suited to one another.

Grace apologised to Rose and Alf for not letting them know she was getting married, explaining that, as time was short, we had decided on the spur of the moment. Alf replied by saying that they could not have come anyway as it was the same day that they had moved out from Lewisham. When we were all sitting down to lunch, it occurred to me how suprisingly easy it was for some people to take to each other without too much effort. This was a case in point – it seemed as though we had known each other for a long time.

While eating, the subject of cars came up and they laughed when I told them how I had sold my car to the policeman on the motorcycle. I asked Alf what he was going to do with his car when he joined up, to which he replied that, as Rose could not drive, he supposed that he would leave it in the garage. I had a suggestion to make and proposed that I could keep it, tax and insure it and maintain it in perfect working order so that Alf could have it when he was home on leave. Alf pondered for a moment and asked Rose what her opinion was – she said without any hesitation that she thought it was a good idea, and willingly gave her consent. Arrangements were made for me to pick up the car the following weekend after Alf reported for RAF service. The car was a 7 horsepower Jowett saloon, powered by a twin-cylinder, horizontal, air-cooled engine. It was a roomy car and very economical to run, covering around forty-five miles to the gallon.

Once Alf had left for his war service, I collected the Jowett and drove it back to Hayes. As I had no garage, it had to stay on the road, parked in the cul-de-sac outside our flat. Because of the scarcity of petrol, I did not use the car a great deal during the winter, preferring to save my petrol ration for the better summer months. Grace and I did occasionally go to Ealing Broadway for a shopping trip, just to give the car a run. As I had promised, Alf had the car for his leaves and embarkation leave when he was posted abroad. He had no trouble picking up the car, as he was stationed just further down the Great West Road. When he called for the car, he always stayed for a while, usually having a meal with Grace and I and talking about Rose and the baby.

As Alf was leaving after he had collected the car for his embarkation leave, he said his farewells, gave Grace a friendly kiss and shook hands with me. I reminded him that I would be down to collect the car when he had finished using it and asked him to send our love to Rose. That was the last time Grace and I saw Alf until after the war was over, as he was posted to a North African Gladiator Squadron as a gunner, observer and wireless operator. Their main task was spotting enemy tanks. He was eventually commissioned and survived the war without any personal injuries.

In the summer, Grace and I would visit our favourite places near the river Thames, at Cookham and Marlow, two delightful riverside towns. We had some fantastic times, picnicking on the river bank, boating in a punt, and generally trying to forget about the war. The workers at the factory were officially allowed one Sunday in four off – this was worked on a rota basis between sections.

At work, I was still having trouble with my chargehand, who was the son-in-law of the shop foreman – it seemed he was still being jealous of my earnings. It came to a climax one day when I had finished a batch of work and was put on 'waiting time', this being customary whilst waiting for further work. The chargehand instructed me to sweep up the floor while I was waiting. This was a deliberate attempt to provoke me who told him in no uncertain terms to do it himself, saying forcibly that I was a tradesman, not a labourer. I followed this by stating that I would go and get the shop steward union man, to see what he had to say. I set off to find the union man – it was one of the terms of employment that one had to join a union. Strikes were illegal during the war so workers had the option of paying union dues or the equivalent to a nominated charity. When I went off to find the union man, I noticed the chargehand go into the foreman's office, getting himself in a lather. After a while, the foreman sent for me, and I attended his office with the union man.

The chargehand was standing there with a smirk on his face. Before a word was said by me, the foreman stepped straight in and said that I had been insolent to the chargehand, and he was putting me on a three-day suspension, starting straightaway, for misconduct. As the foreman was making his speech, I again noticed the smirk of smug satisfaction on the chargehand's face. The foreman was not the least bit interested in anything I or the union man had to say, and neither of us was given a chance to speak at all. The union man advised me to forget about it, as there was nothing I could actually do about it. As I walked back to my place of work, I mentally thought there was something I could do about it – one way or another I would knock that smirk off his face.

I collected up my tools, with the idea of taking them home. Inwardly I was boiling at the injustice of not being able to tell my side of the events that led to my foreman backing his stupid son-in-law. Up to then, the foreman and I got on well together – it was out of character for him to take this attitude. It was early afternoon when I arrived home. My wife was still at work, so I made myself a cup of tea, sitting down at the kitchen table to drink it and, at the same time, formulate a plan of action in my mind. There was no way I was going to accept this without some form of action. The years in the charity home had taught me how to look after myself to my own best interests. After finishing my tea, I decided to go down to the Labour Exchange to see the manager. I had to wait a while before being shown into the manager's office and spent the time clarifying my thoughts. We shook hands and I was offered a seat. The manager asked what he could do to be of assistance and I explained in detail what had happened. In fact, the manager was not very helpful, offering no specific advice about the actual incident. While I was explaining, the manager was making notes. I asked if I could appeal against the misconduct suspension as I thought it would be a black mark against my character – the foreman had over-reacted and the chargehand had clearly acted beyond his authority. The manager looked up from his notes said that I clearly had the right to appeal and that he would let me know the date of any hearing. I added that I did not particularly want to return to Fairy Aviation to work and asked if it would be possible to have a card for Air-Works at Heston. The manager could see no real reason why not and asked me to wait outside while he attended to it. After a while I was given permission to change my job, and an application to apply for a job at Air-Works.

During the war years, the Ministry of Labour had wide, sweeping powers. If a worker was reported to them for persistent lateness or taking too much unofficial time off, or for reasons of serious misconduct, the Ministry had the authority to take whatever action they thought fit or appropriate. If a worker did not take heed, he could be transferred anywhere, even to the coal mines and, in exceptional cases, into the armed forces. Being in a reserved occupation was no protection. If a worker appeared before a tribunal, their decision was final – there was no appeal.

I went along to Air-Works that same afternoon and after a short interview, I was offered a job immediately, starting the next day. Feeling exceptionally pleased with myself I made my way back home. Grace was in when I arrived home, so I explained to her the events of the day. She gave me a kiss of welcome, realising why I was home a little earlier than usual. While eating our evening meal, I told her of the details leading up to my change of job – I was not sorry to leave, as the chargehand was making my life intolerable.

My hearing came up, which I had to attend, and the charge against me was dismissed. I was told by the Chairman of the tribunal that I could sue the company for lost wages if I wished and also that I could apply for reinstatement. I had no intention of going back – my life would be hell back at Fairy. I had been at Air-Works for about a month before the hearing was set and I informed the Chairman of the tribunal that I was quite happy where I was. I only wanted to clear my name, and I respectfully requested that I might be allowed to stay at Air-Works. The tribunal were all in agreement that I could stay, and so I was given permission to do so. When leaving the hearing, I was thinking to myself that it was a very pleasing decision, as the work was much more interesting, with no boring repetitive tasks, the money was better, even though working hours were just as long. As events turned out, the chargehand, being the jealous fool he was, had unwittingly done me a favour.

Sometime later, I saw the chargehand in a pub with his father-in-law, the foreman, and I could not resist the temptation of going straight up to them and shaking their hands, thanking them warmly. They both showed considerable surprise at my actions, especially when I explained that they had done me a great favour, because, not only was the money better but the work much more interesting. I wanted to knock the smirk off the chargehand's face, and I succeeded. Turning to the foreman, Mr. Pilgrim, I said how astonished I was at his backing the jealous idiot of a son-in-law. The foreman didn't say a word, the expression on their faces said it all. I pushed my point home further by adding that I had won my appeal and had been told that I could sue them both for intimidation and misconduct. I wanted them to squirm and I was really enjoying watching them fidgeting in their seats. I told them that I would not be taking any action, as I could not be that vindictive towards other people. I concluded my confrontation with one final word of warning – if either of them pulled such a stunt again against any one of their workforce, it would be them appearing before the tribunal. Turning to the chargehand, I challenged him, saying that, if he was jealous of the workers' money, he should ask for a transfer to the shop floor, if he believed he was capable of doing the work, putting this as sarcastically as possible. Feeling a lot happier, I returned to Grace who had been watching from a distance.

By late 1941, I was enjoying my work, being entirely different and varied. I worked with a good team, as opposed to being so much on my own at Fairy. The work mainly consisted of conversions and modifications to Spitfires and Wellington bombers. The Spitfires were being upgraded to Mk 10, and the 'Wimpy' was being converted to carry torpedoes. This being a much faster plane than the Swordfish, it had a better chance of successfully attacking its target, I thought. The Wimpy was to Britain what the Dakota was to the Americans – a 'Jack of all trades'.

It was while working on one of the Wimpys that I got the urge to join the RAF as aircrew. The idea kept nagging at me, and eventually I mentioned it to Grace explaining that it was no sudden impulse, but something I had been thinking about for some time. Grace did not try to discourage me but suggested that as it was such a big decision to make, I should sleep on it for a while. If I felt the same in a month's time, then I should do something about it. It was not that I wanted to be a hero, or had strong patriotic feelings, it was purely the urge to fly, rather than simply working on the aircraft on the ground. Some weeks later, I entered an official application to volunteer for Aircrew duties. By return, I was sent a rail warrant to report before an Aircrew selection board at Oxford.

The selection board consisted of three top-brass Air Force officers. They asked me a great number of questions but appeared to be somewhat cautious, coming to the conclusion that I would be more useful to the war effort continuing with the work I was presently doing. The senior member of the board suggested that I should make another application in three months' time if I still felt the same. In March 1942, I made another application as my feelings were still the same. I appeared before another selection board at Oxford and this time I was accepted. I thought that my determination may have been a factor in influencing them to this positive decision.

When my call-up papers came, I wrote to Rose, making arrangements for the return of Alf's car. Rose responded by letter with an invitation for a weekend visit, when Grace and I saw Rose's baby for the first time, a fine, healthy boy. Rose asked Grace if she would like to be the child's godmother, and she was delighted to be asked, and accepted. Alf was still in the Middle East – Rose had no precise idea where he was as all letters to and from him were addressed via box numbers. He had had a further promotion, which pleased Rose, feeling quite proud of him. On leaving after our weekend visit, I thought that it would the last time we would see Rose for the duration of the war – how long it was to last was anyone's guess.

Although she never mentioned it, Grace was missing her best friend Valerie, and her mother. There were letters but these were never as good as personal contact. The last time Grace had seen Valerie was at her wedding, nearly two years before. Grace had found another job, at a local Ordinance factory. It was an office job, where she struck up a very good relationship with her supervisor, a married woman with three young children, two daughters and a boy. The two of them became very close friends.

CHAPTER ELEVEN

In June 1942, along with my call-up papers came other documentary information amongst which was an instruction to report at Padgate near Warrington, Lancashire. On the momentous day that I was due to leave for active service, Grace went along with me to the London train terminal to see me off. I would have given anything to read Grace's mind, to understand what she was thinking. From the day I told her that I had volunteered for the RAF, she had never mentioned the subject. We simply stood close together on the platform until we took one last, lingering kiss before I boarded the train on my way to a new life.

I arrived at Warrington railway station with several others, where we were met by an NCO with a truck. When all were aboard, we were driven off to an RAF initial training camp at Padgate. This was where we would be spending the next six weeks doing our basic training and being documented, medically examined and inoculated. Any men with long hair soon had it shortened by barbers who, it seemed, were more used to shearing sheep than cutting men's hair. They were not at all fussy about styling – off it came. Financially I was going to be considerably worse off – from taking home about twenty pounds a week, to a mere seven shillings a week, paid fortnightly. I knew this because of what Alf had told me, so I took a reserve of cash with me. Grace's allowance was also seven shillings a week. While I had been at Air-Works, I had been working long hours, seven days a week, earning good money but never having any time to spend it. Consequently our joint savings account had swollen quite comfortably, so I knew that Grace would never be short of money while I was in the services.

The NCO Corporal in charge of my platoon was very tolerant whilst putting us through our paces. The NCOs of each of the six platoons had some sort of competition amongst themselves, with a wager, to see which one of them could turn out the best platoon at the passing-out parade, after the six weeks initial training.

While some of the other NCOs were bawling and shouting at their men, my NCO used the soft approach – he knew he could catch more flies with honey than with water. His tactics paid off, and he was particularly pleased with this and with his platoon when he won the wager. It was ample proof that excellent progress could be made through patience and helpfulness in sorting out his men's problems and greenness. After all, it was a huge change from civilian life to service life. This is where I scored, settling in quickly, as my years in the home helped me to acclimatise quickly to my new way of life, and to discipline.

During the six weeks' training, none of the new recruits was allowed outside the camp at any time. The only exception was the death of an immediate family member, mother, father, brother or sister – no one else, whatever the circumstances of their death. I suspected that, if let out, a few might change their minds and go absent without leave, a very serious and punishable offence.

After the initial training, culminating in the passing-out parade, the whole of the intake, en bloc, were posted to Blackpool of all places in July and August, the most popular seaside resort of the north-west of England. Fourteen shillings a fortnight was hardly going far in such a place and I was thankful that I did not smoke – that was a saving.

All the men were billeted twenty to a billet, in private guest houses, close to the mainline railway station. If all the landladies were like mine, they were on their way to making a fortune. They were being paid full board for each man, but not at any time did the lads receive a decent meal – at breakfast there were two slices of bread and scrape, cornflakes already served out, and a cup of tea. There were no second helpings at any meals.

Lunches and teatimes were just as bad and most of the lads left the table feeling just as hungry as when they arrived. They had to eat what was put in front of them or go without – it was as simple as that – there was no choice of food. Consequently, most of their own money was spent in the NAAFI.

All the men in my billet were complaining bitterly about the poor food, and I was prompted by the others to approach the billet Corporal – there was one to each billet. He could not have been ignorant of what was going on although he had his meals separately from the men, probably with the landlady, so no one knew what he was being offered for his meals. The landladies were not on civilian rations. They had a special allocation of all rationed foods such as meat, sugar, bacon and so on, so no doubt the billet NCO was being well looked after. These NCOs were there permanently, but the rookies were lodged there for only six weeks. Any official complaint somehow would either get lost or mislaid by the time the intake left. The procedure was different in camp – at all mealtimes, the duty officer would make an appearance in the dining hall and, so that everybody could hear, would bellow, 'any complaints?' in a loud voice and take notes. Throughout my stay in Blackpool I never saw a single officer at any time. The routine of the place seemed to be run by NCOs.

After breakfast and lunch, the men paraded outside their billet and a roll-call was made to ensure that all of them were on parade. They then marched off to Stanley Park, some distance away. There, the men in their separate platoons would play sport, do drills of all sorts, negotiate obstacle courses, or run through armament drills, stripping down a worn-out Lewis machine gun, then reassembling it for the next platoon to amuse themselves. There were no guards or duties at any time, so evenings and weekends were free – the men could do as they wished, as long as they were on parade for Monday morning roll-call. To amuse themselves, some of the squaddies would meet the trains at the mainline station on a Saturday, to meet the 'wake' girls. These girls were from the mill towns, coming to Blackpool for their annual holiday, for just one week, with money in their purses and the intention of having a good time. The squaddies would offer to carry their baggage for them to their digs – if a girl took a fancy to one of them, with a bit of luck he could have a good time at the girl's expense. He would then see her away on the following Saturday, and wait for the next gaggle of girls to arrive. Some of the lads struck lucky, some did not – it was one way to pass the weekend away.

Generally the local people were very good to the servicemen, knowing that they did not have a lot of money to splash around, especially if they went to the Tower Ballroom, the centre point of the town. This was a very popular place to pass leisure time, and one where the locals would offer drinks and cigarettes. In order not to offend, the boys would always accept their hospitality, although at times it could be a little embarrassing.

Eventually the six weeks were up, and the new recruits awaited their respective postings to different parts of England, to continue their training as aircrew. Some others and I were sent to a wireless/Morse code training camp at a place called Yatesbury – this was the same camp that Alf had attended when doing his course. Here we learnt how to send and receive Morse as well how to operate the transmitter.

The camp consisted of all wooden, military-type huts, each sleeping twenty men with separate accommodation for the NCO. The huts were set out in orderly fashion, with concrete pathways connecting each hut to the main road within the camp.

I had no trouble learning the Morse code itself. Being an isolated camp, there was very little for the men to do in the evenings in their spare time, except learn the Morse code or play cards. My trouble was when I listened to the Morse through the ear-phones at the training school. The learners sat at a desk, just like in school, with earphones plugged into a socket attached to the desk. As we listened, we had to write the code down in a book provided. When the Morse came over my earphones, to me it was a complete jumble – I just could not decipher the dots and the dashes. There was nothing wrong with the equipment – it was me. The transmission was only four words a minute, not fast for a beginner. I was given three tests on my own, and failed each one. I explained my problem to the instructor and was given a verbal test to see if I knew the code. This presented no problem and I scored high.

It was essential that a cadet had to send and receive Morse to pass out, and go on to further training. As I could not comply with the Morse training requirements, I had to appear before the Technical Commanding Officer, who explained that an essential part of Flight Engineer training was to be able to transmit and receive Morse. As I had failed, he had no choice but to curtail any further training, and recommend me for a course for rear gunners, known in the RAF as 'tail-end charlies'. I saluted, then left the office, a little dejected – this was not what I wanted. While waiting for a posting, I was put on camp duties. When it eventually came through, it was to another seaside town on the south-west coast, Torquay – not quite as popular as Blackpool.

It was spring when I arrived in Torquay for the next phase in my training. I had to make my own way from the railway station, carrying my kitbag. I found the Orderly Room, situated in one of the hotels on the seafront. After reporting, I was taken to another hotel also on the seafront, as my billet – there was no camp as such, just a series of hotels the RAF had taken over for offices and accommodation for the airmen. There were no drills or parades, just a basic roll-call in the mornings, and I found that discipline was very relaxed. This was just a holding centre until such time as there were vacancies in the gunnery school.

To fill our time, we squaddies were given dinghy drill in the afternoons, in the sea, wearing full uniform, boots and a 'Mae West'. We were taken out to sea by boat, with a dinghy in tow. When the boat stopped, we were instructed to jump overboard and make for the dinghy, practising getting in and out. To add a degree of realism, one of the platoon had to act as if he was injured and the rest of us had to drag him into the dinghy as quickly as possible. At this time of the year, the sea was very cold and most uninviting. The official reason for this drill, the instructor informed us, was that many aircrew were being lost in the North Sea, mainly because very few crew members knew how to use the dinghy properly, once in the sea.

I had been in Torquay for just over two weeks when I developed a thumping headache and felt that my chest was going to burst. I went to bed early hoping that I would feel better by the morning, but I hardly slept at all that night, feeling no better in the morning. Dragging myself out of bed and dressing in some pain, I decided to report sick to the MO. After a thorough examination by the duty Medical Officer, I was rushed straight to a hospital, one solely for RAF personnel, where all the nursing staff were RAF Medical Corps. I was suffering from pneumonia, although fortunately only one lung was infected. I was put to bed and promptly passed out for two days, immediately being put under twenty-four hour medical care. At about this time, a new drug came onto the market to deal with pneumonia, simply known as M & B (May & Baker, the manufacturer). It was exceptionally effective against the fever and I was one of the early patients to be treated with it. When I came round after my long period of being unconscious, Grace was sitting by my bedside – I made the stupid mistake of asking her what she was doing there, sitting on my bed. It was customary practice for the RAF to notify the next of kin, whenever they were dealing with a seriously ill patient. Of course, I was pleased to see Grace, but I wished it had been under different circumstances. Grace stayed for three days until the fever was under control, and the worst was over – the RAF had provided free accommodation for her for the length of her stay. Visiting times were very relaxed and we were able to spend a good deal of time together, with Grace being able to provide a much needed stimulus for my recovery.

After Grace had left, I was in hospital for a further ten days. There was one poor squaddie sharing my ward who had double pneumonia – he nearly failed to make it through, he was so badly ill. I could not help wondering, while lying in bed recuperating, if the dinghy drill was such a good idea. How many cases of pneumonia there were in other wards, I was not sure – the one consoling factor was that no one died. On my discharge from hospital, I was to be given fourteen days sick leave, being instructed to report back to Torquay afterwards. I had already been told by the ward doctor I would be sent home on sick leave, the date being dependent on my recovery. As soon as I had the information about sick leave, I wrote to Grace, telling her to expect me home within a week or so, for fourteen days sick leave. I told her not to worry as I was now feeling much more like my old self. I was sorry that I could not give her the exact time and date but I assured her that, whenever it would be, I was greatly looking forward to seeing her so that we could have some time together. On my discharge, I would have to report to the Orderly Room to collect a railway warrant to my home town.

When Grace arrived back home after visiting me in hospital, she thought that my mother should know about my illness as quickly as possible. The next day, after finishing work, Grace went straight over to Peckham, braving the blackout and possible air raids. My mother answered the door to Grace's knock but, when she saw Grace standing on the doorstep, without any niceties like a simple 'good evening', she merely said, "What do you want?", in a very unfriendly manner. Rather nonplussed, Grace explained that she thought that Het ought to know as soon as possible that her 'Bun' was seriously ill in hospital. My mother asked no questions about my welfare, merely telling Grace that I was her responsibility now, at the same time slamming the door in her face. It was late evening by this time and Grace had to make her way back to Hayes in the blackout, a one and a half hour journey. She felt angry and annoyed at my mother's attitude, but she chose not to tell me about the incident for some time afterwards. When she eventually did tell me, I was not too surprised, knowing my mother. Grace thought that the least my mother could have done was to send a 'Get Well' card – how could a son deserve such a mother?

As soon as I was fit enough to travel, I was sent home. When I arrived home after a tiring journey from Torquay, I was surprised to see Grace talking to Elsie, who wanted to move back into her flat. She was explaining her reasons for wanting to do so – it seemed her younger sister had got herself in the family way. Being a single girl, their mother made it quite clear she didn't want her living at home. Elsie wanted to help her sister and the only way to solve their problem was to move back into her flat. I knew I had no legal right to stay, and it had been agreed before renting, that Elsie had the right to move back in at any time – she had let it on this understanding. Elsie did suggest that Grace could stay on if she wanted to, with her and her sister taking over the main bedroom and with Grace moving into the smaller bedroom.

When Grace and I were alone that evening, Grace decided she was going to move back to London. I was not too keen but Grace was determined – she wanted to be amongst her family, saying that she felt isolated and lonely being on her own in Hayes. There was no real reason why she should live there, now I was in the RAF – the bombing had eased off and there was in fact very little war activity day or night. I could see I was not going to change Grace's mind so we decided to go in to London the following morning.

Grace telephoned Gloria, her supervisor, telling her that I was home on sick leave for fourteen days. She also mentioned that we had to find new accommodation. Grace had saved her holiday days, preferring to take them when I was on leave, so she asked Gloria if she could have some time off. There was no problem with this and Gloria agreed that she had time owing and she wished her good luck. In the morning we set off for London discussing as we travelled in where we would like to live. It was agreed it had to be within easy reach of Peckham. Finding a place was no problem, as in most streets there were many properties with 'For Sale' or 'To Let' boards outside them. Many occupiers had left London during the height of the Blitz and air raids, for more peaceful rural areas. After looking at several available properties, Grace decided on a top-floor flat overlooking Goose Green in Dulwich, south-east London, within easy reach of Peckham. We were shown the flat by the occupiers of the middle-floor flat, a middle-aged, married couple.

The flat consisted of two bedrooms, one very large, overlooking the back garden. A fair-sized sitting room looked onto Goose Green, a very pleasant view. There was also a kitchen at the back of the flat, which was nicely compact, once up the stairs.

The Green itself was not a park, but a very large fenced-off green. There were pathways through it from the houses to the main road the other side of the green – a lot of people used it to exercise their dogs. Grace liked the flat and the scenic outlook. It was her decision, so I went out to telephone the landlord at the number given to me by the middle-floor lady. The landlord owned and ran a boy's prep school in Purley. I told him I was interested in the flat and asked if he could come over, as soon as possible, to approve and finalise the letting. He was obviously keen to have some new tenants, as he arrived within thirty minutes. In the meantime, while waiting, the middle-floor tenant offered us a cup of tea and biscuits. In making this offer, which was gratefully accepted, I assumed the intention was to find out what sort of upstairs neighbours she was going to have. At the same time, she gave us some very useful information about the locality.

The landlord arrived, a tall, distinguished-looking man in his middle forties. He shook hands warmly with Grace and me. He explained it was his mother's house before she died. She had lived in the basement flat, which was empty and would remain so. Terms were agreed, and he suggested that I should have another front door key cut, sending the landlord the bill. I paid a month's rent in advance, in return for which he gave me a key to the front street door and a receipt. Before leaving, he told Grace and me that he came over personally every fortnight to collect the rent. He again shook hands with us both, wished us a pleasant stay and left us to decide how to organise the flat to our liking.

The house itself was a three-storey, Victorian, semi-detached residence with a basement flat. The whole street consisted of some fifty houses, all the same. Each had a small front garden, enclosed by a low brick wall and a hedge, with a flight of concrete steps leading up to a heavy glass-panelled street door, set in a brick porch which was a part of the house. The back entrance led to a very long garden, and coal bunkers.

The house was ideally positioned for shops and public transport, with a mainline railway station within five minutes' walk. The only disadvantage that I could see was that the bathroom and toilet were shared by all the tenants. The water for the bath was heated by a multipoint gas heater, the gas being supplied via the basement flat, which the landlord owned. The rent included all other charges and was very reasonable considering the location and facilities.

After we had concluded all the final arrangements, we went over to see Grace's mother. For old time's sake, we decided to walk across Peckham Rye, where I had vivid memories of the time when the bombing of London started just as I was on my way to see Grace before we were married. For a moment, standing there, I could almost hear again the drone of the bombers and see the lurid light from the burning areas of east London.

We gave Grace's mother quite a surprise at our unexpected arrival, but she greeted us very warmly, being pleased to see us after such a long while. Grace was extremely happy, as she had feared the worst when she received the telegram while I was in hospital – it was such a relief to see

I was making really good progress. She explained to her mother that I was on sick leave, which was why we were around to visit her during the day. The two of them had a long chat, catching up with the family's news. Grace told her mother that we had to leave our flat at Hayes, because of the problems that Elsie was having, but we would be much closer to her as we had, that morning, arranged to rent a flat at Goose Green, and would be moving in as soon as possible. Her mother was pleased to hear this news. Grace asked her mother if we could stay with her for a couple of nights, while we got the flat ready for occupation. Her mother was very pleased to help out in this way and Grace gave her mother one week's ration card of my entitlement.

The following day, I made arrangements with the carriers to collect our belongings from Hayes, and deliver them to Dulwich. In those days this service was available, providing, as in this case, there were only a few items to be moved. Later the same day, I went to the Government office where coupons were issued for wartime utility furniture. This service was primarily available for bombed-out people to set up home again so there was a ready supply of household furniture, at Government-controlled prices. I explained to them that my wife and I were moving into an empty flat at Goose Green, from a fully furnished, rented flat, so we needed furniture to set up home. The people at the centre proved to be extremely helpful, giving me coupons for a double bed, four dining chairs and a table, an occasional table and a sideboard.

There was no choice of style, as all utility furniture was made exactly the same, under strict Government control of design and retail pricing, to prevent black marketing. I took the coupons to a large, local departmental store where they were able to supply all our needs except for the dining table. These items were paid for and a delivery time and date were arranged – the goods could only be delivered at certain times, due to petrol rationing.

I then visited a local, secondhand furniture store and as luck would have it, we found a solid oak, gateleg table for £9 which I paid for, making arrangements for delivery. This was indeed a lucky find and although it was slightly scratched, possibly war-damaged, I was not worried about this as I had learnt how to French polish by helping Bert Greaves, my pre-war friend. During the war years, wood imports were strictly controlled by the Government and most timber went to the makers of utility furniture, working closely to Government designs. These pieces were very sturdy but austere in appearance, nevertheless serving the purpose for which they were made.

The flat was taking shape. This made Grace extremely happy – in fact, she was in seventh heaven to have her own home at last. She was thrilled and I was very pleased to see her so happy. While Grace was busy around the flat, cleaning and scrubbing, I went over to Hayes, to settle up with Elsie, and supervise the move.

While waiting for the men to arrive with the van, I joined Elsie in having a cup of tea. Elsie was petite in size, with a full figure – she had wonderful curly, shiny black hair, and the biggest brown eyes I had ever seen. She was most attractive, except for her rather thin lips, which slightly spoilt her otherwise good looks. She was very pleased with the way Grace had looked after her furniture and other items around the flat and she asked me to pass her thanks on to Grace. Elsie asked if there were any bad feelings and I assured her that there were no such difficulties and that she had actually done us a favour. I described our new flat, not far from Grace's mother, having which was a blessing in disguise.

I helped to load the van with our possessions. I was surprised when the driver told me that delivery to Goose Green would be in two or three days' time. I offered him a pound note saying that there would be another one for the delivery man, if the load was delivered at any time the next day as someone would be there to receive it. The message clearly got through as the goods were promptly delivered next morning. I gave a hand to unload and when all the bits and pieces were upstairs in our flat, I gave the driver the pound as promised. I had never seen Grace so happy – she was in a dream world, the transformation since leaving Hayes was fantastic. During my sick leave, we managed to get the flat all spick and span. Not surprisingly, there were a number of things we still wanted, but we agreed that we would have to wait for a while longer for some of them. Moving into an empty flat from fully furnished accommodation meant starting from scratch.

Grace preferred to cook by gas but new cookers were very hard to acquire. We visited a local showroom but found that there was a long waiting list with little prospect of buying a new one. As our need was urgent, we went to a secondhand store where they had a good selection of used cookers. This was Grace's domain and she saw what she wanted, made arrangements for delivery and connection to the gas mains, saying to me that it would have to do until after the war. In fact, we had been so busy, we had little time to read the papers or listen to the radio, forgetting that the war was still on.

On our way home from the secondhand store, Grace and I visited a local market street. Here we were able to buy a kettle, a 65-piece canteen of cutlery, and a dinner and tea service, having to make two journeys to transport it all home. For the time being, we took our main meals at Grace's mother's house. She was most interested in how we were coping at setting up home, offering us a great deal of advice and useful hints. As the flat was on the top floor, Grace was not all that worried about curtains and she decided to buy the material and make them herself, being very handy with needle and thread, making most of her own clothes, although she had an 'off-the-peg' figure.

While we were sitting down having an evening meal at her mother's, I asked Grace what she was planning to do about her job at the ordinance factory, as she would have to give it up, living some way away now. Grace said that she really did not want to let Gloria down but I pointed out that it looked as if she would have to. I reminded her how I had to make the journey from Forest Hill – Grace would have a little further to travel – and she knew how shattered I was by the end of a long day. That was in peace time, and now there was a war on, anything could happen, I continued. Although it has been quiet for a while, there was no certainty that it would stay that way. In any case, it was unlikely that Gloria would expect Grace to make the journey. I suggested that she would understand if Grace wrote to her, and I offered to go to see her if that would help sort the matter out. Grace asked for a while to think about it and I was happy to let it rest for a while as long as I had an answer before my leave was finished.

Grace was particularly quiet for the rest of the evening, obviously turning over in her mind what she should do. While laying in bed that night, she told me that she had come to the conclusion that she would have to give the job up. She planned to write to Gloria explaining her new circumstances, and the difficulty of all the travelling involved. It was a great relief to me, hearing this – I turned towards Grace giving her a long lingering kiss, and a loving hug. After a few days, Gloria responded with a letter of understanding, saying that she would miss her and asking Grace to keep in touch by phone or letter. She hoped that they would be able to see each other at some time in the future and she wished Grace good fortune – it was a friendship that lasted well after the war.

CHAPTER TWELVE

My sick leave was up. Travelling back in the train to Torquay where I had to report, I was thinking about how fate had played its hand – if I had not contracted pneumonia, I would not have been home at just the right time. It would have been very unlikely that I would have been given compassionate leave just for moving house. That would have meant Grace staying where she was – a very unhappy thought. She would have had to wait until I was owed some normal leave, sometime in the future. As events turned out, it all happened for the best and I had recovered very well from my unwanted illness.

I reported to the Orderly Room and was fixed up with sleeping accommodation. I had been told before going on sick leave that I would have to have a thorough medical examination on my return. With all my travelling around and the effort involved in moving and fixing up the flat, I felt perfectly fit. I was not the least out of breath or suffering any tiredness all the while I was exerting myself – in fact, I felt as fit as a fiddle. I went before the medical board, who gave me a thorough going-over. As I dressed, I was told to report sick in two days' time for the results of the tests. This was normal procedure for trainee aircrew who had suffered a serious chest illness.

I reported sick as instructed, and saw the normal duty medical officer who told me to sit opposite him, on the other side of his desk. When the medical officer had finished reading the notes, he looked a bit glum, peered at me over his half-framed glasses and informed me quite straightforwardly that the prospect of becoming aircrew should best be forgotten. I was really shattered when I heard this news – was it fate playing its hand again? I explained to the officer what I had been doing during my leave, and that I felt perfectly fit and healthy. The MO seemed to disregard this and told me that he would make arrangements for me to see a psychiatrist. Immediately, I asked him why – I certainly wasn't a headcase. Whether this had anything to do with the Morse code business, I was not sure – I was certainly puzzled. This meant the end of my aircrew training, I thought, so what would I do now? Perhaps it was a blessing in disguise, as I felt the RAF was responsible for what happened to me.

While in Torquay waiting for a gunnery course, I had longed for the possibility of becoming a member of a bomber crew as a 'Tail-end Charlie' in a Lancaster bomber squadron. It was the rear gunner's job, not only to protect the tail-end of the plane, but also to inform the pilot of any possible enemy attack from the rear. He and the rudders were the prime targets for enemy fighters – these were the vulnerable points. If the rudders were put out of action, the rest of the aircraft was made easier to finish off.

I felt deeply disappointed at not becoming a member of an aircrew, and not unnaturally felt that fate was against me – first the failing of the Morse code and the medical, apart from suffering pneumonia. After a few days, I was given a rail warrant to report to a place in Lincolnshire. When I arrived at the railway station, a truck was waiting. The truck met all trains to transport RAF personnel to our respective camps and this one proved to be a God-forsaken hole. It was some sixteen miles in any direction from the nearest town, well hidden in the Wolds of' Lincolnshire.

On the way from the station, for quite some distance, I could not help noticing that the wide grass verges alongside the road were stacked two-high with huge bombs. No doubt the appropriate authority took precautions to protect these monsters, I realised. If the German Air Force had successfully targeted these with their bombs, a good part of England would have disappeared without trace. It was an unbelievable sight to behold, and I ruefully thought that I would not want to be on the receiving end of those monsters.

My interview with the psychiatrist was arranged. Why I had to be subjected to this indignity I had no idea, but thought I would soon find out. The psychiatrist was a professional-looking man, dressed in an RAF uniform of the medical corps. He sat at his desk with pen and paper ready to make notes. He asked me what I felt was a mass of stupid questions. One of the most surprising was when was the last time I had wet the bed. Most of the questions seemed to me to be totally irrelevant to my case, and to make no sense at all. Puzzled by all this, I decided to ask a few questions of my own, but I just received grunts for answers. Some time later I found out this was just a formality, in case I applied for an invalidity pension – I never did.

After a few days, I was given a rail warrant to Eastchurch on the Isle of Sheppey in Kent. I was extremely pleased to leave the camp in Lincolnshire, thinking that I would have turned into a real nutcase if I had stayed there much longer. I had been writing to Grace three times a week to keep her up to date with my movements, although I could not receive mail in return, because I had no fixed address. I was wondering how Grace had settled into the new flat, how she was coping and whether she had found a new job yet.

When I arrived at Eastchurch, I soon settled in, adapting very quickly to my new surroundings, and wondering what the future held in store for me, now there was no hope of becoming aircrew. While at this camp, I noticed a number of chaps wearing their aircrew wings and half wings, but with no stripes denoting a rank. This appeared a little odd to me, but after a while, I found out that they had been permanently grounded. I was also surprised to discover that they had all been reduced in rank to AC2, the lowest rank of the RAF, with an associated drop in pay in accordance with this rank. The official jargon for the reduction of rank was 'lack of moral fibre', a phrase which could have been interpreted as cowardice. It appeared that many of these men had done one tour of operations, others more, and that they had just cracked up under the physical and mental strain. All this was kept strictly hush-hush. I suspected it was easier to do this than try to sort out their psychological problems. The RAF could now afford to be fussy who they kept – fully trained aircrew were now coming from Canada and Rhodesia. I wondered what would be written on the grounded mens' discharge papers, should they survive the war.

This explained to me why the place I had just come from was in the wilds of Lincolnshire, in the heart of RAF Bomber Command operational aerodromes. These cases could be dealt with without too much fuss, and no publicity.

There was very little to do at this camp, while awaiting one's fate. After roll-call in the morning, we could do as we wished within the confines of the camp, for the rest of the day. There was very little chance of anyone going AWOL because there was only one way on or off the island by a bridge, which was closely guarded by the police. We were allowed out of camp after 6pm. As long as we were on morning parade for roll-call, there was no curfew.

I had been at this camp for just about two weeks – it was August and corn-cutting time. The local farmers were asking for volunteers to help with gathering the corn, paying them a shilling a day. I thought that I would volunteer to relieve the monotony. The day I worked was a burning scorcher and I finished up with sunburn, my arms blood red where the corn stalks had dug into them. The corn had to be stacked into stooks, ready to be transported to the threshing shed. I dared not report sick as sunburn was a punishable offence and for two days and nights, i suffered agony.

A few mornings later at roll-call, with me still feeling a bit sore, but nevertheless better, names were read out – mine was one of them. Those listed had to remain on parade when the others were dismissed. Those that remained were told to report to the guardroom at 12 noon, with their kitbags.

A meal had been laid out in the dining hall at 11.30am and no one seemed to know what was going to happen. As usual there was plenty of speculation – some, like me, had volunteered from a reserved occupation, so they were expecting their discharge back to civvy street. All duly reported to the guardroom, where there was a covered RAF lorry was waiting. After a check, we were all told to clamber aboard with our kitbags. Some of the men were still wearing their flying badges. When all had been accounted for, the lorry was on its way, travelling for about four hours non-stop. No one was allowed off, not for any reason, until it reached its destination. The lorry turned into an Army Camp at Bury St. Edmunds in Suffolk. The tired passengers all thought it would be an overnight stop, with the journey continuing in the morning.

Everyone was thankful to leave the lorry as sitting down for that length of time on slatted seats was not too kind to our buttocks. When we were clear of the lorry, we were told to line up for a roll-call. The army NCO instructed us to take our kitbags and remove all personal possessions by the morning. After being shown our sleeping quarters, we were directed to the dining room where a meal had been laid on – any food at all would have been welcome.

In the morning, instead of continuing our journey, as we all thought, we were marched to a huge Bolero – a Nissen hut is a midget compared to one of these monsters. On entering at one end, we were told to dump our RAF kitbag and an empty Army one was given to replace it. Moving along a very long counter, the kitbag soon began to fill up as each man was issued with full regulation army equipment – uniform, socks, pants, boots, puttees, the whole lot. Any thought of going back to civvy street was soon dispelled by the Army.

When the whole group had been kitted out, we left the huge warehouse at the other end and were told to go back to our billet and change, leaving our RAF gear there. Those with flying badges were told they could sew them on the Army uniform if they wished – some did and some chose not to. The air· was rather blue with what some were calling the RAF. All were now enlisted in the Army – like it or lump it – on basic pay. For me and the others our RAF days were over. I had served one year and 324 days, with nothing to show for it but a few bitter memories.

When our Army pay books were given out, we were informed that our RAF service would count towards our demob number. We were excused drill and parades – it would have been rubbing salt into sore wounds if we had been subjected to drills. Some of our time was spent having our Army issue altered. After the RAF shoes, the heavy clodhoppers of Army boot issue felt like Frankenstein's monster walking around.

It was still August. I reflected how I would have felt if I had been one of these chaps, being punished merely for being human. I had made friends with one of these men, a bomber pilot. I told him of my own experiences and he then opened up, talking about what had happened to him. He had finished one tour of operations, and was part way through the next when he was returning to base after a successful mission. Suddenly, out of the blue, he encountered enemy fighter action – his plane was badly 'shot up', and in the skirmish, his best pal had been killed. One minute he was talking to him and the next, he was dead. His death had naturally unnerved him. He brought the plane successfully back to base where he asked his CO if he could be stood down for a couple of operations. The RAF reacted by stripping him of his rank, and he had finished up in the sad group that I was with. The man's only interest had been in the safety of the other crew members. His nerves were a bit jagged.

CHAPTER THIRTEEN

During all the time I had been moving around, I had only been able to keep in touch with Grace by letter and she had eagerly awaited and received every one. As I had no permanent address, she could not reply. When Grace received my letter telling her I had now been transferred to the Army, she though I was pulling her leg. I now knew I was not going back to civvy street – there was no point in being miserable about it, there was nothing I could do but to accept what had happened to me. Eventually, my posting came through – I was given a rail warrant to report to a barracks in Brighton, Sussex, another seaside town, but not before an extremely welcome seven days' leave.

Grace was very pleased to see me home, giving me a warm and loving welcome. I was just as pleased to spend some time with my wife, but I puzzled about the fact that she never mentioned or commented on my Army transfer. Perhaps it was too sensitive a subject to talk about although she probably guessed how I must have felt about it. The one comforting thought was that he was still alive. Grace had found herself another job, as secretary to the Commanding Officer, at a local Territorial Army barracks. Her mother was now living next door to Grace, in a basement flat, which was much easier for her to keep clean, and with no stairs to climb. Grace was able to help her by doing her weekend shopping.

I was pleasantly surprised to see how Grace had transformed our flat, making it look welcoming and cosy. The curtains were now up – she had chosen a chintz material, a near match to the sitting room carpet. Looking out of the sitting room window, I noticed a large purpose-built air raid shelter on the green opposite. I asked Grace how long it had been there and she told me it had been built about two months previously. I commented that at least we would not have far to go if there was an occasion to use it.

There had been quite a lull from air raids over the last few months and people were just becoming used to the idea of peaceful nights and sleeping in their own beds, when the Germans reminded the civilians that there was still a war on. They were now sending over what became known as 'Doodle Bugs'. At first, no one quite realised what they were – on first sight they seemed like small, pilot-less aircraft – but they carried around one ton of high explosive. They had a distinct droning noise. People felt quite safe all the while they could heard the engine, but when it cut out, they had cause to be apprehensive, as it would then dive, unpowered and in eerie silence, to explode where it landed. This was pure and simple indiscriminate bombing. With London being so large, it was impossible for the Germans to miss it – wherever the Doodle Bugs fell, they caused the utmost confusion and damage. By good fortune, none of these appalling weapons fell very close to us, although we heard quite a few which exploded on impact in the distance.

By a strange coincidence, three of the premises we viewed when looking for a flat suffered damage, either by the bombing, the Doodle Bugs, or the rockets that followed. These were a very different proposition. The RAF was shooting down many of the Doodle Bugs over the English Channel, before they even reached the mainland – the Spitfires were faster than their prey, so their task was made a lot easier. The RAF had no answer to the rockets which just dropped when they exhausted all their fuel. These terrible flying bombs could not be seen or heard, making life difficult for the civilians. One of these did drop only about half a mile away, on a Saturday afternoon, but fortunately no one was killed or injured. If it had happened during the busy shopping hours, it would have been a different story.

Grace and I decided to buy a three-piece suite – we chose a rich maroon colour. At one time, anything else needed for the flat was going to wait until after the war, but we decided to enjoy a little comfort while we were still alive and able to enjoy it. Our philosophy was that, if we were going to get blown up, we might as well do it in style. When it was installed, it completed the room, complementing the chintz curtains and carpet. The curtains Grace had made herself – she was expert with a needle and thread, and was also blessed with good taste.

Grace got on well with the lady in the flat below. They were a very quiet couple, and she was a very pleasant lady. There were no problems sharing the bathroom or keeping it clean. Meeting on the stairs one day, she was a bit surprised to see me in Army uniform as she thought I was in the RAF – I laughed and said it was a little complicated to explain in a few words.

My leave came to an end all to soon, and I was obliged to set off on the next phase in my military career. Reporting on time to the Brighton barracks Orderly Room, I was shown to my sleeping quarters. In the morning, I reported once again to the Orderly Room after parade, to be told that I was now in the REME and was given shoulder flashes to sew on. All soldiers were given, as part of their kit, a 'housewife' – a compact of needles and thread, and wool for darning socks. I was also informed that as from the next day, I would be attending Brighton Polytechnic for a three months' course, along with several others. The REME (Royal Electrical & Mechanical Engineers) was a new regiment, not long formed, to take over all transport maintenance and repairs, including tanks and heavy guns. When I next wrote to Grace, I told her that I was now in the REME, saying that it was no wonder I had not been discharged, because with my knowledge of electrical and mechanical skills, I was a prime candidate for transfer into this new regiment.

All REME were called craftsmen, being classified as Class III on enlistment. We were excused all guards and barrack duties. The Polytechnic was only a short distance away from the barracks and after morning parade we made our own way there, reporting in by 9am. It was a five days a week course, from 9am to 5pm, with a one-hour break for a midday meal at the barracks – we were taught by civilian instructors. Being excused all regimental duties meant that we had our weekends free and, as there were no weekend passes needed, this meant I could go home. As long as the soldiers were back for the morning parade on Monday, everything was in order. I was beginning to think that, if I had to stay in the service, this was an ideal way of doing so. I knew that I would see Grace at the weekends for the next three months.

She was overjoyed at the prospect of me being home so often. The weekends gave Grace and I ample opportunities to contact old friends and relations. It was not so hazardous going out, as the Doodle Bugs were not the menace that they were at first, many being destroyed before reaching the mainland, or being shot down over open country before reaching London. I made enquiries at the café, but Chris had either sold the business or he had been called up. It appeared that all contact with my pre-war friends was lost – I was hoping and praying they were still alive. One weekend, I called round to see Bert's mother – I knew she would speak to me. We had a long chat over a cup of tea and she said that she was really worried about Bert. He had always thought the world of his mother, and they enjoyed a close relationship since his father had died. Teddy, Bert's younger brother, was there – being a diabetic, he was excused all wartime duties. Their younger sister was at home growing up to be a fine-looking girl. Bert was still sending his mother money from time to time, but she still did not know where he was or what he was doing. Not knowing where he was, his mother found very hard to bear, causing her so much anguish. I thought it would help if, at least, she knew whether he was fit and well.

On the occasional weekend, we would go over to see Grace's twin sister – for twins they were as different as chalk and cheese and one would not have thought they shared the same mother. Her sister was expecting a baby – her husband was excused military service, on account of his bad eyesight and flat feet. He was, however, required to do air raid precaution (ARP) duties, which consisted of helping bombed-out victims, assisting the fire and ambulance services, fire watching and helping to extinguish fires started by incendiary devices. These duties were carried out on a strict rota basis, usually with a retired ex-serviceman in charge. In London, when the bombing was at its height, the ARP were frontline operators. Many were killed doing their civilian duties, which they performed as well as following their normal employment.

Grace and I found time to visit Rose, to see how she was coping. She and the baby were fine, but missing Alf a great deal. During war years, babies were allowed a special allocation of pure orange juice, strictly controlled by the Government, to prevent rickets. Alf had received further promotion and Rose felt really proud of him. If she only knew where he was, she would have been more than happy. All letters were censored and posted via forces' box numbers.

My mother-in-law was now comfortably settled in next door. After our initial upset when I married Grace, we were now on the best of terms, realising it all happened for the best. Her son was somewhere in England although his exact whereabouts, like thousands of other troops, was secret because of the preparations for 'D' day and the invasion of Europe from 'Fortress Britain'. Grace kept in touch with her brother's wife, who lived in another part of Peckham, within easy reach of Goose Green. Having two young children to bring up on her own was no easy task during the war years, but she and the children were managing to keep fit and well.

The only personal consequence of enemy bombing was my mother being bombed out three times. Fortunately she was uninjured – all through the bombing, she slept down the Anderson shelter in her back garden – a bomb had landed on her front doorstep and had blown the front of the house apart. The whole of her street had suffered that night with both sides of the road receiving severe damage. My mother had lost most of her possessions, but still remained in Peckham, in defiance of the German Air-Force. She was offered safer accommodation, but preferred to stay put. In spite of the way she had treated me, I did not wish her any harm. She seemed to have a Jekyll and Hyde personality – towards other people, she was friendly and nice, towards her son any show of love or affection was non-existent. This always puzzled me – I could remember that she never kissed or cuddled me as a toddler, as most mothers do with their children. Why, I never knew. Maybe when my father died, she had the chance of marrying one of her cricketing friends, but blamed me for the lost opportunity. As a child, I remembered my mother's long auburn hair, down to her waist. She had a perfect complexion, and beautiful white teeth which she always cleaned with soot and lemon skin twice a day. She was always smartly turned out for work in her black uniform with clean white collars and cuffs each day and she always wore her hair in a bun when at work. She must have taken someone's fancy – at her job she was the best. I was convinced that she definitely deserved someone better than Tom. I used to muse over how it was strange the way some women picked their men – Tom was a no-hoper and a dead loss as a man and a provider.

When my three months at the Polytechnic were up, I passed my trade test with flying colours, receiving almost maximum marks. Of course, this was made easy for me by my previous experience in electrics and engineering. I was made up to a class I tradesman, skipping class II. This made a difference in pay for both Grace and me, of an extra seven shillings a week each, duly entered in my pay book. I was told by the Commanding Officer of the barracks that it had been decided to send me on another course to learn about refrigeration – I was the only one to be selected. For the first six weeks, I would be based at home, travelling to Dartford to work and learn about refrigeration at J & E Halls for five days a week. Afterwards, still at home, for another six weeks at Lightfoot Engineering Ltd., an equally well-known refrigeration firm at Wembley in North London. The army supplied season tickets for my travelling.

Before I left the CO's office, he congratulated me on my high marks for my trade tests. I replied by saying that my civilian work had been a great help although I realised that the subject of refrigeration was going to be entirely new. The CO responded by telling me that they thought I was the best candidate for the course, a comment that pleased me enormously. I was told to report to the Orderly Room to collect the necessary papers, after which I would be free to leave whenever I wanted to. I gave the CO a cracking salute and left the office for yet another step along my way.

Although my knowledge of refrigeration was nil at the start, I learnt quickly and found the work interesting, and thought that another trade would serve me well in finding work after the war. There were no exams on completion of these courses, or extra pay, just extra knowledge. I was wise enough to recognise by now that I was best suited to doing practical work with my hands.

After the completion of these courses, I was posted to an Ordinance camp at Bicester in Oxfordshire. I very soon decided that this must be the worst camp in the whole of England. It consisted of many boleros scattered over a wide area – they were used as sleeping quarters, stores, offices, workshops – there were no brick buildings to be seen. The working day for the REME was stripping down 251b shell guns, then re-assembling them, in a unheated bolero, really boring work.

The camp's Regimental Sergeant Major was a small man, aged about 45 years. However, what he lacked in height, he made up for with his authoritative voice and he knew he was the boss of the camp, including the officers. He was a real 'pig' and would have been more suited to working in a concentration camp. Being a REME did not excuse me from guard duty, although, during my stay at Bicester, I only did one camp guard duty, and that was quite an experience. This was the only camp, as far as I knew, where the camp guard duty detail was personally inspected by RSM. It would usually be done by the NCO in charge of the guard.

The eagle eye of the RSM was always on the lookout to keep his 'jankers' book full. At Bicester, guard duty was from 6pm to 6am, seven days a week, based on two hours on and two hours off. The two hours off was spent in the guardroom keeping an eye on the soldiers under detention, escorting them to the toilet and back – most times just to allow them to have a smoke. Soldiers were under detention for many reasons, the most common cause being absent without leave (AWOL). Others had been detained for selling army equipment, swearing at or causing bodily harm to an officer or NCO.

One night, I had been detailed for guard duty and, after coming off patrol at 2am and while having a cup of tea in the guardroom, the RSM entered, a little unsteady on his feet, baton under his arm. He crossed to where the soldiers under detention were sleeping in their bunks, one up, one down, and started banging with his baton on the bunks, waking up the soldiers. He barked at them to get dressed in full uniform. While they were doing so, he returned to where the other 'off duty' men and I were sitting, not saying a word. He picked up the full ashtrays of cigarette butts, took them over to the fire buckets full of sand, and emptied the dog-ends into them, giving them a stir with his baton. By this time the soldiers were fully dressed. He made them stand to attention at the end of their bunks and inspected each man, taking his time looking at every one up and down. After the inspection, he made the soldiers empty the fire buckets onto the floor, instructing them to pick out all the cigarette butts. When this was done to his satisfaction, he ordered them to clean and polish the brass on the buckets, refill them with the sand, and then clean up the floor. Once this was completed, he made them stand to attention by their bunks, while he gave them a lecture on how to become good soldiers. Only then were they allowed back into bed – the whole process took about an hour. Whether this was normal practice in other camps I did not know – what I did know was that it was never made easy for any soldier under detention. The Army took the view that one dose of medicine would cure any further misdemeanour. When the RSM left the guardroom, what the soldiers called him could not be repeated – 'pig' would be a very polite word.

Another of the RSM's favourite tricks was to try and catch a patrolling soldier smoking, or failing to make the correct challenge. If this should happen, he would be given a long lecture on the correct way of challenging, demonstrating it by using the soldier's rifle and giving him a further guard duty for future practice.

All the boleros were of single-skin construction, so condensation was rife during the winter months. It was always a problem for us to keep our clothes dry as there were no lockers. The only way we could try to keep our clothes dry was in our kitbags. The risk of catching bronchitis was always a possibility. In each sleeping bolero there were twenty-five double-tier bunks on each side, with just four large combustion stoves to help keep the building warm. These were spaced out against an outside wall. These were the only means of heating allowed. They were all right for the evenings, but if left to go out overnight, in the mornings it would be like being in a refrigerator. If they were stoked up before lights out, they would still be alight in the morning, so consequently, there was always a scramble if one of the bunks near these stoves became vacant. Running the length of the bolero, in between the rows of the bunks, were tables and forms used for leisure purposes, when the men were off duty. Those on 'jankers' had the job of cleaning out the stoves, and getting the fuel in ready for later use. The RSM always made sure there were plenty of men available to do this chore. The stoves were not allowed to be lit in the sleeping boleros before 4pm on any day, including weekends, no matter what the weather was like outside in the winter.

In the ablutions, there was no running hot water to wash and shave in the mornings. When on morning parade, if the RSM noticed that a soldier had not shaved, his name would be entered in his little black book and he would receive seven days jankers, with no appeal, and an extra guard duty. Many men got around this by heating some water on one of the stoves, and having as close a shave as possible, before going to bed. With luck, there could be a modest amount of hot water on the stove in the morning for washing purposes, by using one of the fire buckets. The ablutions were unfriendly places, virtually exposed to the elements. No one wanted to spend more time there than they had to – prisoners of war probably had better conditions and facilities, I thought. I also wondered how the RSM could get away with it. The answer, on reflection, was quite obvious, no one dared to complain as all applications for an interview to see the Commanding Officer had to go through him – there was no short cut. If any of the officers knew what was going on, they made no attempt to stop it.

News was coming through that the war in Europe was coming to a successful conclusion although the Pacific war had yet to be won. I began speculating on my future. On parade one morning, the men were told to keep their eyes on the order board. There was a mixed bunch of regiments at this camp and, despite it being winter, there were men under canvas. A few days later, orders were posted. The names listed were told to have their army issue laid out on their beds, for full kit inspection – any shortages were noted to be paid for at the next pay parade. After the inspection, all kitbags were to be handed in at the stores, with the exception of some soldiers who were instructed to be on another parade at a stated time.

I was on parade with a few other REME and all of us were given fourteen days embarkation leave with strict instructions to report to platform one, at Victoria Railway Station, London, at a stated time and day. No one knew for sure where we would be going, but as usual, there was plenty of wild speculation.

I had been at Bicester just on three months during the worst of the winter. I had been home on the occasional weekend and was pleased to find that everything there was quiet and peaceful. With the invasion of Europe, any further threat of bombing in England had ceased. Grace was a little perturbed at the prospect of me being posted overseas – she had been so used to me being home regularly, she wondered what life would be like without me, and for how long. I persuaded her that speculation would not help and that we should enjoy what time we had together. It was early spring in 1945 – a time to enjoy freedom from Doodle Bugs and rockets. The uncertain, untimely death threat had now ceased for the civilians and fear of being killed or maimed by these weapons of war was over.

While on leave, Grace and I went over to Putney, on a surprise visit to see Valerie, Grace's pre-war best friend. She had done well for herself by marrying s publican. As usual, she was dressed up 'to the nines'. Being a publican's wife seemed to suit her. She was never flashy in her dress, but had a good dress sense, with a style all of her own. Maybe it was her natural red hair that set her off – she knew how to enhance her looks to her best advantage, to make the pub attractive to the male customers.

It turned out this was the first time the two girls had met for nearly five years, so naturally they had plenty to talk about, to catch up with the latest news. We all had a pleasant evening and it was agreed that after the war was finally over, we would meet up again. We shook hands with her husband, George, kissed Valerie, wished them both well for the future and left to catch the bus back home, almost door to door.

We had a wonderful two weeks – I did some necessary jobs around the flat, now looking very attractive and nice. Grace was overjoyed with the results of our labours.

We even had time to visit other old friends and relations. I toyed with the idea of seeing my mother. As much as I wanted to see her, I thought better of it – it would only have finished up with a battle of words, not so much because of myself, but because of the way she had treated Grace, after taking the trouble and exposing herself to personal danger, to let her know that her son was seriously ill in hospital.

At the end of my leave, I kissed and embraced my wife, saying our goodbyes at home. Therewas no point in Grace seeing me off at Victoria. The station would have been full of other troops. Victoria brought back some happy memories of the time when I met Grace there to go on to Chiswick, before we married – this time, the visit there was for a very different purpose, one which I still did not know.

CHAPTER FOURTEEN

At Victoria Station, there were about 200 men in the draft from a variety of regiments, and at roll-call, suprisingly, there were no absentees. We were all shepherded into a waiting train whose destination was the docks at Dover. The lads were placing bets on our eventual destination, with Germany or the Far East being favourite choices. I settled myself comfortably in the train for the journey and my thoughts went back to Grace – now that the European conflict was nearly over, I could go to wherever my posting was taking me with some peace of mind, knowing that she would be safe from further threats of war. She was blissfully happy and safe in her own home and I recalled how emphatic she had been when living in Hayes, about moving back to London. Her insistence on moving proved to be right, although at the time, fearing for her safety, I had not been too keen on the idea and was somewhat apprehensive. Luckily however, although the house was shaken a couple of times, we did not suffer any serious damage during the worst of the London bombings.

When we arrived at Dover Docks, we found a ferry waiting – when all the troops were aboard and accounted for, the ferry left the docks on its way to France. A cooked meal was provided during the crossing for those that could manage to eat it – the sea was very rough, with the ferry being tossed around like a cork and everyone wondered whether it would reach the French coast safely. The weather could not defeat the ferry's captain and we eventually arrived at Calais where another roll-call was made to check that all were aboard and accounted for. We were hurried straight from the ferry and onto a waiting train. As we were boarding the train, every man was given a book of coupons for cigarettes, drinks and refreshments. These were to be used at the stated time, to prevent a stampede to a special buffet carriage that had been attached to the train. The coupons were stamped MEDOC, although I had no idea what that stood for or meant. The train pulled out of the station and travelled non-stop to Milan – those soldiers that had bet on Germany lost their money.

As the train pulled into Milan Station, the platform was packed with Italians of both sexes and all ages, and they all wanted to barter or trade with the British soldiers, for cigarettes and chocolate. No one was allowed off the train during the short time it was stationary at the platform and whilst the crew were changing the engine. Then the whole train set off again, but where to was anybody's guess. More bets were made now that Germany was out of the running as a destination. The train had been travelling for a while, when it slowed down to a crawl, and we all started thinking that this was where we were to get out. It did not stop, but passed slowly through Rimini – from the train's window we could see that the town was completely flattened as though a squad of bulldozers had passed through. Rimini was of strategic value to the Germans as well as the Allies and this was the result.

After passing through the appalling ruins of Rimini, the train gathered speed again, eventually stopping at Bari, further down the east coast of Italy. This was the end of the train journey, and we were all extremely thankful to get off and stretch our legs, a welcome relief after sitting for such a long time on the wooden seats, certainly not made for comfort on long journeys, but probably the best that could be done under the wartime circumstances. The entire group was transported to a local barracks, where, during the course of eating our Italian-style meal, we were told that it was only a temporary stop until a ship was available to continue our journey. We were still not told where we were heading for, so speculation was rife again.

The barracks were really terrible, like the rest of the place – a prison would have been more comfortable. British barracks were palaces compared to these. It seemed to me that this stopover had been prepared in the shortest possible time. We were told that if we wanted money, we could obtain this after finishing our meal – those with English money could change it for British Military currency. This was the only currency recognised by the Italians and British alike. The exchange rate was set by the British Government in the hope that it would curb black market activities.

We were told to behave ourselves – if we wanted a drink, the only drink available was vino, a cheap Italian wine, very dark in colour, but tasty and not all that expensive. I found that I could buy a good measure for a few coppers. We were still speculating where we were going – would it be Palestine or the Far East?

In spite of the Italians being on the losing side, they treated the British extremely well with what seemed like a 'let bygones be bygones' attitude. We were told that the southern part of the town was strictly out of bounds and the signs were clearly visible. We were promised that anyone found inside the forbidden area would be picked up by the Military Police, and be confined to barracks until the ship sailed – no excuses would be acceptable.

In the city itself, there was not a great deal for us to do, because, like the rest of Italy, they were suffering from the aftermath of war with shortages of almost all everyday things. Twelve-year-old boys were offering egg and chips, and also touting their teenage sisters to the Tommies, but not for cash – the only currency they were interested in was chocolate or cigarettes. It was pitiful to see these children having to do this to be able to survive. At the time it was the way of life for most of them. I was relieved to leave the place – I had never witnessed anything like such poverty, even when I compared it with my younger days.

After a few days, we were paraded, and taken to the docks after yet another roll-call. Waiting there was a 'liberty ship', ready to receive its passengers. On embarking, we were told we could sleep anywhere, except the crew's quarters. After looking below decks for a place to sleep and finding no bunks but only hammocks slung wherever a hammock could be slung, I decided to make myself comfortable on deck as the weather was quite warm. I managed to find myself a sheltered and reasonably cosy place at the stern end of the ship.

Liberty ships were the first all-welded American ships, with a displacement of around 2,000 tons. They were known as the 'maids of all work' and were certainly not made for comfort. The ship went on its way although none of the passengers knew its destination. When leaving the shelter of the harbour, the sea was quite calm and the weather was warm with a slight sea breeze, and remained that way for the duration of the journey. The ablutions and the eating arrangements left a great deal to be desired, and were, in fact, appalling. Philosophically, we all agreed that we could not really expect cruise liner standards on a free trip like that. I asked one of the crew members where the ship was heading for, to be told that the destination was Athens, which was the end of the voyage as far as the sailor was concerned. Even my inquisitiveness could not draw any more from the man, so we might travel on or not – no one knew.

Athens it was – the ship entered Piraeus harbour at about nine o'clock in the morning. The sun was just rising, giving the place a picture postcard look. Eventually the ship docked, and we disembarked, thankful to be back on dry land once more. The Military Police were on the quayside waiting to supervise the new arrivals. When all were accounted for, the Military Police organised everyone to be taken to our respective barracks.

The REME were kept separate from the others and taken to a barracks just outside the city centre. After being shown our sleeping quarters, and settling in, we were told that our stay was for only one night, and that a meal would be laid on at a stated time. Afterwards, we could do as we wished for the rest of the day. Those who wanted to write letters were asked to use the special mailboxes provided. For once, letters could be sealed as there was no censor, and we were given a special box number to use in the letters, so that replies could be forwarded to where we might be posted. I wrote to Grace – I had plenty to say after being eight days on the move.

I and another REME, Nobby Clarke, from Manchester had been together since our days at Brighton. To pass his hours away, Nobby spent most of his time burnishing and polishing his boots to a mirror finish – one could safely use them for shaving, they were that bright. If the British Army had held a competition for the brightest pair of boots, he would have won it hands down, putting any Guardsman's boots to shame. After spending the afternoon writing, I had a shower and shave and Nobby and I decided to have a look around the city after our evening meal.

When we reached the city centre, it was like fairyland. The shops were all lit up, with flashing neon signs outside and the streetlights were all on. What a contrast to poor old London, I thought, where folk were still suffering from the effects of the bombing and the blackout. There did not seem to be any apparent war damage to be seen, in spite of the Civil War between the Royalists and the Communists that erupted on 4th December 1944.

When the Germans vacated Greece, it left a political vacuum. That was when the British Government stepped in, at the risk of upsetting the Russians. It was unthinkable that the world's oldest democracy should fall under Communist influence, like the rest of Eastern Europe, Bulgaria, Hungary, Romania and other countries. One of the first actions the British Government had to take was to stabilise the Greek currency. To do this, British Military paper money was issued, set at 400 drachmae to the pound sterling. This was the only legal currency – unlike the Germans' approach, when they issued half-million, one million and other denominations, completely destabilising the drachma.

The following morning, we were taken to an assembly point where we saw, neatly lined up, a convoy of twenty vehicles of all types, including a recovery lorry. I was told that I was seconded to the 17/21st Lancers of the 4th Indian Division as co-driver and mechanic on the recovery vehicle, based at Salonica, on the north-east coast of Greece, where the convoy was heading for. My driver for this journey to Salonica was a ginger-haired RACS chap in his early twenties. He was one of the original militia boys, aged 19 on enlistment – he had seen action in North Africa, and a part of the Italian campaign. Being one of the first to be called up, he was looking forward to his demob, having a very low number. I knew him as Harry.

Once the convoy was complete, the ASM (senior in rank to an RSM) gathered us around him to inform us that our destination would indeed be Salonica. We would make an overnight stop at Volus and if all went well, we should be there before night. There would be two official stops on the way, the length of time depending on what progress we made. The field kitchen men would brew up and give out dry rations on the journey. The ASM wished us good luck and asked if there were any questions. One bright spark asked where Salonica was and the ASM, being in a jovial mood, told him that he would find out when he arrived there. He added that the expected time of arrival would be the next evening. With this, he dismissed us, telling us to go to our vehicles – he led the way in his jeep.

The first part of the journey went without incident, travelling towards Lamia, then on to Volus, making it in good time. On the way, we took a few rest stops for a brew, to stretch our legs, and to have a cigarette. The scenery on the way was absolutely gorgeous – we were seeing it at its best. The convoy carried all necessary supplies for the journey, including petrol, tinned food and water in a water-bowser, which was unsuitable for drinking unless a chlorine tablet was used, although this made the water taste awful. Arriving at Volus on time, in the early evening, there was time for the field kitchen men to prepare a meal, before we bedded down. The REME had to check all the vehicles for water, oil, and petrol, and to ensure that all was in order for an early start in the morning.

After breakfast consisting of porridge, bread and butter (bought locally) and tea, the ASM made a final check before starting the convoy on its way again. The worst was yet to come, driving through the mountains. Some distance from Volus, one of the Dodge trucks started playing up, before coming to a complete halt, bringing the rest of the convoy to a standstill. The convoy was at this time in mountainous country, making it very difficult to pull off the road. The ASM approached me and asked me to find out what the trouble was. I walked over to the corporal driver of the broken-down truck to see if he knew what had caused the breakdown. He replied that the engine had started to splutter and then faded completely when pulling hard. While I was talking to the driver, the ASM ordered the brew-up team to make use of the unofficial stop.

In the meantime I had lifted the bonnet but all seemed to be in order. Going back to the driver, I asked if he had plenty of petrol and the corporal checked to find that his tank was half full. While I was talking to him and carrying on with my examination of the engine, by a stroke of luck I noticed that the petrol filter bowl was half full of water. The filter was bolted to the chassis, directly under the driver's door. I released the glass bowl, making sure I did not damage the cork washer, and emptied the contents, cleaned the bowl and filled it with clean petrol. Replacing the bowl, I asked the driver to start the engine – it started immediately and roared strongly. I told the driver to keep revving, to make sure the fault I had found was the only one. As they were checking that I had indeed cured the problem, the ASM and Sullivan, the recovery driver, came up to ask what the trouble had been. I explained what I had done and the ASM was surprised that the problem had been solved so quickly. Judging by the expression on Sullivan's face, he was very relieved as he did not want the job of towing a heavy truck for the next hundred road miles, in that sort of mountainous terrain. The ASM told me and the driver we had five minutes to get a cup of tea, before the convoy started on its way again.

The convoy had travelled quite a long way farther before coming to a stop again. My truck was sixth in line. The hold-up this time was to cross a narrow ravine – the original bridge had been destroyed and a temporary one had been put in its place, but with no sides to it. When my driver went up to see what the hold-up was, and saw the ravine and the method of crossing, he returned to the truck and became quite nervous. The ravine had to be crossed – there was no other road to Salonica. It was a very busy road and the hare-brained Greeks were up and down the road all day during the hours of daylight. For safety's sake, it was decided to cross one vehicle at a time. When it came to my driver's turn to cross, he just froze, and completely lost his nerve at the prospect of driving over the narrow crossing. I tried to talk him round saying that the others had crossed without problems. All Harry did was to mutter his demob number. I noticed in the driver's mirror that the ASM was approaching us very quickly. Harry was still sitting in the driver's seat motionless – I had never seen a man so scared. With some quick thinking, I pushed Harry over to the passenger seat, sitting in the driver's seat myself, just as the ASM got to the door. He bawled a question at us about what the hold-up was and that we had to be in Salonica before dark. I responded by saying that there was no trouble, but Harry was not feeling too well and I would be driving. The ASM barked that he did not care who was driving as long as someone was and the convoy started moving again. We all crossed the ravine without incident – the recovery truck being the last to cross, a five-tonner with all the recovery gear could have been a problem. Sullivan, the driver, was a regular soldier, a 'Desert Rat' of the Western Desert and a part of the Italian campaign, and he was game for anything. Having crossed the ravine safely, everyone gave him a cheer and he doffed his hat in acknowledgement. My driver thanked me for not letting on to the ASM and agreed to tell me when he felt like taking over again.

It was still some way to go to Salonica – the remainder of the journey was uneventful and the convoy managed to keep to the time schedule the ASM had set. The ASM was based in Salonica and had been detailed to go to Athens to take charge of the convoy as he knew the road and what problems might be encountered on the way, hoping the convoy would make it before dark. Harry recovered from his fit of nervousness and resumed driving – he was a good driver, so consequently I felt comfortable with him at the wheel. Eventually the convoy arrived at the outskirts of the city where we were met by the Military Police and the Town Marshal, who lead the way in his jeep to where the convoy had to end its journey.

The brick-built barracks were not far from the city centre and were already occupied by other Army personnel. The convoy arrived safely at its final destination in daylight, giving the drivers time to park their vehicles and have a clean-up, before sitting down to their first cooked meal for a couple of days. All meals were prepared and cooked by the field kitchen team, who were not expected to cook a proper meal en route, as it would have taken far too long. At the barracks, all cooking was done out of doors, at all times. The device they used was like a big bread oven, with pressurised blowtorches providing a very effective heat. Following a very enjoyable cooked meal, and hot drinks, we were shown our sleeping quarters – the barracks were only for recreation and sleeping purposes.

Although I had heard unofficially that I was to be Sullivan's mechanic and co-driver, the ASM confirmed this in the morning. When out on a breakdown, what we could not fix on the spot had to be towed back to the workshops.

I had been writing home to Grace regularly, in spite of being on the move after leaving England. Incoming mail was a little more difficult to receive while in transit. It was a tremendous surprise to us all to discover mail waiting for us in the Camp Post Office. Grace was surprised that I was in Greece, but all the same very relieved that my posting was not for the Far East, and I felt the same way. When we were all on parade, the Commanding Officer of the Camp addressed us, telling us to keep a low profile out on the streets and in the cafés. We were warned not to get into any political discussions with anyone, not even amongst ourselves. We were there to keep law and order and to prevent clashes between the Loyalists and the Communists. If trouble did erupt between ELAS and EOKA, our task was to nip it in the bud as soon as possible. One could guess which side the British were on. The Brigadier finished his address by saying that anyone found breaking this order would be severely punished. During the eighteen months I was in Greece, I never heard of any disturbances of any consequence in spite of the political vacuum that existed at the time.

The CO, a professional soldier, was regarded as 'one of the boys' – he was a gentleman, firm but always fair. He found the time to talk to the men under his command, irrespective of rank, making sure that they were as happy as possible. I had the responsibility of keeping his official car and jeep in good repair, a job delegated to me by my ASM. There were three workshop mechanics, one of whom was Nobby Clarke. Nobby and I were not buddies although we enjoyed the occasional evening out to have a drink and a meal together. Mostly we talked about our respective families – Nobby was not married, but he was engaged, hoping to marry when he was demobbed.

A corporal was in charge of the workshops and he attended to all the paperwork, as well as being in charge of the stores. The ASM was in overall charge of all transport, including the vehicles, stores and the equipment locked away in the German Compound. He was a regular soldier, like Sullivan, and they had been together since the Western Desert Campaign. Summer was coming and the CO, with his Adjutant, set out one day to find a suitable location in the mountains for a summer camp. They selected an area about forty miles from Salonica, not far from the Bulgarian frontier. Whether the CO named the place, or whether it was its right name I don't know but it was called Ali Baba.

Sullivan and I got on well together as a team – Sullivan had an easy-going nature and he was good at his job. While out on the road, we had some good times together, Sullivan always making light of any situation with his comic personality. We were kept busy rescuing broken-down vehicles. The road to the summer camp was partly a dirt road and the men of the Pioneer Corps had the never-ending job of filling in the potholes.

Although the recovery service and workshops were still based at Salonica, Sullivan and I spent a great deal of time at the summer camp, where most of the officers and men were. This camp was not too popular with the men, as there was no nightlife, there were no cafés or bars, and more importantly, no women.

To my knowledge, there was only one fatal accident, when a soldier was returning to camp in the darkness and ran off the road, down a precipice. It was particularly important to keep a safe distance from the edge of the road as there were no crash barriers, in most cases just a sheer drop over the edge. Many of the Greek drivers were maniacs and most of their vehicles were held together with anything from nails and rope to parts salvaged from unattended military vehicles. Spares were in short supply, which made it imperative for the recovery team to hurry to the broken-down vehicle as soon as possible and before there was only the plundered body shell left to tow away.

When summer really arrived, with temperatures of 30°C, the men who had to stay in the city were ordered by the CO either to stay in their billets between the hours of 1pm and 4pm, or go swimming. I had the use of a jeep, so with Nobby and the two other mechanics, I went sea swimming as often as possible. I had found a pleasant, sandy beach, with a vineyard almost down to the water's edge. On one of our first visits, I went off to find the owner, asking him if I could buy some grapes. The kindly owner gave me a whole bunch and even though I offered to pay, he would not accept any money. He told me that he was only too pleased to be of service and told me to be his guest. I thanked him for his generosity, saying that I would rather pay as we were likely to go there quite often. The man would not hear of it and insisted that I should just help myself, even if he was not there. I washed the grapes in the sea and then left them to dry while going for a swim. The water was beautifully warm, more like having a bath. We had to try and avoid the jellyfish lurking in the shallow waters although it was impossible to miss them all – they were only small, but if one did get stung it was only like brushing against stinging nettles, just a nuisance. We stayed as a foursome as often as possible, relaxing on the beach after our swim, eating the grapes, large black ones, delicious and sweet.

On some afternoons after our swim, we would wander farther along the beach, for something to do to pass the time, and generally to admire the marvellous view across the gorgeous bay. One afternoon we wandered a little farther than usual and came across a purpose-built airstrip, most of it projecting out to sea. Judging by the length of it, it was intended for heavy bombers. There were no tyre marks or buildings near or on the airstrip, so I assumed that it had not been completed before the Germans had been forced to leave Greece. We could only speculate as to why it had been built, possibly to attack targets on the Black Sea or maybe further afield to the oil fields in Persia, as it was known then. Whatever it was built for, it gave my swimming friends and me a very good diving platform for the lazy afternoons. The next time I saw the vineyard owner, I asked him about it but he was not too sure what it was for, but he did say that it had been mainly built by forced labour. We agreed that the Germans had possibly done Greece a favour by providing what could, in years to come, be used as Salonica's International Airport.

Chapter Fifteen

Sullivan had a soft Irish accent. He was in his early twenties, short and stocky in build, with powerful shoulders that proved to be a great asset when driving the recovery vehicle. He was blessed with a full head of sandy-coloured hair which could have been the result of his Army service in the Western Desert campaign, in the early 1940s. His warm smile and his hazel eyes with their roguish glint, together with his mischievous sense of humour made him a very likeable person. Sullivan was a career soldier, enlisting in the regular army at the age of eighteen, having been a boy soldier cadet from the age of fourteen. I was uncertain if he had any family – he never spoke or mentioned anyone, so I assumed he may have been an orphan. Sullivan and I were becoming quite pally, as far as our respective jobs were concerned, recognising the need to be dependent on each other.

One day out on a recovery call, Sullivan pulled off the road to have a leisurely smoke – he would never smoke whilst driving as the recovery vehicle took all his concentration. I took the opportunity to ask him why he was allowed a live-in girlfriend. Sullivan explained unashamedly that, due to his sexual needs, he spent a good deal of time in hospital with some sort of venereal complication. For this reason, the CO officially gave his permission for him to cohabit with his girlfriend. He added with his roguish grin that he supposed his CO thought he would be more useful to the Army out of hospital rather than in it.

His current girlfriend, Mellissa, was an extremely nice girl, definitely not a camp follower. I came to know her quite well, discovering that she was a war orphan, hoping to marry a British soldier. Mellissa's mother was Greek, her father a British soldier – they met in the First World War in Salonica. She was a nurse, he was a patient recovering from wounds suffered during the Allies' ill-fated attempt to gain a foothold on the Turkish mainland. Mellissa was the result of their relationship. They were both very much in love and hoped to marry after the war, but fate decided otherwise as he was killed in action on the Western Front in France. Her mother died when Mellissa was a young girl, so, having no living relatives, she went to live with a girl friend's family. The two girls were about the same age and they became very close friends – more like sisters. She was a striking-looking girl, not beautiful but extremely attractive.

The Army employed local civilians – Mellissa was employed as an office worker and interpreter. Because of her relationship with Sullivan, she was on Army rations, having all her meals provided free. One evening Mellissa invited me to join her and Sullivan to have a meal and a drink at one of the many cafés and restaurants close by the waterfront – a very popular haunt for the Greeks as well as servicemen, with its varied selection of cafés and bars. Mellissa led the way inside to a vacant table – although it was a warm and humid evening, she preferred to eat inside. They had only been sitting there for a short while, when the most gorgeous girl came over to chat to Mellissa and Sullivan. She was introduced to me as Maria. Mellissa explained to me that she lived with Maria's family before moving in with Sullivan. She must have mentioned me to Maria at some time previously because the newcomer said in very good English, "So this is the friend you spoke about?" She was invited to sit down and join us and stayed for the rest of the evening, talking, eating and drinking – all greatly enjoying each other's company. I could not stop myself from admiring her beauty, in many ways reminding me of my wife, with her dark complexion and black hair.

I learnt that Maria was in her early twenties and unattached and, to be fair, she did have the edge when it came to looks. She had sparkling brown eyes, shiny black hair hanging loosely to her shoulders, very little make-up – just a hint of lipstick – and a figure most girls dream about. About 5' 7" tall, she wore a light floral cotton dress, with a halter neckline, which showed off her figure to perfection. I suspected this was a pre-arranged date and indeed, Maria seemed to be attracted to me but no more than I was to her. Mellissa was trying to do a bit of match-making, although at the time neither Mellissa nor Sullivan was aware that I was married.

During the course of the evening, it was suggested that all four should go to the local cinema one evening the following week – apparently there was a good film showing that both girls wanted to see, an American film with Greek subtitles. I was a bit reluctant at first, but after a little coaxing from Mellissa, I agreed. A date and time were set, providing we were not called out to a breakdown. In case of an emergency after duty hours, Sullivan and I had to leave information in the Orderly Room about our whereabouts so that we could be contacted. On one occasion while we were watching a film at the cinema, a message was flashed on the screen we were wanted for an emergency breakdown. There was no other recovery vehicle or crew in the area so we were virtually on twenty-four hours standby duty.

We all met at the café, at the arranged time, arriving there early so we could have something to eat and drink, before setting off to the cinema where there were two performances each evening, at 6pm and 8.30pm. Preferring the late show, we had booked our seats in advance. We left the café for the casual fifteen-minute stroll to the cinema, Mellissa and Sullivan leading the way with Maria and I following behind. For some reason, I felt very proud walking with Maria, with her arm through mine. We all sat together in the cinema, just talking before the light dimmed to herald the start of the film. Once the lights were out, Maria made herself comfortable by snuggling up to me – to be honest, I was uncertain how to react – I did not want to lead her on by reciprocating her warm affectionate nature, so thought it best to let Maria make all the moves. To my relief, she was quite content just to nestle close to me.

Our meetings continued and, after a while, Mellissa confessed to me that Maria really liked me. When I heard this, I realised that I had a tricky problem on my hands. As a foursome we spent many happy hours together, swimming, dancing and looking around the shops that were now being filled up with goods and merchandise after the years of scarcity.

It was now late summer and the evenings were warm and balmy. This did not help my problem one bit – although as long as we stayed together as a foursome, I felt quite safe, not from Maria, but from myself. I always made sure I was never alone with Maria because that could have proved fatal, pushing temptation beyond human endurance. The spark was definitely there – I did not want it to develop into a flame of uncontrolled passion. When saying goodnight, I was sorely tempted to kiss her fervently on her well-shaped, inviting lips, but settled for safety's sake with a modest peck on the cheek. Somehow I managed to control my feelings, wondering what would have happened if I had succumbed to the temptation. In all my service days, this was the closest I came to cheating on my wife. There had been a WAAF at Yatebury, the wireless school – although very attractive, she had come nowhere near the temptation I was fighting against with Maria.

On the occasional Sunday, Maria would invite the three of us to meet her mother and father, at her home, for a meal and a chat, with Maria having to act as interpreter. I greatly enjoyed these visits. Their flat was in a small tenement building, on the first floor, reaching it by a beautiful marble and metal ornate staircase.

After a great deal of thought and not a few nights wrestling with my conscience, I thought it best to be honest with Maria, before our association went to the point of no return. Very gently, I explained to her that she was the most attractive girl I had ever met, she was good company, very desirable, and I felt flattered to be in her company. I went on to say that I had a wife in England and took a small photograph out of my tunic pocket to show her. Her response was to ask whether we could remain friends, even so. Of course, I was relieved at this response and the two of us remained good friends all the while I was stationed in Salonica for the next eighteen months.

The recovery vehicle was never easy to handle or drive. Occasionally Sullivan would pull off the road for a breather and to enjoy a leisurely smoke. It was on one of these occasions that I spoke to Sullivan about

Maria, saying that, if I had been an unscrupulous person, I could have easily have led her on but I liked her too much to take advantage of our relationship. Sullivan, puffing away at his cigarette, told me that Mellissa had said that Maria really enjoyed my company, and liked me a great deal. I confessed to Sullivan that I was enormously attracted to her too, but no one had any idea what mental torment she was causing me. To me, it was a question of mind over body and that was the part of me that was going to win. I desperately wanted a physical relationship, whereas the more logical part of my mind was telling me to be more cautious and to think of my wife back in England, whom I loved very dearly. I sensed that Mellissa was eager to see our relationship blossom. To me, it was not the question of just a summer fling – Maria deserved something better than that. If I had been single, I would have taken my chances as there could possibly have been a future for us together. I continued by saying somewhat ruefully that it was an idea best forgotten about, as I was a married man. I had no doubt that I would always remember her and, in the meantime, we would remain the best of friends. By this time Sullivan had finished his cigarette, and drove off without saying a word. The Army never made it easy for a serviceman to marry a local girl, both having to go through a lot of red tape, making it as difficult as possible to marry – a test of true love.

When calls came in from broken-down vehicles, the drivers were under strict instructions not to leave their vehicles unattended for any reason, until the recovery team came on to the scene. Sullivan and I were also under orders to inspect the vehicle for any missing parts, no matter what, with the driver being held responsible for any loss. Spare vehicle parts were bringing big money on the black market and they were always a temptation. The spare wheel was the favourite until it was discontinued. All vehicles had a complete history sheet back at the workshops. It was the driver's responsibility to check his vehicle before taking it out, against the workshop file sheet to see if anything was missing. There had been a considerable amount of pilfering going on, so this rule was religiously enforced. In the city, if a vehicle was left unattended, no matter for how long, it would be stripped of parts, in some cases the whole vehicle, just like a plague of locusts going through a cornfield – tyres and spares were bringing big money.

Sullivan and I were not too popular with some of the drivers. Our philosophy was, why should we stick our necks out for those that wanted to take the risk of making themselves a few extra drachmae. To my knowledge, there were at least six soldiers awaiting Courts Martial, for either abandoning their vehicles, or selling parts from them. The Army took the view there must have been collusion with the driver if it was stripped, or if parts were taken from it. It was up to the driver to prove he was the innocent party. Outside the city this problem was not so bad.

On one hair-raising occasion, Sullivan and I were called out to attend a breakdown after dark, up in the mountains. We found the vehicle without too much trouble and Sullivan pulled up behind the truck, leaving his headlights on, and climbed out of the recovery vehicle to investigate the trouble. I was sitting in the passenger seat close to the verge. It looked to me as though the vehicle in front was pulling away, but it suddenly dawned on me that it was the recovery truck gradually moving backwards. When I realised this, I reached for the handbrake, and at the same time tried to smash the vehicle into gear. Sullivan realised what was happening and rushed round to the driver's door, opened it and reached for the handbrake to yank it fully on. It was unlike him to forget to apply the handbrake and to make sure it was fully engaged. I quickly scrambled out on the driver's side to find that the rear wheels were mere inches from the edge and a sheer drop – another yard could have proved fatal. Sullivan chocked both rear wheels, gingerly clambered into the cab, started the engine, leaving the door open for a quick exit, if need be. Very slowly, he moved forward away from the edge, and danger.

Needless to say, Sullivan was nowhere near his usual self for some time afterwards, but neither was I, we both had anxious moments. Sullivan had a smoke to calm his nerves. In the event, the recovery truck was safely turned round, and we managed to hitch the broken-down vehicle to it. The recovery was equipped with a hoist, jib and winch. It was too risky to tow in the dark, especially up in the mountains, so Sullivan hitched it to the hoist – the driver of the truck sat with us in the cab for the journey back to Salonica. When back at the barracks, Sullivan invited me into his billet to have a stiff drink to steady our nerves, and I stayed for a while talking to Sullivan and Mellissa. During our conversation, nothing was said about Maria. I noticed how orderly their billet looked – a vast improvement with the women's touch, as against the usual drab appearance of most billets. I remarked how cosy the room looked and Mellissa was pleased that I had noticed and had made such a comment.

Demobs were now taking place – the Pacific War was over and demob numbers were coming up quickly. My number was 39 – I knew it was not far away and coming up shortly, possibly in a week or so. When group 39 came round, the others in the group were released but my name was not on the list – naturally, I wondered why. Later that day, I had a word with my ASM but he just shrugged his shoulders and suggested that my name had merely been overlooked. When the next list was posted, my name was still missing. This time my ASM explained it by saying that my replacement had not arrived. The next time it happened, I asked for an interview with the CO, making my application through my ASM as was the normal procedure.

Grace was beginning to think all sorts of things – was I in trouble? Did I want to come home? I wrote to my wife, giving her the reasons and excuses why my demob had been deferred – I thought she only half believed me, causing a little friction between us. Demob numbers had by this time moved up to 49. After constant stalling by my ASM, I finally got my interview with the camp's Adjutant, a young Captain. We had met several times before in the course of our respective duties. The ASM marched me before the Adjutant and I was told to stand easy. It was customary for an officer hearing a case to be primed on the subject before an interview was granted, so I was puzzled when the captain asked me what the trouble was. Patiently I explained that I thought my wife should be informed why my demob was continually being deferred, saying that it was causing some friction between us. She knew what my demob number was and where the system was up to at that point, well past my number. I said that I believed that she thought I was in some kind of trouble, although I had written explaining the circumstances as I knew them. I asked for an official letter to be sent. Both the Adjutant, who was twisting his pen in his fingers, and the ASM who was standing by the desk, were attentive to what I was saying. The Adjutant sympathised and agreed a letter would be sent in due course. With the interview over, the ASM pulled me to attention, saluted the officer, turned about and marched out of the office. When outside, we both went our separate ways, without saying a word to each other. A letter was eventually sent and this did help between me and Grace. I had a sneaking suspicion that the ASM had something to do with my deferment – he was within his rights to do so if the ends justified the means, but only for a short time.

There was very little that I could do about my deferment. I thought I had done all I could to hasten things along, so there was no point in getting annoyed with my ASM. One day not long after the meeting with the Adjutant, the ASM asked me if I was doing anything special that evening. No arrangements had been made with Sullivan even though we never seemed to tire of each other's company, either working or going out socially when off duty. I held no grudge against the ASM, but at the same time wondered why I was being asked. I was instructed to pick the ASM up at 7.30 that night at his billet.

The ASM came out of his billet in his best uniform, with well-polished Sam Brown and shoes, looking really smart and pleased with himself. His batman must have spent a great deal of time pressing his uniform, putting knife-edge creases in his trousers, for this special occasion. As he stepped into the jeep, wiping the seat before he sat down, I started the engine to be on our way. Once out on to the street, the ASM gave his instructions where to go and I made a mental note of the route, eventually pulling up in one of the side streets, outside a rather splendid villa. It stood in its own grounds, protected by a high brick wall, with an entrance to the villa through oriental iron gates from the pavement. As the ASM alighted, he told me to pick him up at midnight, thrusting a fistful of banknotes into my hand and telling me to go and have a meal and a drink. I was mightily pleased with this and said that I most certainly would do as instructed, stuffing the money away at the same time as trying to get a glimpse of the lucky lady. The property was well laid back from the street, the front door partly hidden by the pavement trees and the garden shrubbery – I never did catch a glimpse of her. This happened on several occasions and each time the ASM gave me money, the sort of money that could never be spent normally – I wondered if it was conscience money.

I decided to take Sullivan, Mellissa and Maria to wine and dine at one of Salonica's smartest restaurants – one that had a floor show. My friends did make a few remarks about my extravagance, but I casually said it was my thirtieth birthday, so I felt like celebrating. A very enjoyable evening was had by the four of us and, as usual, Maria was looking adorable. When seeing her home, she thanked me for the wonderful evening, coming up very close to me to give me a parting kiss. I just managed to turn my head in time, to avoid a kiss on the mouth – if this had happened, there was no telling what might have followed. I often wanted to gather her up in my arms and kiss her as a lover, for I was truly in love with her, and from all the signs, Maria was in love with me.

Of course I could not confide in Sullivan, or anyone else, about the money that started to pile up, causing me problems about the best way of spending it, without drawing too much attention to myself. The problem was made more difficult by being told by my ASM to draw my pay fortnightly, so as not to arouse suspicion. To make matters even more complicated, the British Military money was changed and revalued unexpectedly, in the hope of keeping black marketing activities down to a minimum. I could only change to any new money, an amount equivalent to what I drew on my last pay day. Civilians were given a week's grace to change to the new money.

I thought about what I should do with the cash – I could possibly have changed it with Maria's help but decided otherwise, and then I had a brainwave. I went to one of the best jewellers in Salonica and bought a pair of silver filigree earrings with small cameo inserts, a cameo brooch set in gold with a gold safety chain, and a twisted multicoloured coral necklace. With the remainder of my surplus cash, I bought Maria a farewell present. I asked the jeweller for small individual boxes in which to put these items of jewellery.

When back at the barracks, I carefully wrapped them in tissue paper from a toilet roll, put them into a registered envelope and posted them to my wife with a covering letter. I also enquired about sending flowers to England by Interflora – this service was reintroduced after the European war was over – and arranged to have a beautiful bouquet sent to my wife. Getting rid of all my extra cash was quite a relief. When I was having this money thrust upon me by my ASM, it had not occurred to me how I could explain how several thousand drachmae had come into my possession. If I told the truth, it was possible that my ASM would have denied all knowledge. I could have been in real trouble, simply by doing my ASM a favour – this could have further delayed my demob by at least three years. I suspected that my ASM was acquiring his extra cash from doing deals over the stores and equipment in the German compound. He was in sole charge, whilst waiting orders from the War Office, about how best to dispose of them. Whether there was an inventory, I did not know – I had never seen one. I guessed why the ASM was getting rid of his spare cash – he had probably got wind of another change of currency. He never asked me how I managed to spend the handouts.

On the next occasion when I was in the café with Maria, Sullivan and Mellissa, sitting around a table enjoying a meal and a drink, I handed my farewell present to Mellissa and my special present to Maria. When she opened it and saw what it was, I could see a tear of joy sparkling in her lovely eyes. Not only did she say how pleased she was, she came round to where I was sitting and sat on my lap, giving me a lingering kiss full on the mouth. I just sat there and enjoyed it – it seemed that she was determined to have a farewell present of her own, a kiss of love and appreciation. Showing her thanks made me a little embarrassed, especially in front of the other customers – she had a very affectionate nature, catching me completely by surprise. When I got my breath back, I told them that my demob number should be coming up shortly, so this was my farewell presents to the girls. I said, with real feeling, that it had been more than a pleasure knowing them both, and of course, my partner Sullivan. I had gathered memories I would always cherish for many years to come.

I thought that if I had not been married, there might have been a future for me and Maria – there was no doubt that I was in love with her, and I felt sure that she loved me in return. Discretion being the better part of valour, I realised it was best not to pursue my feelings towards her – a lost opportunity maybe, but at least I could return to Grace with a clear conscience. It was very difficult at times to keep our relationship on a platonic basis as I thought on numerous occasions that Maria wanted to become more involved. I thought it best to have a clean, sharp break although feeling absolutely wretched by doing so.

I was beginning to wonder if I would ever be released. The ASM offered me my sergeant's stripes but I just thanked him, saying that I would have said yes a year before, but now it was too late – they would not make a great deal of difference. The ASM could rely on my discretion, besides being trustworthy and reliable, confessing to Sullivan he did not want to lose me – I was the best mechanic he had ever had.

It was approaching summer again in 1946 and swimming was the order of the day for the city soldiers, but now with a different bunch of chaps. They could not understand why I was still in the army – I should have been out months ago. The new men coming into the Army were National Service men, only in for two years. One night I became quite paranoid over my demob, so I decided to go out on the town, leaving the jeep behind, with the idea of getting drunk – not paralytic but just enough to relieve my feelings. I found a quiet bar and indulged in a heavy session, staying off the Ouzo. I had seen many squaddies doing strange things, and heard of some accidentally killing themselves whilst hallucinating, drinking it like scotch, instead of adding plenty of water as the locals did. Somehow, I managed to stagger back to my billet and collapsed onto my bed, passing out for the count. In the morning, I was still not feeling too good when Sullivan came looking for me. Seeing me in that condition, he said that he could manage without me, telling me to keep out of sight until later. Relieved, I fell back on the bed and promptly went back to sleep to sleep it off.

Apart from the demob business, I was missing my wife – the affair with Maria, although under control, was nagging at me. I thought maybe I was being punished for being too good at my job. However, I cheered up quite a lot when I received a letter from my wife saying that she had received the jewellery safely – it had not been opened by the customs. Grace was also feeling depressed, not having seen me for such a long time. She had so looked forward to my homecoming on my demob, and was sorely disappointed when I was prevented from leaving the Army at my due time. The presents and the flowers had arrived at the right moment to cheer her up.

One morning in early September, the ASM came to me while I was making my bed. He told me that there was no need for me to do that, but instead, I had one hour to return all my gear to the stores, pack all my personal belongings and be down at the docks by nine o'clock sharp. On hearing this, I could have kissed him. I had no time to say goodbye to anyone, especially Sullivan and Mellissa, and of course, my precious Maria. I wondered if the ASM had been rumbled and wanted me out of the way – the ASM himself took me to the docks, and accompanied me onto the gangplank ready to embark, after I had been checked off. He gave me a warm handshake and wished me well. When I got to the top of the gangplank with just my personal belongings, I hoped fervently that I had not forgotten anything in the scramble. I turned and waved goodbye to the ASM, who returned my wave – I had to pinch myself to make sure that I was not dreaming. During the eighteen months I served the ASM, we had enjoyed a very good relationship – there had not been any cross words. In fact, Sullivan and I had been given virtually a free hand for the smooth running of the department. I decided that I would write to Sullivan when I was back home, to explain the haste of my departure.

The ship was heading for Marseilles in France – there were no other ports of call on the way. After docking and once all the formalities had been dealt with, I caught a train going straight on to Calais. There was no stopover there and I was whisked off the train, onto a waiting ferry. Everything seemed to be going like clockwork. I had wanted to send a telegram to Grace, to let her know I was on my way home but the journey was so swift, I could not find a single opportunity. While on the ferry, a cooked meal was provided free, so I arrived in England well fed and relaxed. On reaching Dover, again there was no delay – off the ferry, straight to a waiting train. Before boarding, I had my name and military number checked by the Military Police, but still there was no time to send a telegram. The train started on its way, running straight through with no stopping or changing, eventually arriving at Beeston, Nottinghamshire, my Demob Centre. So I was back in England at last. At Beeston, I was fed and bedded – arriving late at night, there was no way I could let Grace know of my homecoming. In the morning, I tried to find the time to send a telegram, but the Army was sticking to a tight schedule. After my last Army breakfast, I was taken, not marched, with the others of my group to the Demob Centre. Here we were all issued with civilian clothes, certainly not made to measure. We were allowed to keep what Army issue we wanted, entering at one end of the stores as Army, and out at the other end as a civilian. I recalled a similar process when I moved swiftly from RAF to Army.

I was given a rail warrant to my home station, and gratuity money for 28 days paid leave. My discharge papers and any money owing would be sent on to me at my home address. I managed to change my drachmae for English money, but still could find nowhere to send a telegram. I could not phone Grace at her office, as I had no note of the number and there was no one I could contact to pass the message on, so I resigned myself to wait, hoping for the best.

We were taken to the mainline railway station. While waiting for my train, I made mental comparisons between my life in the Army and the RAF – I came to the conclusion my life in the Army had been better. The only blemish was the demob business. I was eventually demobilised with group 53 – my number was 39. I also wondered why I had been sent on a refrigeration course, as it must have cost the Army a lot of money to give me the comprehensive knowledge I gained. While in Greece, I never saw a fridge, let alone serviced one. In most Greek butcher shops, the meat just hung up on display – whether it was ever refrigerated I doubted – I had no idea how it was kept fresh.

Eventually I arrived home at 6pm, let myself in, and climbed the stairs to the flat. On my way up, I met the lady from the middle flat. She greeted me warmly and said that Grace was not in, having returned from work and then gone out again. Being midweek, I doubted whether Grace would go visiting. I dumped my gear and took a careful look around the flat. In her letters, Grace had kept me informed of the improvements she had been making by adding other pieces of furniture and some interesting ornaments and decorations. She had certainly made the flat homely and comfortable. I wondered if she would be next door with her mother, so, after having a quick wash and shave and a cup of tea, I went next door.

When Grace's mother responded to the knock on the door, she had difficulty believing her eyes. I greeted my mother-in-law with much affection and explained that I had been travelling for the last six days and was feeling a little tired. I asked her if she knew where Grace was, hoping that she might have been there with her She responded by saying that Grace had said something about going out for a drink with a friend, but she did not know precisely where. All this conversation took place on the doorstep, so I asked if I might go in to have a talk. The old lady invited me in and I started to tell her how hastily I had been despatched, with no time to send a telegram. Her view was that telegrams can bring good news as well as bad – one often wondered what the contents might be before opening it – at least in this way, it could be more of a surprise.

My mother-in-law said that Grace had been getting all worked up over the demob business. I said that I too was very irritated by it, making it clear that I had not stayed on by choice. If the Army decides to keep you, I explained, there is not much you can do about it. I had done all I could to hasten my demob – the trouble was that I was too good at my job.

I complimented my mother-in-law on the way that she had made her basement flat nice and cosy, with plenty of light. Grace had been a great help in settling her in, she said. Over a cup of tea, she spoke about the family – all had survived the war. There was a time when she thought that she would not make it, at the height of the bombing. Daisy, her third eldest daughter, lived only a short distance away, moving after her house was demolished. Her husband and young daughter were down the shelter at the time, escaping any personal injuries. They had to be rehoused, in Ashbourne Grove, only five minutes walk from the old lady's flat. She went on to say that her son, after his demob, had volunteered for a four-year, short-term commission, and was promptly sent to Palestine. His wife, Joan, with two small children, was furious – after coping on her own for four years, it was more than she could bear. The prospect of another four years of separation was too much and in the end, it led to their divorce.

CHAPTER SIXTEEN

While I was waiting in the flat for Grace, I decided to write to Sullivan, telling him why I had left Greece so suddenly and reminiscing a little about the good times that we had shared over the years.

Grace returned home at about 9pm and was totally surprised to see her beloved husband waiting to welcome her – she became very emotional seeing me standing there and tears of joy clearly showed in her lovely brown eyes. "Yes – it is me!", I said, as we greeted each other. We had two years of separation to catch up on. We melted into each other and spent the next few hours remembering how good it was to be together and what we meant to each other.

As soon as Grace had come home, I noticed that she was wearing the earrings I had had sent from Greece – they looked superb and suited her extremely well. I had some more presents, but decided that they could wait until morning. After breakfast, Grace went out to telephone her boss, to explain my sudden homecoming and to ask if she could have two weeks off. When she returned to the flat, she was delighted to be able to tell me that her boss had agreed to her having time off. She also mentioned that sometime in the near future she would have to seek other employment. While Grace was out making her call, I had finished off my letter to Sullivan, explaining my sudden departure, and lack of time to say goodbye. I thanked him for all the good times we had had together and the pleasant memories I had brought away with me. I asked Sullivan to give my love to Mellissa, but decided not to mention Maria. I did wonder what her reaction might have been if I had said goodbye to her personally – perhaps it had been better that way. Whether she shed a tear on hearing of my sudden departure, I would never know.

As Grace had arranged her holiday, I told her I was going out to acquire a car. After all we had been through, we both deserved a break, and to be alone together for a while. I explained that, as we did not have a honeymoon when we married, Grace was going to have one just as soon as I could hire or buy a car. I suggested that Devon and Cornwall was an idea that appealed to me and, I hoped, to Grace as well. She thought it was a marvellous plan, because it was now mid-September and people said it was the best time to visit the West Country, to see the gorse in bloom and the carpet of heather. Before I went out car-hunting, I asked Grace to pack a case for ten days. I discovered there was very little choice in the car market – all that was available were the pre-war models. I eventually settled for an 8 horsepower Ford Popular, already taxed, insured, serviced and ready for the road within two days.

We said goodbye to Grace's mother, telling her to expect us back in ten days' time. The cases were put in the car, and away we went. On our second day, at Weston-super-Mare, Grace became covered in an uncomfortable rash and I thought it would mean the end of our trip. Wondering what to do, on the off-chance, we called into a chemist's shop where Grace showed the chemist the rash. When he saw it, he just smiled and said in a reassuring way that there was no need to worry as it was just a pollen rash. He handed Grace a tube of ointment advising her how to apply it and stating that he thought it should do the trick. He was right, the rash disappeared as quickly as it came, much to my relief, as I did not want anything to spoil this trip – a trip to be remembered for a long time afterwards. We resumed our journey, following the north Devon coast, seeing some of most spectacular scenery nature has to offer. I spoke to the landlords where we were staying and arranged candlelit dinners in the evenings – I wanted to make it as romantic as possible, as though we had just been married.

I recounted to Grace all about the events that had happened in Greece – all the stalling by my ASM over my demob, and the money I had been given. Grace enjoyed all the stories about Sullivan and I told her that he had made the imposed deferment of my release more bearable. I confessed that I would not have known what to do if it had not been for Sullivan and his cheery disposition, making light of any situation. For obvious reasons, I never mentioned Maria – I had no guilt to hide so my conscience was clear. I could see that, as we travelled around, a real transformation was taking place, Grace becoming her old self once again, carefree and light-hearted. It pleased me to see this change taking place as I had thought that there was still some doubt in Grace's mind as to why I overstayed my demob. Now that I had explained it all to her, it had removed any doubts she had.

We travelled down as far as Penzance – although I had travelled this way many times, it was the first time for Grace, taking in the magic splendour of the scenery. The one place she really fell in love with was Polperro, on the south coast of Cornwall.

Whilst driving back to London, thoughts of Bert Greaves came to my mind, thinking I should go and see his mother. On the day we got back, while Grace was sorting out our things, I said I was going round to see Bert's mother. Answering the door, she really looked old – the war years and the worries about her son had left their mark. I managed to persuade her to give me Bert's address – at least she knew where he was living now, somewhere over in Fulham in south-west London. I made a swift decision to call on my old friend and told his mother that I would be going over the next day. She asked me if I would give Bert a letter.

The following morning, I took Grace to work in the car and kissed her before leaving to drive to Fulham. From my A–Z street guide, I found the address with little trouble and noticed that the street had not suffered any bomb damage. I knocked on the door and heard movement inside the house. Eventually the door was opened by a middle-aged lady sitting in a wheelchair. She did not say a word, as though she was not too sure what to say, seeing a stranger on the doorstep and wondering who he might be. I broke the silence by asking if Bert Greaves was in, announcing myself as his old pal. She looked confused, but still did not say a word as though she was wondering what to say. Just then the door opened wider and standing there was Bert – but not the Bert I remembered. He looked really old and haggard and I supposed this was because of the constant worry of avoiding the police, and the hassle of being caught as a deserter.

Bert showed me through to the kitchen-cum-dining room, offering me a cup of tea which was most welcome. He introduced his wife, the lady in the wheelchair. Memories came flooding back as I remembered and visualised all the girl-chasing, and the capers we had cut, Bert's wonderful dancing, and the amazing times we shared together. It seemed ironic to me that Bert should marry a lady in a wheelchair, suffering from multiple sclerosis, a semi-cripple. It took me a little while for all of this to sink in. We never spoke about old times and, in fact, there were lapses of silence between us – not a bit like the Bert I used to know, never at a loss for something to say. I waited for a cue from Bert to arrange a further meeting but this was not forthcoming, so I assumed that there would not be any future meetings. As we walked to the front door, I gave Bert the letter from his mother – we shook hands and I left. That was the last time I saw Bert, the last of the gang, my pre-war mate and best friend. While driving back home, I wondered if it had all been worth it – he might just as well have taken his chances in one of the services. Not being able to see his mother in all that time must have caused enormous mental strain, quite apart from the life he had had to lead, to avoid arrest. Although the war was long over, technically, in the eyes of the law, he was still a deserter, an absentee avoiding call-up. Some years later, the Government did offer a pardon, or amnesty for those that avoided call-up, but whether Bert turned himself in, I never knew.

A few days later, I went along to the café with the hope of finding out the whereabouts of my pre-war pals and friends, but the new owner of the place was little help – I wondered if they were dead or alive. They had all played an important part in forming my character. The years in the home had given me self-reliance and the years in the services had taught me comradeship and discipline. I felt ready to face my future with confidence.

CHAPTER SEVENTEEN

A NEW BEGINNING

I heard from Sullivan. He confirmed that the ASM had indeed connived to keep me as long as possible. He wished me all the best for the future.

I went round to see my mother on my own. She was fit and well although there was still a frosty reception towards me – I was puzzled to know why. As all my pre-war friends had now faded from the scene, I hoped that with Grace I would have a long and happy marriage.

Now demobbed, I was settling down and slowly adjusting myself back into civilian life. I was preoccupied immediately with the dilemma of making a most important decision concerning my future, finding the means of making a good living for myself and Grace. On Government orders, certain vacancies had to be left open for returning servicemen, who had to be taken back if they applied for reinstatement of employment, to jobs they held before being called up for active service. I did not want to return to factory life – I wanted a more varied, outdoor employment.

In my later years of Army service life, while in Greece, I had worked on my own initiative, made my own decisions, and had freedom of movement – that was what I still wanted. I had three trades to choose from – I was skilled in two of them. I dismissed the thought of working in a garage, although that knowledge would come in handy for doing my own car repairs, or for members of the family if they sought my advice and help.

Although my knowledge of refrigeration was limited, I somehow felt my future lay in that direction. In the late 1940s, only about one per cent of households had a domestic refrigerator, but the future development of commercial refrigeration had to be a good opportunity after five years of war. The principles of refrigeration were surprisingly simple – liquids like sulphur dioxide or methyl chloride, which boiled at very low temperatures at normal atmospheric pressure, were used mainly for domestic and small commercial installations. In later years these two were superseded by a non-toxic refrigerant, freon 12 – other refrigerants were used in industrial installations, although the principle remained the same.

There are basically two moving parts in a mechanical refrigerator – a compressor of special design and an electric motor as a means of driving it. The compressor converts a low pressure gas into a high pressure gas which is passed through a condenser, either water- or fan-cooled, converting the gas into a liquid. The action of the compressor forces the liquid through a small orifice, known as the expansion valve or restrictor. The sudden release of pressure allows the gas to expand, becoming a latent heated vapour, resulting in a chilling effect as it is drawn back to the compressor, so starting the cycle again. The only factor that will stop this cycle is a loss of refrigerant, so all systems have to be completely leakproof. To detect leaks of freon and methyl chloride, a special lamp is used which shows a colour change in the flame if there is a leak.

Grace had left the Territorial Army office and had successfully applied for employment in the Civil Service, being appointed supervisor of the typing pool at the Weights and Measures Department of the Board of Trade at Millbank in south-west London, not far from the Tate Gallery. Grace progressed very well, eventually becoming the Departmental Head's private secretary, after teaching herself shorthand, obtaining a speed of 140 words a minute. While she was learning, I helped her by dictating at that speed in the evenings at home. I was pleased to help her, taking on this daunting task, as she became fast, efficient and accurate.

There were few available electricians' jobs that interested me although there was a demand for factory maintenance electricians, most of whom were on shift work – this had no appeal to me. Bomb damage and rebuilding had not yet started in earnest, so I came to the conclusion that I would seek work as a refrigeration engineer, building on the skills I had learnt at Brighton Polytechnic. The refrigeration industry was in its infancy, but it could offer better prospects, combining the two trades in which I was skilled.

I talked it over with Grace, but her only comment was whatever I decided would be agreeable to her – she was content to let me make the choices for our future. Although I knew the fundamental principles of refrigeration, I had never had the chance to put my knowledge into practice. This did not deter me from applying for a job with Hall's in Bermondsey in south-east London, in spite of my inexperience. I had no trouble getting an interview, or the job. The outfit consisted of a small workforce of four engineers, one of whom was the boss's son. The firm's main source of work was repairing and servicing ships' refrigeration plants, while they were docked in the port of London. At the time, the London Docks were bristling with activity, unloading and loading cargoes, to and from all parts of the world. The ships were bringing food to replenish England's empty larders after five years of wartime food rationing. People had not seen a banana in five years, most children not at all.

The refrigerated ships that my firm serviced were mainly from Australia and New Zealand, England's main suppliers before she decided to join the Common Market, for supplying meat, butter, cheese and other dairy products. Bacon was mainly home produced. During the war years, and for a short time afterwards, the Government offered subsidies to anyone one who could rear and produce pig meat. Consequently, it was not unusual, in towns and country, to see pig sties in people's gardens, although before doing so, they had to be licensed by the Ministry of Food.

There were always two engineers sent on each ship assignment. The work was awkward and heavy – most times I went with the boss's son who was about thirty-five years of age. He was clean-shaven and well-built, with light sandy hair, and was of pleasant disposition and easy to get on with. He had served in the Navy during the war years, so he knew about ships. Although green at that type of work, I soon caught on to what had to be done. There was little variation of plant from one ship to another, so I soon swung into the rhythm of working. As most ships were obliged to make a quick turnaround, and other ships were waiting downriver for a berth, work had to be done quickly and efficiently as well as to the satisfaction of the ships' Chief Engineers. They had to sign the work certificates saying that all work had been carried out to marine standards and specifications. Most ships' Engineers kept a log while at sea, noting any faults and recording cold-room temperatures which had to be read, checked and logged twice daily.

A part of my firm's contract was to make sure there was a full bottle of refrigerant, suitable for their plant, on board and firmly secured for emergency use while at sea. I found the work interesting and rewarding, even if the money was not all that good. I had placed my foot on the bottom rung of the ladder, which I hoped would lead to better rewards later on when I had gained more experience in the various applications of refrigeration.

One day I was sent by my boss to attend to an emergency breakdown at a private butcher's shop. At the time, I had no way of knowing that this visit was going to change my whole future life. I was greeted by a sorrowful-looking butcher, the owner of the shop. I was given the facts of the problem, and shown the poor condition of the meat. The butcher explained to me that the fridge had been under repair for some time by another engineer, and although it had worked satisfactorily for a while, it was not long before it went wrong again. He felt that he should seek another opinion, because he had been obliged to trim far too much meat away, causing unnecessary waste. Meat was still on ration and the butcher had to have his fridge functioning properly and efficiently, to keep waste to a minimum. I asked him whether he simply wanted a report on what was found to be wrong, or did he want me to put it in proper working order. It was a clear case of immediate repairs, as the butcher needed it working for the weekend. The poor man had to have a reliable refrigerator, adding that in its present condition, it had given him a few sleepless nights, not knowing what to expect in the morning.

From what the butcher told me, he had a shrewd idea what the trouble might be – a loss of refrigerant. I set to work straight away, connecting up the high- and low-pressure gauges. I could see immediately that the system was short of refrigerant, and that the compressor was not functioning as it should. I gave the whole of the plant a thorough diagnostic test, looking for leaks – I found two.

I had became a fully competent engineer, gaining a lot of knowledge working for my employer on all types of equipment, and the case I was examining was quite clear to me. I made notes of all the faults I found – the whole unit was in poor shape, requiring replacement of some parts to get it back to proper working order. I checked in the van to see if I had all the spares available. I had to tell the butcher that it would be an all-day job, showing him the list of faults I had found. I asked if I could telephone my boss, to explain all the problems – my boss replied by saying that I should continue and do what I had to do. My boss gave a monthly bonus to the engineer who had the fewest repeat calls – I had won it twice, so he knew he had a good engineer out on site.

The van carried a comprehensive range of spares for most makes of refrigerator. Hall's were very protective about supplying servicing spares to other engineers, but during the war years this rule was relaxed, so I had on hand all the spares required. Having done a part of my initial training at Hall's, I was familiar with their plant. I informed the owner that I might have to work after the shop closed, if that would be in order. The butcher was pleased with the idea that he might at last have his unit working properly, so he would have agreed to any suggestion.

I carried out all the necessary work, recharged the plant with refrigerant and tested it once again for leaks, making a few minor adjustments, so that the cold-room temperature would drop to the level the butcher was needing.

My boss lived in the same area as the butcher's shop and, passing the shop on his way home, he noticed the van outside, so decided to call in. He asked me how the job was going and was pleased to hear me say that I was just putting the finishing touches to it. While the three of us were drinking a cup of tea, the butcher explained how disappointed he had been with the other engineer, admitting that I seemed to know what I was doing. I asked my boss if he would mind me calling in first thing in the morning for a final check – he agreed it would be a good idea and left me to gather up my tools and gear to put into the van.

The following morning I called in as arranged and was greeted by a smiling and happy butcher, quite a contrast from the previous day. The man told me that the refrigerator was working perfectly. Just for a final check, I connected up the gas bottle and pressure gauges, to make sure all was in order. While I was checking, a rather tall man entered the shop and walked over to where I was working. He did not speak to me but just muttered to himself as he walked across to the butcher who was standing by his counter where they went into conversation. It was of no concern to me what they were discussing, but had a shrewd idea – this was the man who had been servicing this plant with poor results.

When they had finished talking, the man left the shop, going to his car parked outside, where he just sat in the driver's seat, without driving away. I collected up my tools and gear ready to put in the van. The butcher never volunteered any information about the tall man, but just gave me a package saying that there was something for my tea. I thanked him, and said that I would see him in a couple of days' time, for a final check. We shook hands and then I left. I had put my tools in the van, and was about to get in to drive away, when the other man suprised me, coming up to me and asking if we could talk. Puzzled, I asked him what it might be about and the man assured me that it was not to do with the butcher's shop he had just left. Suggesting a chat over a cup of tea, the man indicated the café across the road. He seemed to be quite calm and did not seem to be too upset, so I agreed, wondering why he had made the invitation.

Sitting down drinking our tea, I was soon to find out – he said to me that I seemed to know a lot about refrigeration, and offered me a job working as his assistant. He introduced himself as Ernie Morris, a self-employed refrigeration engineer and handed his business card to me, continuing to explain that he had found it difficult to cope with his workload. That was the reason why he could not spend too much time on any one job – what he tried to do was give a unit a charge of refrigerant and hope for the best. I realised immediately that this was not the way to run a profitable and successful business. Morris went on to say he had no one else working for him on service work, mainly because he could not find an experienced engineer, although I seemed to fit the bill. I looked at his business card and noticed that his workshop was only a short distance from where I lived at Goose Green. I did not bring up the subject of money in the conversation, but Morris spoke about it first, offering me two pounds a week more than I was getting. Although I was quite happy working for my present employer, the money was not my main concern, but something was telling me to take the job. Morris pointed out he would do all the emergency calls at the weekends and my working hours would be from 8am to 5.30pm and 12pm on Saturdays, these times being subject to overtime. I asked for a couple of days to think about it saying that I would give Morris a ring the next evening at about 7pm, if that would be agreeable, to give him my answer. We shook hands and left the café, although I was still pondering what to do.

When I arrived home that evening, I gave Grace the package the butcher had given me, containing two choice lamb chops. Grace set about cooking them for our evening meal, as we had not yet bought a fridge for ourselves, this being one of my priorities. Once we were seated for our meal, I mentioned to Grace about my new job offer, but Grace was non-committal – the only time she expressed an opinion was when discussing anything for the home. Grace always left it to me to decide about our future – she knew I would do the right thing for our mutual interest – there were times however, when I needed reassurance that I was doing the right thing. After I had finished my very tasty chops, it was still daylight, so I thought I would walk round to see Morris's workshop – it was only a few minutes' walk from our flat. I left after giving Grace a kiss, saying I would not be long.

The workshop was situated at the end of an alleyway which was the back entrance to the main road shops, entered from a side road. The workshop was a two-storey brick building – there was no sign board denoting what it was being used for. I did not venture up the alley, but just looked at it from the road end. While I was standing, thinking and looking, a tubby man dressed in a khaki-coloured working coat asked me if I was looking for Ernie Morris. I told the man he had guessed correctly and explained that Morris had offered me a job and that I was wondering what sort of person he was. The tubby man said that he was an easy-going type of person, always seeming to be busy, popping in and out all day. He then offered to introduce himself, shaking hands with me. He was known as Evan and owned the dairy shop around the corner, looking after the milk round side of the business while his brother David ran the shop with the help of their mother. He explained that they took Morris's daytime messages which either he collected at lunchtime, or they pinned them up on his workshop door. Walking back to my flat, I was deep in thought, wondering what I should do – my present job entailed a lot of heavy lifting when working on the ships.

By the time I got home my mind was made up and once indoors, I told Grace I had decided to take the job, saying I could not explain it, but my mind was made up for me. The following evening, I phoned Morris to ask if the job was still available and if so, that I would take it as offered. In our earlier conversation, when we were in the café, Morris had asked me if I had a car and whether I was prepared to use it. He offered to pay a mileage allowance when I was using it on service calls – a mileage allowance which was generous. After a brief conversation, I agreed to his offer and when all the loose ends were tied up, a time and date were agreed when I could start working for my new boss.

I gave my notice in at Bermondsey. My old boss gave me a glowing reference – I had worked there for two years, learning a great deal while in his employment.

CHAPTER EIGHTEEN

I reported for work for my new boss and Mr. Morris showed me around the workshop, pointing out where everything was stored and kept. I took it all in, recognising the tools and materials and making a mental note of where things were. Then I received my instructions for the day, kitting myself out with the necessary gear – I had brought my own tools. I still had the Ford Popular that I bought after my demob and so far had had no problems with it. Morris had a similar car, but not so well cared for.

Morris explained that any necessary heavy equipment was transported by the carriers at the corner of the main road, saying that he found this arrangement better than having his own van. While in the workshop, I had a good look around – it was illuminated by fluorescent lighting, and held a good stock of spare parts. There was a good, solid ten-foot workbench, a small combustion stove, a vacuum pump, a small spraying plant and a good selection of V-belts used to drive the compressors. There was also gas welding equipment on the premises. Morris further explained that all his work was commercial, working for butchers, grocers, cafés, restaurants and so on, with very little call for servicing domestic appliances. Generally, domestic refrigerators were mostly pre-war, imported from the USA, and most were sealed or semi-sealed units, impossible to repair. Not many domestic refrigerators were made in England before the war – it would be some years before these became widely available to the general public.

After I had been working for Morris for a few months, he became a little irregular with my wages – on some occasions this stretched to three weeks. Most of my work instructions came via the dairy – it was only occasionally that I saw Morris himself. Evan bought the messages over, or pinned them to the door. If I was in, he would stay a while for a chat. He mentioned to me that he was courting a publican's daughter, from a pub situated in Kennington, not far from the Oval cricket ground in south-east London. He suggested that Grace and I should call at the pub one evening and have a drink with them. His girlfriend and her mother ran the pub, but she was able to have Tuesday evenings off, so I responded that I would check the idea with Grace and let him know, although it would have to be after 8pm. Evan thought that that would be fine – we could sit in the bar and have a chat over a beer – I jotted down the name of the pub and its address, together with instructions how to find it.

A few days later, Evan brought over a message from Morris, asking me to go over to the stated address to help him with the installation of a new cold-room. I found the address quite easily – it was a butcher's shop. The makers of the sectional cold-room had assembled it and it was now ready for Morris and I to install the refrigeration equipment. When it came to connecting the compressor unit, I was surprised to see that it was very old, and had obviously seen many years' service elsewhere. This was supposed to be a completely brand new installation. I asked Morris what refrigerant he intended to use, to be told it would be methyl chloride. The compressor was not designed for that refrigerant – it was intended for a low-pressure operating refrigerant like sulphur dioxide. Installing such a mismatched unit was really courting trouble, I thought, but Morris was the boss. He knew he was doing wrong – his aim was to get the plant working so he could ask for his money. As though Morris was reading my mind, he said that he intended to change it when the proper unit arrived and that it was only a temporary arrangement. I could only believe him but at the same time I felt uneasy about what Morris was doing.

I found out a little later that Morris had acquired the equipment through the 'back door' of another refrigeration company in south London – the storeman there was a close neighbour to Morris. For this installation, Morris had been sold a 'pup' by this chap. Over a period of time, Morris had also received spares and compressor units by the same means. After a while, the storeman's nefarious deeds were rumbled and he was promptly sacked. One day this chap turned up at the workshop. I had not seen him before, so really did not know who he was. He introduced himself as Bill, saying that Morris had sent him over. I asked him if he was working for Morris, and Bill explained that it was only for as long as it took for Morris to give him a reference so that he could get another job. He felt that Morris owed him a favour. He also described to me what he and Morris had been up to, skimming off items from his stores. Morris had promised to pay him a weekly wage, but I thought to myself that if Morris had problems paying me, how was he going to find the money to pay both of them? At least I was earning money for Morris – Bill would just be a passenger, doing nothing.

During the evening, I phoned Morris, and told him that I was very unhappy about Bill hanging around the workshop doing nothing. I stated very clearly that I did not want to get involved with his shady dealings and added that I was only an employee doing a job of work, so if the police caught wind of it, Morris would carry the can alone. I asked Morris to tell Bill to stay away or I would hand in my notice, leaving the choice to him.

The following morning, Bill roared into the workshop in a blazing and very bad temper, his eyes full of fury, shouting that I had been on the phone to Morris. I told him that I had made it quite clear that I did not want him hanging around the workshop doing nothing. While I was saying this, I noticed that Bill was clenching his fists menacingly. I stayed my ground and told Bill in no uncertain terms that I had no intentions of being a part of their shady dealings, a point I made crystal clear to Morris – either he stayed away or I would quit. I added that it would be no good Bill turning nasty with me as there was a Police Station just up the road – if he had any intentions towards me, he would soon be up there, so he should think before doing anything stupid. With this, Bill cooled down, hung around for a while and then left, much to my relief. That was the last I ever saw of him.

I was a little worried about what was going on although I knew that I could not be implicated, so I decided to carry on working for Morris. My pay, or lack of it, was by this time overdue by eight weeks, so I decided to go over to see Morris after work that evening. I pulled up outside Morris's house, climbed out of the car and walked up the pathway leading to the front door. I noticed straight away that there were no curtains up at the windows and there was a hollow sound when I knocked on the front door. The man next door was working in his garden, so I asked him if he knew where Morris might be. The man alarmed me by saying that they had moved out some time the previous week – I had a feeling that something was seriously amiss, my work messages were becoming fewer and fewer.

I assumed that Morris had done a moonlight flit. I had wondered why Morris employed me in the first place as the last few months had shown me that there seemed insufficient work for two full-time engineers. If the two butchers' jobs were anything to go by, Morris must have lost a lot of business, through bad servicing or over-charging.

On my way back to the workshop, after my abortive trip, I called in the butcher's shop where I had helped to install the unsatisfactory compressor unit. The butcher explained to me that Morris had given him a real sob story, and feeling sorry for him, he had paid him in full. In spite of Morris making promises to put the installation right, he paid him £450. He said he had phoned Morris a couple of times but there was no answer so he had also decided to go around to his house, to find it empty. He told me that he had issued a summons for the return of his money but I said I thought that would be a waste of time and expense. When I asked him how the fridge was working, the butcher gave the reply that I expected – that it was not very satisfactory. I told him that I suspected he would have severe trouble with it, but it was not for me to say anything at the time, merely being the employed fitter. I asked him if he intended to have it put into perfect working order and he ruefully agreed that it would have to be done, adding that he was completely satisfied with the cold-room, an excellent job. I made a quick calculation in my head and suggested to the butcher that it would cost him around £150 for a new compressor unit although the electric motor could be used again as it was the only serviceable part – using it would help to keep the cost down. The rest was scrap.

The butcher asked me if I knew that Morris had done a moonlight flit and I admitted that I had only just found out, adding that, if it was any consolation to the butcher, he owed me eight weeks' wages, plus expenses. The butcher asked me if I could supply and fit a new compressor unit. I agreed to give him a quote for supplying and fitting a brand new compressor unit, with a year's guarantee, using the existing electric motor, assuring him that it would give many years' trouble-free service. I added that the butcher could keep the old unit, getting what he could for it as scrap. I emphasised that if he accepted my quote, he should not judge me the same as Morris, who I always thought was a bit of a conman.

On my way back to the workshop, I dropped into an ironmonger's to purchase a really stout padlock, to replace the one on the workshop door. This was a precaution in case Morris made a midnight call to collect all his gear from the workshop. I was not so much worried about the eighty-odd pounds Morris owed me in lost wages as I knew the workshop equipment and stock were worth far more.

When I was demobbed, thoughts of being self-employed did not enter my head but now that the opportunity presented itself, why should I not take the challenge? I would not be starting from scratch – there was a solid base to build upon and develop. As the cold winter season was about to begin, it would give me a period of time to consolidate, using my knowledge of Morris's clients. When I returned home, I prepared a quotation for the butcher. I explained to Grace the events of the day, and my momentous decision to go into business on my own account. Grace did not show any great enthusiasm, as usual. Undeterred, I said I was confident that I could make a real success of my new venture. To reassure Grace, I said there was plenty of scope and demand, and that here I hoped was my first order, pointing to the quotation still in the typewriter. All I was asking for was her support, but as usual Grace was her non-committal self. In the morning, I called on the agent for the workshop's landlord. The agent informed me that Morris owed him eight weeks' rent, so I asked whether I could take over the workshops if I paid off the arrears. The agent could see no objection to this idea which would please all concerned. I did have one other request – I asked if I could have a seven-year lease with an option on a further seven, if the rent was agreeable. The agent recognised that he was dealing with a very serious young man and asked me to call back in three days' time, to give him time to make the necessary enquiries and discuss it further.

I called in as requested at the agent's office. The landlords had agreed to the seven-year lease, provided that I paid both solicitors' fees. I agreed to do this, and so set the ball rolling to take over the workshop.

Now I was assured of the workshop, I gave Grace an outline of my future plans. First I had the tricky problem of asking Grace if I could have a loan of £150 from our savings account, to pay for the compressor unit I needed for my first quotation. I emphasised that the money would be the foundation of our future and it should be looked on as an investment. I had quite a task, trying to convince Grace, while at the same time seeking her approval. Grace was insistent in her questioning about whether there was a future in refrigeration and I showed her that I had no doubt about it, as it was in its infancy in this country, and the scope and opportunity were wide open. I eventually managed to reassure her and she agreed that I could have the loan, but that would be all. She reminded me that we were saving for a special reason – I gave her a kiss, saying I promised her that she would not regret it.

CHAPTER NINETEEN

On December 4th 1949, I became a self-employed refrigeration and electrical engineer.

I drew the money from the Post Office so that I could purchase the equipment to fix the butcher's fridge, as he had accepted my quotation for the work. The wholesale company knew me when I was employed at Bermondsey, as I often called in for spare parts. When they saw me, they said that they had wondered what had happened to me and they crowded round asking me about my health and my work. I gave them a brief outline of my time working for Ernie Morris and one of the office staff commented that he hoped he did not owe me money, as he had done a moonlight flit. I explained that that was why I was there, having just taken over Morris's business and consequently finding myself in need of supplies.

The wholesalers had just received a consignment of compressor units delivered from their American parent company. I paid with cash on that occasion but asked to open a monthly account, in the meantime paying cash until the formalities had gone through. I was accepted for my monthly account within a couple of weeks, with no problem at all. By that time, I had refitted the butcher's fridge – my first job as a self-employed engineer. I explained to the butcher it was a special price, and a favour, as we had both been left in the lurch by Morris because of his sudden disappearance. I had called on the butcher a few days later and he was highly delighted with the finished result, the cold-room working to perfection. He paid me immediately and I subsequently did more work for him over the years.

When I arrived home that evening, I showed Grace the cheque and asked her to kiss it for luck, saying that it was going to be the first of many. I decided to open a bank account the very next day. I had decided on a trading name, which I duly registered, but for banking purposes, used my own name when signing cheques.

About a month after I went into business, I was cleaning my car outside the workshop – a job I left for a Sunday morning, together with any odd jobs needed on the car to keep it up to scratch. Whilst I was lathering away, another car with a trailer attached, came up the alleyway. The driver, who I had not seen before, stepped out of the car with a piece of paper in his hand. He gave this to me, saying he was the brother-in-law of Ernie Morris and explained that he had been sent over to collect all his gear from the workshop. The list of items was typed on one of Morris's old bill heads. At the time, I had not unlocked the workshop.

I read the list and told the man, who had not given his name, to tell Morris to come over himself if he wanted his gear and tell him also to bring the money he owes. Until then, I said very meaningfully, the stuff stays here. No money – no gear. The fellow was also told to tell Morris that there was no point in his coming in the middle of the night, as I had put another padlock on the door. I felt rather sorry for the man who had been sent on a false journey. As an extra shot, I added that it might cheer Morris up to know that the Ministry of Labour was looking for him, as he had not stamped my cards since I had been working for him. I did not have to spell out the seriousness of that offence. I did tell him, however, that I had taken a lease out on the workshop, and paid the back rent, so if Morris should show up, he would be trespassing. I wanted Morris to realise that I was not quite the fool he had taken me for – I was astonished at the gall of the man. While I was talking to the brother-in-law, I felt uneasy, but could not put my finger on the reason why. As the man was getting back into his car, I added the fact that the cold-room people were looking for Morris as they wanted their money. He had brought all this on himself with his shady dealings. I wished the man good day and watched him drive back out of the alley – that was the last I ever heard of the dubious Mr. Morris.

I became busy going round to all the customers I knew. Not many had a good word to say about Morris and his work. They had very little choice when it came to repairs – in the war years, they had to get anyone who could fix their fridge, engineers being so scarce. In fact, one butcher told me that before the war, Morris had been a car mechanic and as he had a caste in one eye, he was excused call-up. He heard there was a shortage of refrigeration engineers so he set himself up in business. That accounted to me for his lack of the finer points of the industry and his inexperience to carry out satisfactory repairs – a sort of hit and miss attitude.

I had spoken to the Hughes brothers seeking their permission to put their phone number on my business card. Not having a telephone at home, this was a lifeline as far as my business was concerned – without it, I could have had a few problems. I had approached the GPO but no lines were available until the new exchange was built and they gave no promise when this would be.

It was now approaching Christmas. Butchers always get nervous at that season – if the weather should turn mild with all their poultry hanging up in the shop all the time until it was gutted and dressed, then it had to go into the fridge or cold-room. As very few people had their own fridge, this meant that their orders were not collected until Christmas Eve. Some called me out on false alarms on the grounds that it was better to be safe than sorry. Most of the trouble was because many fridges were overloaded, causing an increased demand on the already overworked compressor unit. With luck the butchers survived Christmas without serious trouble – most were pleased when the festivities were over, and they could revert to normal business.

I spent a great deal of time thinking about what I should do for my future. The real money would come from making and supplying domestic refrigerators and deep freeze conservators. Repairs and servicing was just the bread and butter means of a living. I decided to concentrate on supplying the domestic market. During the war years, the general public had been deprived of many small luxuries, like ice cream. After the war, it was common to see people of all ages and sexes, walking along, even in mid-winter, sucking an ice cream or an ice-lolly. For most ice cream vendors, it was impossible to keep up with demand, especially in the warmer weather of the summer.

After a while I built up a good clientele – I had contracts with many Italian makers of ice cream, supplying them with new equipment. The demand for ice lolly and ice cream storage was very high. Fats and sugar were still on ration although most seemed to get around this problem. For my first year in business, I fared much better than I had anticipated, building it up on a firm foundation and ploughing all my profits back into the business. I gained a lot of new customers, chiefly by recommendation.

I received an enquiry from one of my customers for a deep freeze. On my way there, I was near the butcher whose fridge I fixed when working for my Bermondsey boss and I decided to call in, on the spur of the moment. As soon as he saw me, the butcher approached me, extending his hand for a welcoming handshake. He told me that I had done an excellent job as the unit had been working perfectly ever since. I explained I was now in business on my own account although I chose not to go into detail about my experience with Morris. While drinking tea the butcher had made, he asked me if I could supply a deep freeze. I replied enthusiastically, saying I made them to order. The butcher then pointed to a recess in the wall and asked me if I could make a freezer to fit it. I took out my expanding ruler to measure the space and, after a quick calculation, suggested the maximum estimated internal cubic capacity. That was perfect for the butcher, exactly what he had wanted. About this time, Britain was importing from Australia and New Zealand a substantial amount of frozen offal, liver, hearts and kidneys, besides whole sheep carcasses, taking the demand for freezers to stretching point.

I promised to prepare a quote and drop it in on the following Monday, together with the specification. As we shook hands before I left, I felt very pleased that I had decided to call in. I then carried on to the other butcher from whom I had the enquiry – it was a very large shop, like the one I had just left, on the fringe of a huge council estate of well over a thousand dwellings. Two elderly men ran the shop in partnership.

Their main problem was that they could not make up their minds what size freezer to have – they kept bickering at one another so much that I mentally called them Mutt and Jeff. In the end they came to a compromise and gave me a good order.

Making these two deep freezers, plus my contract servicing work and doing workshop repairs kept me so busy that I wondered how I was going to cope. Poor Grace only saw me in the mornings before she went off to work. In fairness to her, I always took Sundays off, no matter how hard-pressed I was for work. I normally worked up to 10pm at night to keep abreast of work, from Monday to Friday and usually until 6pm on Saturdays. Before going home, I would often call at the local greengrocer's because it was easier to take the heavy loads in my car – a chore I was pleased to take on.

One day not long after I was puzzling about coping with my workload, I was working in my workshop, when a tall middle-aged man walked into the workshop, asking for Ernie Morris, as though answering my dilemma. I told him that Morris was no longer there and asked if there was something I could do for him, at the same time wondering who he was. The tall man said he used to work for Morris part-time but had been off sick for a while. When I asked what he worked at, he replied that it was mostly stripping down compressors, lapping in valve plates, and general workshop work. He did confess that he could use some extra money. As I was turning over in my mind what to do, Evan entered with a message and saw the man standing by the bench, greeted him as Jock and asked quite genuinely about his health. The man, Jock, told him that he was now fully recovered and had called in to see if there was any work. When I asked what he had been paid and for what hours, the man said ruefully that it was a case of when he was paid rather than what. I just smiled at this remark, knowing the feeling – £2 a week for fifteen hours part-time. Jock expected me to understand what coppers' hours were like – he was a policeman as his main job. He explained that he could do mornings on some weeks, afternoons on others, to fit in with his shifts on the beat. I asked him if I could rely on those hours as I really did need to plan my work and had to have someone I could depend upon. Jock was certain that he would not let me down.

I agreed that I would pay him £2 a week, plus forty pence an hour overtime, and he could work whatever overtime he wished. Jock eagerly replied that that would suit him fine. His money would be paid every Friday and any overtime the week after. I was keen to know when Jock could start and was pleased to hear him say the very next day. I promised to have another workshop key cut for him, but insisted that he should keep it in his possession, and certainly not simply hang it up on a nail as it used to be. I also emphasised one other thing – if he should go over to the café, he was to make sure to lock up the workshop. Once all the arrangements were satisfactorily sorted, we shook hands, agreeing to meet at 9am the next morning.

I met up with Jock in the morning and spoke about the work that was in hand, but decided not to go into details about Morris – I thought it best to let sleeping dogs lie. I suspected that Jock had got wind that Morris had left the scene – if that was so, then it could have been why he suddenly turned up. As far as I was concerned, it could not have happened at a better time. After all, no one wants to work for nothing.

I asked Jock if he could do welding and braising and was pleased to hear he could. The previous evening at home, I had made out two sketches for the two deep freezers I had orders for. I had to go and purchase some angle iron and asked Jock to tidy up the workshop while I was away as we would need all the space available. When I returned to the workshop with the angle iron, I handed the sketches to Jock to cut off the required lengths and promised to show him how to round the corners off. I was adamant that we wanted modern-looking cabinets, not boxes on wheels. I had made contact with a self-employed sheet metal worker who agreed to make the interiors to my precise specification.

Within a week, we had both cabinets in the workshop, ready for spraying – another of Morris's legacies was the portable spraying plant. When the crisp, white enamel paint was completely dry, the compressor units were fitted within the cabinets making them self-contained and easy to move, having fitted castors. The freezer units were now completed and ready to be put on test, for any final adjustments. I arranged for the carrier to deliver both units, following on in my car to make the final installation in the two shops. Jock was amazed how everything had panned out and was very impressed by the way I had organised the work. I stated very clearly that we did not want any of Morris's slapdash ways of working – I was in business to make money, and have satisfied customers. I made sure that my thoughts were known to Jock and I was fairly sure that my new assistant echoed my sentiments.

More work followed with enquiries for various types of refrigerators. I was making a name for myself as well as a healthy bank balance. It did mean working long hours, to fulfil my commitments, beavering on up to 10pm on most nights, except Saturdays and Sundays. These were Grace's two nights for whatever she wanted to do, without question. Sometimes we would go down to see Rose and Alf who had three children by that time, two boys and a girl. On other weekends, we would go and see her wartime friend Gloria, who had now moved down to a south-east coastal town. She had bravely taken on a boarding house, offering full board to her summer visitors. The town was still a restricted area, mainly because of the wartime defences, so one had to acquire a visitor's permit, with certain restrictions. Driving through the Medway towns was an ordeal, taking up precious time, but it was always rewarding when reaching our destination, to see the smiles when greeting each other.

Occasionally we would opt for a trip into the country on a Sunday afternoon, especially when the blackberries were ready for picking. Grace envied the people that lived in the country, often saying that she would like to do so herself. The weekends gave us time to relax, and recharge our batteries for the busy week ahead. Grace had always had a hankering to have a dog – while living at home before marrying, her mother always had one. After Grace and I married and lived at Hayes in the early war years we did have a dog for a short while. The night our pup was born, the German Air Force decided to pay Hayes a visit. Their possible target was HMV's (EMI) electronics factory. There were a few other large factories on either side of the mainline railway line – if their bombers missed one target they were bound to hit another. During the raid, a piece of shrapnel came flying through the dog owner's French windows, facing the railway, and lodged in the wall mere inches above the mother of the pups' head. Had she been sitting up, without doubt she would have been killed. I spotted the shrapnel embedded in the wall, when I went along to collect the pup from my colleague, who also worked at the Fairy Aviation factory. The owner said he was going to leave it there, as a memento.

Grace only had the dog for a short while, before it caught distemper and died – we never bothered about another. In our present flat, at Goose Green, a large dog would have been out of the question and Grace was not all that keen on small dogs, so it was decided to wait until we moved, sometime in the future.

As my business expanded, Grace decided to employ a daily help for two mornings a week – this would give her more time to do my clerical work. I attended to the typing of the quotations, because of the technical content – they had to be word-perfect. Grace never queried my long hours of working. Her way of relaxing was to do jigsaw puzzles, make dresses, or finish off the cryptic crossword, if she had not had time during the day.

On one special occasion, we were invited out one evening to a Freemasons Ladies' night. Grace's twin sister's husband was the Lodge's chairman for the forthcoming year. Naturally, Grace wanted to look her best, so she spent the whole of one Saturday afternoon visiting all the women's fashion shops, and three department stores. At that time, Rye Lane in Peckham was south-east London's main shopping area. She had set her heart on a dress with sequins and she saw a dress she liked, a red off-the-shoulder calf-length dress, but it did not have sequins. She bought it anyway, together with a box of red sequins. When back home, she sewed on over a thousand sequins – her patience was astounding. The dress was tight at the waist, ballet style, but flared from there down so when she turned, the skirt billowed out making the sequins sparkle with the light. Grace was an ardent ballet fan especially if Margot Fontaine was performing in London. Her dress was styled in this fashion and it really looked fantastic. Being slim it suited her, causing a few comments from the other ladies at the dinner.

I had two priorities at home, a fridge and a telephone connection. I wanted to surprise Grace with the fridge – new ones were still not available. The telephone was a different matter – I had made many enquiries but all the replies were the same. No lines would be available until the new exchange had been built and no one knew when that would be. Before the war and for some time afterwards, only one per cent of all households had a fridge. Home deep freezers were non-existent. Those households that had a larder made do with a slab of marble to keep their perishables fresh, usually with a fine mesh fly cover. Those without a larder had a perforated zinc meat safe, either in the kitchen, fixed to a wall or an outside one on a shaded wall. Most people shopped every day, so as to have fresh food.

On one of my rare free evenings, I was looking through a national newspaper and noticed that there was going to be a Government auction sale near Nottingham in a few weeks time – I sent off for the catalogue. When it arrived a few days later, I looked at it with a great deal of interest, making notes of the lots that appealed to me. Amongst the lots being offered were a number of brand new sealed refrigeration systems by a popular American manufacturer and some six cubic feet domestic cabinets, in plain metal with no working parts. My curiosity got the better of me and I decided to make the journey to Nottingham to see for myself, thinking nothing ventured, nothing gained. Time was precious to me, so I had to plan my work accordingly.

The day before the auction, I saw the Hughes brothers, telling them where I was off to first thing in the morning and that I did not expect to be back until late evening – Jock would call over for any messages. When I saw Jock later on during the day, I briefed him along similar lines and gave him work instructions, asking him to nip over to the dairy for any messages.

The following morning after a 6am start, I arrived at the auction in good time to have a thorough look around, making notes of the lot numbers. The sealed systems were all brand new, and separately packed with a quantity of copper tubing. The catalogue said the units were originally destined to be used as water coolers for field X-ray machines, used in conjunction with a field generator. Being American, they were made for 110 volt AC current – this was no problem as one could buy a separate transformer to reduce 240 volts to 110 volts, for around £2.10.0 each. The domestic cabinets were of modern design and an ideal size. When these lots came under the hammer, there seemed to be a lack of interest from the other bidders and I finished up buying the lot, all the sealed systems and cabinets at absolute give-away prices.

Feeling very pleased that I made the journey, I went to the cafeteria for a drink and something to eat and to reflect on my good fortune. While I was sitting there, another man came and sat down at my table opposite me, asking me how the auction had been for me. I admitted that it had been better than expected, upon which the other man said, beaming all over his face, that he had just bought one million contact breakers. I asked him in a whimsical way what on earth he was going to do with a million contact breakers. He asked me whether I had any idea how much platinum there would be, once he had separated the breakers and of course, I did not have a clue. The fellow reckoned that he could retrieve about one and a half ounces of the precious metal, which at current prices would represent a good investment, an idea which clearly made him smile in smug satisfaction.

My next problem was how to get my purchases back home. I was lucky enough to hire a self-drive van from a local hire firm and I found help from one of the porters, to whom I gladly gave a good tip. When back in my workshop towards the end of the afternoon, Jock was still there – he had waited for me to come back. Together we unloaded the van and Jock was quite surprised at what I had bought. I was very pleased to hear that there had been only one call and that was not urgent. When the van was unloaded, I parked it on the concrete patch outside the workshop, locking it securely. Before parting for the night, I explained to Jock that I would have to make an early start in the morning to return the van. I asked Jock to remove the wooden frames from the sealed systems, taking care when doing so, in case I was not back in time. I decided to walk home – after driving for around two hundred miles, it was a welcome change. I ended the day's work by making a phone call on my way home, in response to my customer's call. Once settled in the comfort of my chair at home, I decided to keep Grace company for the rest of the evening – a pleasant change for both of us. In the morning I made another early start to return the van and collect my own car.

Once back at the workshop, I took a good look at what I had bought. I removed all the copper tubing attached to the sealed systems with extreme care, stacking the coils up on the Morrison for the rag-and-bone man. Although brand new, it was of no further use for my work as it had been specially shaped. The rag-and-bone man called as usual on his weekly visit, normally looking for offcuts and anything made of brass or lead. I pointed to the stack of copper tubing and asked the man what he would give me for the lot. The dealer could not believe his eyes and repeated my question as though he was bemused. I repeated the question as the man removed his cap and started to scratch his head as though in deep thought. Putting it back on, he said he thought he would not have that much money with him, but around £30 would seem fair. I encouraged him to find the cash and said he could take it there and then – the man produced the money. While this was going on, Jock was smiling to himself, enjoying the bartering. Jock and I gave him a hand to load his barrow, which he wheeled away with some difficulty. When he was out of earshot, we both laughed – that amount had been broadly what I paid for the whole lot of the units and cabinets and the deal helped to pay for the hired van. I explained to Jock what my plans were for the new goods and gave him a five pound bonus – he had been working hard, and deserved the extra.

My first priority was to prepare one of the cabinets for Grace and myself so Jock and I busied ourselves preparing the cabinet for spraying. In a week we had it completed and on test. I arranged with the carriers to deliver it one afternoon to our flat as I wanted to surprise Grace when she came home in the evening – she was completely unaware of what had been going on. When I arrived home that same afternoon, I installed the fridge, ready for my evening meal. Grace was so completely surprised and overwhelmed, I had to wait for my meal. After eating I showed her how to use it. Putting my arms around her waist, I said that that was number one taken care of, but how I was going to organise a phone connection, I had no idea. I had been waiting two years and we wondered how much longer we'd have to wait.

Sometime later, I was on my way back from Catford and passing through Sydenham. As I was feeling thirsty, I called into the Dining Rooms, for a cup of tea and a bite to eat. I had passed it many times before, but usually waited until I got back to the workshop for my break. This time for some unknown reason, I decided to call in – it was about midafternoon – and found myself a seat. The owner, somewhere in his mid-fifties, was a big tall man, with curly, greying hair, and sporting a clean, crisp white apron. I gave my order and the man served me. As there were no other customers in the restaurant, he came and sat with me, saying that his name was Ben. As I was a stranger, I assumed Ben was curious to know who I was. During our conversation, Ben mentioned he was a retired telephone linesman and that he had taken early retirement as he got too wet and cold doing that type of work. He mentioned he still saw and kept in touch with his old colleagues who at times would call in as customers when they were in the area. Ben went on to explain that morning and lunchtimes were their busiest – it was easy to see that the afternoons were dead slow. He thought he could use his time more profitably doing an ice cream round, as his daughter could look after the shop in the afternoons. So far I had not said a word, I just listened to Ben as I ate my cakes and drank my tea. Ben continued by saying that he was looking out for a van and an ice cream conservator, to start an ice cream round. I suggested that perhaps we could help each other and I asked what the New Cross telephone exchange was like. Ben admitted that it was terrible, with no new lines available for years – the reply I dreaded. Undaunted, I pressed on by asking whether it was possible to have a phone connection and Ben said cautiously that it depended where it was needed. When I said at Goose Green in Dulwich, Ben merely smiled and asked how I could help him, so I explained that I was a refrigeration engineer and made deep freezers to order, giving Ben my business card.

On hearing this, Ben asked whether I had a minute to spare and he led me out of the shop to go to his garage. The shop was situated on a corner of the main road, the garage in the side street, next to the dining rooms. We entered and Ben pointed to where he would like the conservator positioned and I agreed that it would be a perfect place for it. Walking back to the dining rooms, Ben offered another cup of tea to me, asking how long it would take to make a deep freeze. I answered the question with one of my own – how long would it take Ben's colleagues to install a telephone, adding that I had been waiting for two years already. Ben laughed and said rather negatively that I was lucky, some had been waiting for much longer. To resolve this problem, I thought that I would have to take the initiative – I did not want to go into details about how imperative it was for me to be on the telephone. As my business was expanding, it was difficult for the Hughes brothers to keep up with it, and to attend to their own business as well – I wanted to take some of the pressure off them.

I decided to dangle the carrot, with the hope that Ben would bite it. I looked Ben straight in the eye and suggested that if he could get me on the phone within three weeks, I would make him a special offer, supplying and installing a deep freeze for £100 instead of the normal price, at the size he wanted. I hammered the point home with a promise that the offer was only if the phone was on and connected to the exchange. Ben asked what the normal price was, and I made no secret of the fact that it was £125 with a year's free service. I asked for Ben's telephone number so we could keep in touch, and returned to the garage to take the necessary measurements.

A week later, men were outside my flat house digging a hole. There were no visible telephone lines, so I assumed that they had to be underneath the pavement. Within the three weeks, a telephone was installed and connected to the exchange – Ben received his deep freeze at the same time. We became very good friends, meeting once a week to have a drink together, usually on a Thursday night.

With the telephone now connected, Grace was overjoyed, saying that she had always known her husband was a genius. I asked teasingly whether geniuses deserved a kiss and Grace immediately responded by sitting on my lap, putting her arms around my neck, and giving me a kiss of appreciation, saying with a broad smile that it was a gift on account, with an obvious meaning. I felt very pleased with my efforts.

The GPO supplied free of charge, a pack of pre-paid post cards to new subscribers – all one had to do was enter the new phone number and the addressee and post them to whoever needed to be notified that they were now on the phone. Grace was attending to this task, sitting on my lap, making herself comfortable. I said the next item on my list was a television set – these were now becoming affordable to the average family although at the time, few people possessed one. I mused about what the genius could do about that, while having a nibble and whispering in Grace's ear, during one of the few evenings we had together – I was making the most of it. Grace thought it was a good idea to purchase a TV as soon as possible – she wanted to invite a few of her office colleagues home to watch the forthcoming coverage of the Coronation of Queen Elizabeth II, televised live from Westminster Abbey. Only black and white television was available – colour was to come at a later date. As a means to help celebrate the occasion, all Civil Servants were given the day off.

One of Ben's drinking partners was a man named Yorky. He was about 5' 7" tall, around 60 years of age, with mischievous blue eyes, and a crew-cut hair style – he was always smartly dressed. I had met him several times and we had become good friends. During the war years and having money to invest, he bought about twenty fried fish and chip shops, in various parts of London, at give-away prices. Fish was not rationed, although not in plentiful supply. He closed most of the shops, just keeping a few open to give him an income. After the war, he found managers for all of them, fish becoming plentiful and cheap. Yorky seemed to spend his money quite freely. If he found himself seriously short of money, he would sell one shop at a time to any manager who wanted to buy one. Yorky made a handsome profit on each deal.

Ben, Yorky and I would sometimes go to a local nightclub, having some very good times together. I had never seen a man who could drink so much scotch, and still appear sober. Both Ben and I knew when he had had enough to drink – without notice, he would suddenly disappear. At first, we thought he had gone to the gents, but instead he had ordered a taxi to take himself home. Yorky lived alone – in spite of his free-spending ways, I never saw him with any women friends. He never spoke about his past life – whether he had ever been married, or had any children, no one knew. Yorky's membership allowed him to take friends to the club so there was never a problem gaining entry. They would have a few drinks, and a dance. Next to drinking, Ben's greatest pleasure was dancing and, in spite of his fifteen stone, he was a very good dancer, very light on his feet. He never seemed to have trouble getting dancing partners, reminding me in some ways of my old friend Bert Greaves. After a very enjoyable evening, I would often take Yorky home.

As our phone was on a manual exchange, at times it was a nightmare to use, especially when making calls in the early evening. One could hang on to the handset for what seemed like eternity. I found by experimenting, that between six and seven was generally the worst time to make calls – incoming calls were no problem. As the phone was on the window sill in the sitting room, to pass the time away while waiting for a response from the operator, one could look out of the window and watch the traffic go by, to relieve the boredom of waiting.

The young married couple, Penny and Jim, who occupied the hall flat, soon realised that a telephone connection had been made in the top flat, and wasted no time asking if they could use it. Jim would go upstairs at all times to make calls, eventually making himself a perfect nuisance. It did not matter to him that he was interrupting our privacy, or what he was saying while on the phone. Most of the time it seemed to me to be a lot of drivel, as though the telephone was a toy to be used simply for amusement. Usually when he was connected, he would spend long periods talking. Grace did not see why they should vacate our sitting room while Jim was just passing the time away. This was a regular occurrence. In the end, Grace told him that he could use the telephone for five minutes only, after which she would cut him off. I had no wish to be unfriendly towards Jim by not letting him use the phone, but something had to be said. We told him that we would not mind him using it if it was an emergency, but most times he seemed to be chatting about nothing. I explained that the main purpose of having the phone connection was to receive calls for my business – people could not get through with Jim jabbering away about nothing, so I asked him to be more thoughtful and considerate in future. Jim did apologise. Out of generosity, we agreed to call them for an emergency but that would be all. Grace was concerned because he was beginning to become a nuisance – she and Penny were good friends and she wanted it to stay that way. When Grace spoke about it with Penny, there was no problem, and she said she understood.

CHAPTER TWENTY

When I first started in business, I spent quite a bit of time canvassing butchers, grocers, restaurants and cafés, leaving my business card for potential customers. One of the premises I called on was a very busy market street butcher's shop. The butcher was one of the old school – he had sawdust on the floor, and he wore a straw hat and a blue and white striped apron over a clean white working coat. I received a phone call from him asking me to call back, preferably one evening. I returned the call to the number the man had left and fixed an appointment to visit him after shopping hours.

I always kept my appointments as agreed and arrived at the butcher's premises promptly on the due evening, knocking on the flat door – they lived over the shop. I shook hands with the butcher who introduced himself as Eddie Youldon and his wife Rene, who was sitting at the kitchen table. For husband and wife, they could have come out of the same mould – both were robust in build, and both spoke with a cockney accent. Eddie was about fourteen stone, of average height, heavy in jowl, clean-shaven, and with twinkling blue eyes. Rene, his wife, was about twelve stone, well proportioned, with curly, well-kept shoulder-length brunette hair. She was almost as tall as her husband, with a jovial personality, sparkling brown eyes, a small nose and a peach-like complexion. Both seemed to have a good sense of humour – at a guess, I thought they were both in their mid-fifties.

When I asked him what I could do for him, Eddie took me downstairs to a small back room behind the shop, showing me what was left of his cold-room. It seemed that Eddie had a rat problem – as fast as the holes were filled in, more would appear overnight. It was a continuous battle to see who was going to win. It was easy for the rats to get inside as the cold-room was very old, made with match boarding inside and out. From at least two feet from floor level, the wood was rotten – all the rats had to do was to either claw or gnaw through the cork insulation. Eddie asked me to give him a quote for a new cold-room, using the existing compressor unit which was at least twenty years old. I offered to put together three quotes, the first for merely supplying a new cold-room using the existing compressor equipment, the second for supplying a new cold-room and compressor equipment which would be air-cooled as opposed to the present water-cooled system, saving on water costs, and the third for a tailor-made cold-room with all new equipment. I explained that the third option would give him at least another hundred cubic feet of refrigerated internal storage space, without taking up any more floor space. Both the latter would carry a twelve months' guarantee and free service.

Eddie asked in a puzzled way what I meant by 'tailor-made', so I explained that there was limited floor space to use, and he should make the most of it. I pointed out that there was at least a fifteen inch gap round each side of the present cold-room and I could add a bit more height as well, giving him extra storage space, which he would no doubt put to good use. I described the outside of the new cold-room as being covered with galvanised sheeting up to three feet from floor level and being stipple-glazed inside, for easy cleaning. I would lay a concrete cold-room floor, with a fine metal mesh. That, I promised, would be the end of the rat problem, and I confidently stated that Eddie would receive his money back if even one rat got in. With the extra capacity, there would be plenty of hanging space inside, plus adjustable rails and slatted shelving.

I took the three quotes along to Eddie after a couple of days and asked him to read through the quotes carefully, warning him that if he should choose the tailor-made cold-room, it would take at least three days longer from the date of ordering. I suggested weekend working when Eddie's stock would be low. I also said that I could arrange for the cold-room contractors to take the old one away as it was only of scrap value. A few days after I had delivered the quotes, Eddie phoned me to ask me to call in for a talk. I called as requested and was told that Eddie had decided on the tailor-made cold-room – we continued our discussion of the details over a cup of tea. Both Rene and Eddie were great tea-drinkers – she made a lovely cup of tea, just as I liked it. Eddie admitted to me that he had sought two other quotes besides mine, but mine was the only one that mentioned a tailor-made installation. I was glad that he had, adding that Eddie would have the benefit of the extra storage space, possibly for the same price the others quoted for a standard one. When I asked if I had clinched the order, Eddie said of course I had – he would start the ball rolling the very next day and let me know when it would be ready for delivery, so that I could make arrangements for the installation.

The cold-room contractors erected the new one, taking the old one away – as promised, the work was carried out on a Sunday – and I completed all the interior work before the floor was concreted. All the while the work was in progress, Rene supplied the workmen with endless cups of tea, fussing around like a mother hen looking after her brood. Eventually the complete installation was finished and I said that the cold-room would be ready for use in the morning if they allowed the concrete to dry out thoroughly, by leaving the door open all night. Eddie had made arrangements with another butcher to store what little weekend stock he had – he had purposely run down his stock for the changeover. I said I would call in first thing the next morning to make the final adjustments. Now that the installation was complete, both Rene and Eddie were more than pleased, showing their enthusiasm as proud owners, having made the right decision.

I called in first thing on the Monday morning as promised and stayed for a while to make sure the cold-room was functioning properly, leaving it in perfect working order. Eddie asked me for the account as soon as possible and it was promised for a week's time.

When I called three months later for the first free service, Eddie said how pleased he was, adding that he had recommended me to several of his business colleagues. He asked me if I could supply a deep freeze. I told him that I actually made them to order and Eddie explained it was not for his shop, but for his smallholding at Biggin Hill in Kent. Biggin Hill was one of the frontline fighter aerodromes during the Battle of Britain in 1940–1.

A date was agreed for a Sunday afternoon visit, and I asked if I could bring my wife along – we could then go visiting afterwards. I found the place tucked in between Biggin Hill and the village of Downe. We were greeted by Eddie and Rene, and Grace was introduced. Rene responded by saying she had just made a pot of tea and we readily agreed in unison to the offer of a cup. While Eddie and I were talking, the two women paired off – Rene had the knack of making people feel at ease, without any effort. The smallholding was used for breeding rabbits, and for rearing turkeys for Christmas, all of which were sold in Eddie's shop. During the war years, this was a very profitable and lucrative business, neither being rationed. The smallholding covered about two acres, half of which was used for growing cabbages and lettuce for the rabbits which were housed in long wired runs, for one-month-old, two-month-old, and three-month-old rabbits, when they became butcher's meat. All were white, fat and well fed. There were other runs for the chickens and turkeys and also a wartime piggery. Eddie explained to me that the demand for rabbits had died down somewhat and his intention was to deep freeze the skinned rabbits as he still had some restaurants and a few shop customers he supplied. Frozen, they would be ready for collection or delivery.

As a lucrative sideline, Eddie had no trouble selling the rabbit skins and I suspected that many women were wearing rabbit skins, treated to look like more expensive furs. As I mused to Eddie, it was wonderful what furriers could do. I asked him how on earth he managed all the work involved and Eddie explained that he had a man who came in and did all the feeding and cultivating. He did suggest that, although he paid him well, he suspected that he helped himself to the occasional rabbit or chicken. It was impossible to keep a thorough check on what went on and if he questioned his honesty, he would only say a fox got in and killed off a few, so it was best not to say anything, unless he became too greedy, saying this with a broad grin. On the smallholding, there was a fair-size shed divided in half – at one end, a small kitchen, with the other half for personal use. Eddie said when the London bombing was at its heaviest, he and Rene came down to Biggin Hill to sleep, and to use the smallholding as a weekend retreat in better weather, as they were doing that weekend.

The kitchen was equipped with a sink unit, kitchen table and chairs, a small Belling electric cooker and two easy chairs. The other half was used just as a store room although it was a bedroom during the war years. Eddie said that he would like the deep freeze installed in the store and I saw no problem in that. With all the details finalised, Grace and I left after bidding Eddie and Rene cheerio, going on to see Rose and Alf.

During the journey, I asked Grace what the two women were talking about while I was with Eddie. Grace replied that they covered all sorts of things including Rene's praise for me – apparently she was most delighted with the new cold-room, but Grace declined to say any more, otherwise I might get a big head.

The deep freeze was duly delivered and installed at the smallholding. A short time later, Eddie phoned me to arrange a meeting at a house in Herne Hill in south-east London. Eddie explained on the phone he had just bought the house, and was in need of a good electrician to quote for some electrical work he wanted done. A time and date were agreed for a meeting at the house so we could discuss what Eddie had in mind. When I arrived at the house, I found a corner semi-detached, very impressive-looking property in the select part of Herne Hill. Being a corner house, it had the advantage of extra ground, as well as a rear garden at least 200 yards long, running parallel to the side road. The front entrance to the property was approached through a well-kept front garden with lawn and flowers. The front door was of solid oak, with the upper half in coloured leaded lights.

I announced my arrival using the heavy brass knocker. Eddie must have spotted me pull up because, even before I took my hand off the knocker, the door opened, we greeted each other with a handshake and I was invited inside. The entrance hall was all oak panelled up to 9" from the ceiling with a narrow shelf at the top of the panelling, presumably to display ornaments or decorative pieces of china. The staircase leading to the first floor was of solid oak, positioned against the flank wall with a leaded light window over the landing at the turn of the stairs. The stair banister and handrail were also of solid oak. Eddie led me upstairs and described where he wanted the power supply to be – there were three bedrooms, the master bedroom overlooking the road. On the landing between the bedrooms was a large airing cupboard and the bathroom which was one of the old-fashioned type – just the bath standing on its four fancy iron feet. Eddie said that he thought it was awful, but Rene knew what she wanted done – the room was completely out of character with the rest of the house. The electrical installation upstairs was agreed, as Eddie described what was wanted and I made appropriate notes.

We continued our tour of the house on the ground floor with Eddie again pointing to where he wanted the power points positioned, as we went from room to room. At the bottom of the main staircase was a passage that led to a very large kitchen where there was an Aga stove with ovens on either side – it also heated the water for domestic use. There was a fair-size pantry and an enormous ten-foot purpose-built dresser dominating one wall with white painted shelves, and cupboards under the working top, for storage purposes. A back door led out to the garden which was laid out to lawns and brightly coloured flowerbeds with a large kitchen garden hidden by trellis, covered with honeysuckle in full bloom. Eddie took me into the lounge which ran the length of the house, with glazed French door windows overlooking the garden. Apart from being a lovely room, what took my eye was the Adam fireplace in the centre of the dividing wall of the semi-detached house. The walls were covered with expensive wallpaper and the whole of the ground floor up to the kitchen was parquet tiled in light oak.

All the rooms were fitted with light oak moulded skirting boards and I chalk-marked the positions, as near as I could, for all the additional electrical points. In the entrance hall, upstairs landing and master bedroom were to be off-peak night storage heaters. About that time, 13 amp ring-main socket outlets came into use, becoming very popular – it was agreed to use this system of wiring. Fortunately the electric meter could be positioned under the main staircase leading down to a cellar which extended beneath most of the downstairs floor space. Eddie and I sat on the bottom stair in the hall, discussing the work involved. I said that the upstairs work would present no problem – it would be downstairs where I might have a few problems hiding all the cable, as I did not want to disturb the skirting boards or the floor. The cellar was a godsend which would make the installation a little easier. I told Eddie that it would be impossible to give him a precise quote as I did not know what snags I might come up against when doing the wiring. I asked Eddie to take me on trust, or approach another electrician. Eddie was very content to let me carry on as I suggested and said there was no great hurry as they would not be moving in for another three months. He gave me a key so I could come and go as need be.

Eddie explained that he and Rene were thinking of retiring and that he had tried to get planning permission to build on the smallholding but the council had turned it down flat. Although he had appealed, it was a waste of time. Then the house came on the market,, and Rene fell in love with it, so he bought it. He also had permission to build a garage at the bottom of the garden, and as the back of the house faced south, a breakfast room. The lounge and the kitchen would lead into it. That would help to keep the house warm during the winter months, I commented. Rene had always wanted a garden to potter around in, and now she had one. I thought that they would have a beautiful home when it was all finished – whoever had built it originally had spared no expense.

I made many visits to the property until, finally, the work was done to Rene's satisfaction – she was thrilled the way it all turned out. They moved into their new home and settled in very quickly and comfortably. What a contrast this house was to the dingy flat over the shop that had been their home for the last thirty years, with always the smell of meat hanging around. Sometime after they had settled in, Grace and I received an invitation and were delighted to attend a house-warming party held by Eddie and Rene. It was the first tine Grace had seen the house although I had often spoken to her about it, saying how much I liked it – I thought that when she saw it, she might become envious and want something similar. Although she adored the house, making her comment how much she liked it, Grace had set her heart on a country cottage, so she could have the freedom of walking and keeping a dog.

I was a little late in making my last free service call to Eddie's butcher's shop. Both he and Rene, instead of being their jovial Cockney selves, were quiet and glum-looking, as though something was bothering them. They both appeared to have shed weight – I noticed that Eddie was down to around eleven stone and Rene had lost weight too. I was treated more like a close friend than a business acquaintance but it was obvious to me that something was wrong. The customary cup of tea appeared and while we were all drinking, I asked them if they were on a diet, saying that I could not help noticing how much weight both of them had lost, since I last saw them. Eddie explained that it was not diet but the fact that he had the Income Tax people after him – he took a sip of tea and continued to tell me the background. It had all started with a nice polite letter, asking him how he became the owner of the new house – was it a legacy, or did they buy it. Eddie wrote back to say that he had bought it. The next letter from them had demanded nine years back tax, their argument implying that during the war years and after, while meat rationing was in force, Eddie must have dealt on the black market. He emphatically said that that was a lie and said that he felt very offended that they would say such things. The tax people had gone on to say that he could not possibly have made that amount of profit from his meat allocation.

I was most intrigued but did not want to appear nosy and I told them how curious and interested I was, asking them how they thought it had come about. Eddie said he really did not know and could find only one thing he could associate with the enquiry – when he had the garage and breakfast room built, the tax office had to reassess his rates. He supposed that one thing led to another. I asked Eddie if he had paid cash for the house, which he had, and Eddie supposed they had also noted that he was not claiming any mortgage allowance on his tax returns. I asked him if he had an accountant but Eddie confessed that during the war years and afterwards, he had submitted his tax returns himself. They had been straightforward, as he thought.

I decided to pose a personal question because, as a friend, I dearly wanted to offer help and advice. All the while Eddie and I had been talking, Rene had been present, but remained silent, just nipping in and out of the shop to serve customers. I asked Eddie whether he had declared his profits on the rabbits and chickens he had sold in the shop during the war years.

Eddie looked rather woebegone and confessed that he had not done so, as it was just a sideline, in Rene's name. I commented that, sideline or not, they were not talking of just a few rabbits to accumulate that sort of money, and the tax people would be thinking in hundreds, to have enough cash to pay for the house. I said very seriously that my advice would be that they really did need the services of a good accountant – it was no good them trying to sort it out themselves, as the tax people would tie them up in knots and in the end they would have to pay them what they were asking for, just to get them off their backs.

Eddie sheepishly asked me if I knew of a good accountant and I immediately said that I could recommend my own accountant, who was really hot stuff – someone who could talk to them in their own language. I explained that, in my first year of business I managed to recover a repayment of £100 on my wife's earnings. Eddie commented that he had to be good to achieve that and I asked if he would like me to contact the accountant, as a friend helping a friend. Eddie was enthusiastic, but I warned him that, if he should take on their case, they would have to promise that they would be absolutely honest and hold nothing back. He would have to make that promise as it would be for their own good in the long run – I added that if he found out that they were not being completely truthful, he would drop the case like a hot cinder. They would then be back to where they started, and possibly financially worse off. Eddie responded by saying that he wanted to clear the unfortunate business up as soon as possible and he promised that he would not hold anything back. I nodded approvingly. Rene had been listening to what was being said, not saying a word herself, but obviously showing interest. I could see the sparkle coming back into their eyes, as though the light at the end of the tunnel was beginning to show.

I asked them for their home phone number, just in case the accountant should want it, and I promised to contact him the next morning and then telephone them to let them know what his answer was. In the meantime, I suggested that they gathered up all their old accounts and put them in yearly envelopes in date order. That would save the accountant's staff a lot of time and trouble. Also I suggested that they should have some figures ready for the rabbit skins they had sold, as it was more than likely that the accountant would ask for them. I also advised Eddie to prepare some costings for the smallholding, such as wages, cost of seed and fodder, upkeep costs and any other expenditure he might think was relevant. My final piece of advice was to be careful about first impressions because the accountant might seem like the biggest drip on earth but Eddie should not be fooled – he had a handshake like a wet rag, but a brain like a computer – I thought that he was brilliant at his job and if anyone could help the beleaguered butcher, there was no better man. By the time I departed, they were more like their old selves.

Although I had not seen Eddie and Rene during the time the accountant was handling their tax matters, nothing was said about how their problem was progressing. Eddie said he received the occasional phone call to answer a few queries, but they both seemed to be more than happy with the way the accountant was dealing with their problem. A few weeks later I answered the phone at home one evening and a bright and cheerful voice announced that it was Eddie Youdon, sounding more like his old self. He wanted to know whether my wife and I could pop over to the house one evening, suggesting a Saturday or Sunday evening – there would only be the four of us. A date was agreed and a time set, after I had consulted Grace. When we arrived, we were greeted by a smiling and jovial Eddie. As Grace entered the hall, she could not help noticing and admiring a crystal glass chandelier hanging in the hall – this was something new since she was there last.

Eddie showed us into the lounge which was now fully furnished – a large oriental carpet covering the parquet flooring. There were heavy maroon velvet curtains hung at the French doors and front windows, a three-piece Chesterfield suite with other easy chairs and a walnut veneered coffee table. The room was tastefully furnished, showing off Rene's good taste in home furnishings. Rene carried in the tea.

While drinking the tea, I asked Eddie if he had something to celebrate and he replied that they certainly had – he thanked me for my help and advice and quoted my own words by describing the accountant as 'hot stuff'. Eddie said that it had all been sorted out and resolved and, although he knew he would have to pay back tax, the financial wizard had reduced it to a more acceptable figure, with only a nominal amount to pay, far better than he ever anticipated. Eddie said he was feeling very relieved, and extremely happy with the outcome and result – there had been a time when he thought he would have to mortgage the house to pay the tax people. It would have broken poor Rene's heart, he said, looking over towards her, let alone how it would have affected him.

I said how glad I was for both of them and suggested jokingly that perhaps they would now revert to their old weights. "Not on your life!", was Eddie's quick response. He claimed that the one good thing to have come out of the affair was that he had lost a lot of weight – holding his stomach in both hands, he said that he was a great deal fitter and felt better for the loss of weight. The rest of the evening was passed with pleasant conversation. When it was time to leave, I gave Rene a kiss on the cheek, Eddie likewise to Grace. We men shook hands and Eddie declared that he and Rene greatly enjoyed our company and wished the visits to continue. From my heart, I thanked them both.

Chapter Twenty-One

On one occasion, Eddie telephoned me to ask me to call and discuss some work he had in mind and at the same time, he recommended an Italian ice cream maker and vendor in the same marketplace as Eddie, giving his name as Donnarunna. The marketplace was a long road with stalls and barrows along both sides and I had trouble finding the address, so I called in to see Eddie. I thanked him for the recommendation, and asked him where Donnarunna's shop was, and stayed there for a short while to have a chat for old time's sake. I negotiated the busy road, and eventually found the address, pulling into the yard next to the shop.

I knocked on the back door and was greeted with a friendly handshake by the Italian who introduced himself as Carlo Donnarunna, showing me into a very large kitchen-cum-sitting room. The two elderly people sitting in there were his mother and father and Carlo translated the introduction to his parents in rapid Italian. I shook hands with both of the old folk who just nodded their heads in acknowledgement. Carlo explained that they were just going to sit down for lunch, and invited me to join them. While we ate, he gave me some idea what he had in mind to expand his business and make much more ice cream than he was doing at present.

In the kitchen, there was a large black cooking range with a huge iron pot on top, simmering away, full to the top. The table was at least eight feet long, with forms along either side. There was no tablecloth or covering, just the bare boards that had been scrubbed many times over the years.

I was invited to sit myself down while Carlo served something up for me. Although I was hungry, not knowing what was in the concoction in the pot, I suggested that just a small portion would be sufficient – I felt that if I was going to leave any, it would only be a small amount so I would not offend Carlo. When it was served to me, it was spaghetti Italian style, long lengths of fresh pasta, with tomatoes, in a rich meat gravy sauce, garnished with garlic. There were chunks of French bread heaped in a carved wooden basket on the table.

From the first few mouthfuls, I was not too sure whether I was going to like it – it was really delicious, but a little more spicy than I was used to. Nevertheless, I ate it all with the help of a couple of chunks of bread. Throughout the years that I knew this family, the huge iron pot was always on the hob, ready for serving – I had many happy meals there.

Like most Italians, Carlo had a good stock of black hair, kept in place with the aid of a little hair dressing. He was in his mid-thirties, 5' 8" tall, of stocky build, clean-shaven and with a light brown skin. He had a wonderful personality, with a keen sense of humour, making him a very likeable fellow.

Carlo suggested that we should go and see what he had in mind, and said he hoped that it could actually be done. When I saw the ice cream tubs, my first reaction was to forget about it – Carlo noticed the hesitant look on my face, and asked me what I thought about the idea. Slowly giving it some thought, ideas were beginning to form in my mind, and it dawned on me that Carlo's idea could make sense. His idea was to refrigerate the tub, instead of using ice and freezing salt. Carlo's reasoning was that with ice and salt he could only make one laborious gallon of ice cream at a time. The container had the capacity of five gallons. There are two ways to refrigerate, either direct or indirect – the direct way is the method used in domestic fridges and deep freezers, indirect is by means of using a non-freezing circulating agent, such as a brine solution.

Carlo wanted to increase his ice cream-making potential – at the time, with his old-fashioned methods, he could not satisfy his customers' demands, besides having three pitches to supply. He felt he was losing money by not keeping up with demand. Modern equipment was impossible to obtain so soon after the war – it would be a few years before it was widely marketed. His current way was long and tedious, always requiring attention, draining off the water, and repacking ice and salt – the whole operation taking at least two hours for each mix. I measured the amount of brine required with the ice cream container in position, making relevant notes. I then completed some calculations, working out the required compressor size, to make five gallons in thirty minutes. I told Carlo that it could be an expensive job, but somewhat less if he considered making five gallons an hour, rather than ten. I offered to give Carlo a quote for the two systems – five or ten gallons an hour – then he could choose for himself to suit his requirements. Carlo had clearly been making some calculations himself, working out what he would be saving on ice and freezing salt.

Carlo was eager to know whether it could be done, hoping for a positive answer. I assured him that it was distinctly possible – on hearing this, his big brown eyes lit up. I reckoned it would take about a week to have the system up and running, but could be sooner. Carlo put his hand in his back pocket, and took out a wad of banknotes giving them to me. There were one hundred and fifty pounds in the bundle, by way of a deposit, Carlo explained, saying that he had decided on the quicker, half-hour, system. I gave him a temporary receipt on the back of one of my business cards. I shook hands with Carlo to seal the agreement and agreed to see him again the next day. I wasted no time and went straight to the components company to earmark a suitable compressor unit.

I had by now become a good customer to these people, always settling my account promptly. I asked them to confirm my calculations – they were very good with technical assistance – and they made a slight adjustment to the amount of copper tubing required. Within a week, I had it all working and ready for a trial run and test. In theory it should work satisfactorily although it looked somewhat of a Heath Robinson set-up – but it did the job Carlo wanted. While doing this conversion onsite, I was invited daily to join Carlo and the family for lunch – the offering served up each day was from the same pot on the hob. It became little wonder to me why they had such a large pot. Quite a number of people called in during the course of the day and all were served from the same container – family and friends alike, I thought. At the end of the week, I had acquired a taste for this type of food, really enjoying it.

With Carlo making all the extra ice cream, he had to have a place to keep it, so ordered a deep freeze for storage purposes. The tests were completed and the system was working to Carlo's satisfaction. When I left, I said I would call back in two days' time and suggested that Carlo should ring me if he encountered any snags. Before I left, I gave Carlo explicit instructions to keep the cover on the ice cream container – the protective cover for the brine –in its place while making the ice cream, and to stop the agitator when taking the ice cream out.

When I called two days later, Carlo greeted me with open arms, saying that I was a miracle worker. It was working perfectly and Carlo excitedly said that he was now going into the wholesale business, supplying family and friends. He asked for my account and I promised to bring it round in a week or so, in the meantime suggesting that he should let me know if there were any problems. Before I could leave, Carlo produced a large plateful of food, insisting that I eat it. While eating, Carlo said that he might have one of his other tubs converted. He asked me how I had become interested in refrigeration and I gave him just a brief outline of my transfer from aircrew training to the Army, where I learned about refrigeration on a college course they had paid for. I described how I was actually a qualified electrician and Carlo said that that was clear from the way that I had tackled the job – at the time that part of London was on DC mains.

I had not heard from Carlo, so assumed that all was in order and working satisfactorily. A week later I called on Carlo, taking my bill for the money owing me. Carlo greeted me wreathed in smiles and guessed that I had brought the account. Carlo led the way into the kitchen and told me to sit down at the table – he excused himself, saying he would return directly. He came back carrying the largest of biscuit tins and took the lid off, put his hand inside and brought out a fistful of banknotes, handing them to me and asking me to count them. He did the same for himself, and eventually the right amount of money was counted. I happily receipted the account as paid. We both sat there for a while, and Carlo told me that in the winter months, with the same barrow, he sold hot chestnuts. His brother, who I had not yet met, had a pitch at Brixton, doing the same. I said that I supposed I had put on a bit of weight while working for Carlo, who just laughed. Now good friends, we shook hands before I left.

Doing that work for Carlo had brought in a number of contracts from other Italians, all by recommendation. Not one of them ever gave me a cheque – it was always cash. With the money I received, I was able to settle all my outstanding debts and give Grace some extra cash to buy herself some new summer clothes. I also managed to pay Grace back the £150 I borrowed when first going into business. I was quite pleased with the way my business was shaping – all the long hours had paid off.

One afternoon whilst working in my workshop on my own, a scruffy-looking Italian walked in, asking to speak to me. Being told he had the right man, the Italian asked me to spare him a minute and I agreed that I always had time to talk business. The man asked permission to introduce himself and announced that he was known as Tony. He took a piece of paper from his pocket, and put it down on top of the Morrison indoor air raid shelter that was used for compressor assembly work, making an excellent worktop. When I agreed that I had completed work for Carlo, Tony explained that the conversion he had done for him had given him an idea. What he had in mind had not been tried before, but in his opinion, it could be practical. My curiosity was now aroused, and I asked what my part in the project could be. Tony replied by saying that he wanted to go into business as a wholesaler of ice lollies. He pointed to the sketch lying on the worktop, indicating what he had in mind – it was a tank six foot long by two foot six inches wide which, when refrigerated, would produce one gross of lollies an hour or faster, the whole unit to be incorporated in a steel framework, about three feet high, with a circulating pump underneath the tank.

Tony asked what I thought the cost would be and was told that I could not give an exact figure, as the tank would have to be made of copper, by a friend of mine. I suggested a price of roughly £20. I did some further calculations, giving Tony an estimated cost for installation, testing and checking, but not including electrical work, although I offered to make an estimate for that also. Tony also wanted a deep freeze storage unit, giving me the size he had in mind. In all, I suggested, the job would cost around twelve hundred pounds complete and installed, with twelve months' free service. I thought the price would put him off the idea – he did not seem to have that sort of money. Much to my surprise, Tony agreed with the figures I had given him and asked me how soon I could start. In reply, I said that I would have to allow three days for the tank to be made, because until I had the tank there, I could not do much except erect the steel framework. I thought that about two weeks would be sensible although with luck it could be sooner.

Tony put his hand in his back pocket and pulled out a bundle of bank notes, presenting them to me saying that there was five hundred pounds by way of a deposit. Before I accepted the money, I stated that I would like to have a look at the premises and answered Tony's puzzled expression by saying that I needed to check whether the apparatus would pass through the entrance. It would not be a straightforward delivery, and the floor would have to be strong enough to take the additional weight. Tony assured me that he had thought of all those things, and there would be no problems.

I was happy to accept Tony's word and asked him to look me up a week later to see what progress had been made. We exchanged business cards to enable each to contact the other – on the back of mine was a temporary receipt for the money Tony had handed over. To seal the deal, we shook hands and Tony left. I wistfully thought that you should never judge a sausage by its skin – the man looked as if he did not have two pennies to rub together when he first came in. The successful outcome of this contract secured me further work from Tony – he ordered another unit of similar capacity – besides making one for his brother who had a business in Reading.

Chapter Twenty-Two

I had now been in business for just over three years, during which time I had built up a very good clientele, achieved mainly through recommendations and good reliable service. My hunch in concentrating on refrigeration had paid off handsomely – I only accepted electrical work when required for my own installations of refrigeration equipment I supplied to my customers.

One evening while sitting at home, before going back to my workshop, I answered the telephone to be greeted by a woman's cultured voice, a voice I had not heard before. She said she understood that I did electrical installations, and supplied domestic refrigerators – her voice really fascinated me, and I replied that I did both, wondering what it was all about. She continued by asking me if I would be so kind as to call and see her in the morning, giving me her address. I asked what time would be convenient and she suggested any time to suit me, telling me to ask for Jennifer Tait, spelling her surname. I instantly said that I would call to see her in the morning and I wondered what sort of person could have such a lovely voice, without any affectation. I went to the kitchen where Grace was busy, telling her of the telephone conversation I had just had.

I went around to the address at about 10am – it was the office of an estate agent, opposite the lower end of Peckham Rye. I entered the office and asked for Jennifer Tait. The woman sitting behind the desk said it was her and asked me if I was the fridge man. I acknowledged her idea, saying that I was known as Joe, politely correcting her. We shook hands. Her hands were as soft as her voice and she asked me to call her Jennifer as she hated formalities. She was smartly dressed in a charcoal-coloured business suit and a crisp white blouse. As she was standing on the other side of her desk, I estimated her height at around 5' 6" not knowing if she was wearing high-heel shoes. She had keen hazel eyes, shiny brown hair styled to cover a part of her face, and a natural peaches-and-cream complexion, with just a shade of lipstick. I observed her slender figure, guessing her age as the late twenties or early thirties – she wore no jewellery on her fingers, not even a wedding ring.

I asked what I might be able to do for her, as she was rustling through some papers on her desk, muttering to herself, finally retrieving the paper she was searching for and handing it to me. It was a sketch of the internal layout of a house. She asked me if I knew The Warren, smiling and showing her perfect white teeth. I nodded in assent. She had just bought number 28 and was planning to convert the house into bedsits – with a 2 kilowatt off-peak electric heater on each landing, and also a domestic refrigerator, which was where I was to be involved. I told her that I needed to see the house to assess what would be required, and to ensure that I made an accurate quotation. I asked for the keys and she replied, handing me a bunch of keys, that her office manager was away sick, so I would have to visit the premises on my own. She hoped that I would not mind doing it that way, giving me a lovely smile.

I studied the sketch for a couple of minutes and observed that the whole house might have to be rewired. Each room was to have its own slot or check electricity meter. I asked if she would like me to supply and fit the specified sink water heater in each room and Jennifer quickly confirmed these points. I said I would go and inspect the property, and then give her the quotation and specification in two days' time.

Just before I left, she remarked that each bedsit was going to be fully furnished, except for sheets and towels. On each landing there was to be a fully equipped bathroom with hot water supplied to the bath by a multipoint gas heater. She asked me to fit a lock on the landing fridges, with three keys for each, as she did not want people raiding each other's fridges. Finally, I asked if she would like me to quote for supplying a baby electric cooker for each flat. That seemed to be fine and she agreed to my suggestion. As an afterthought, she told me to bring the keys back when I brought my quote along.

The Warren was an area of three-storey semi-detached Victorian houses built around a centrepiece of gardens – middle-class houses for large families, some of whom were prosperous enough to employ servants. There were at least ten fair-sized rooms in each house, making them ideal for conversion into bedsits. When I left Jennifer, I went straight to a local electrical wholesaler to check on prices of materials, also asking if there was a discount on bulk purchases of water heaters and baby cookers. I then visited the house in question – I knew the size of the house as I had done work in the Warren previously. In the evening at home, I prepared the quotation and specification, taking it round to the office a few days later. To my surprise, Jennifer was not in her office. The person who was there was a middle-aged man wearing a black, pin-striped suit. I asked for Jennifer Tait, to be told in a very curt voice that she was not there. I handed the man the keys and the quote asking him to give it to her, stating that it was the quotation for number 28. The man did not offer his hand to me as I was leaving, so there was no parting handshake. Judging by the man's attitude towards me, I thought that that was the last I would hear of the job.

It was therefore quite a surprise to hear the gentle voice of Jennifer Tait a month later, when I answered the phone. She confirmed that the quote was in the office, and said she would be obliged if I would call in to the office as there were a couple of points she would like to discuss with me. We agreed that the next day at around 10am would be a convenient time for us both. I called in the office as suggested – the office manager was present, but I really could not describe him as having a pleasant expression on his face. I shook hands with Jennifer, and said good morning to her manager, which he chose to ignore.

She thanked me for coming so promptly, adding that there was one problem she could foresee – would it be possible to position the electric company's meters outside, so when they come to read the dials, they would not have to disturb any of the tenants? I could see no real problem in this. She also told me that she would be away for three months from the beginning of January and, if any problems arose, Mr. Knight, the office manager would help me sort them out. She would be keeping in touch with the office by telephone while she was away. She handed me the confirmation order for which I thanked her wholeheartedly and I shook her hand, saying how much I hoped she had an enjoyable trip. Fortunately for me, this work came at the right time, at the beginning of my fourth winter, when refrigeration servicing was at its lowest demand, except for the panicky butchers around Christmas time.

I intended to concentrate on refrigeration work in the mornings, doing the electrical work in the afternoons and evenings, except for any emergency refrigeration calls. Jennifer Tait returned from her trip and eventually the house was finished – the builders and carpenters had quite a lot of work to carry out, so that had dragged the job out rather. She was very happy with the finished result. Out of curiosity, I asked her how she first got to know about me. She explained she was in Wales the butcher's, and casually mentioned that she was in need of someone to do some work and he had given her a really glowing recommendation, so she thought that I would be the man for the work she had in mind. That contract was the result. I was pleased with the way that my reputation was spreading and I cheerfully presented my account – and was promptly paid.

As the properties became vacant, Jennifer Tait was buying them up – consequently I completed five more to the same specification as the first, over a period of three years. She was getting more applicants than there were bedsits available. She let them at six pounds a week, excluding supplying sheets and towels and electrical consumption. The tenants had a choice of either shilling slot meters or a quarterly bill. Although the bedsits were only let to single professional people of both sexes, it was on the understanding was that no sharing should take place. Of course, she had no way of knowing if anyone stayed the occasional night or weekend, but suspected it did happen.

I had previously said to Jennifer that if she wanted to get in touch with me to speak to me personally, the best time would be at home after 7pm, or before 8am in the morning. One evening she phoned me at home, asking if I would come round one evening as she needed some electrical work done in her flat. I asked if the next evening would be convenient and we agreed to meet at 7pm. I visited promptly as promised the following evening. Her flat was above the office and could be either entered through the office or via a separate outside street door.

When I entered the office she was sitting at her desk. Immediately she suggested that, before she showed me what she had in mind, we should have a drink to celebrate our successful association and poured out two glasses of wine, offering one to me. I thanked her, but had a feeling there was more to it than merely having a drink. Jennifer took a sip of her wine, then told me that I had done a wonderful job on the bedsits – she was more than pleased with the finished results. I thanked her for the compliment and said modestly that I only did what any other electrician would have done. She said I had done more than that – apparently she had another property before starting on the Warren, where she had more problems than she really wanted. She took another sip of wine and continued to explain that the workmen seemed to resent taking instructions from her as a woman. They took the attitude that a woman's place was in the home, doing housework and looking after children. With me, she had had none of that – the work went smoothly and without problems. Mr. Knight had reported that I never approached him once while she was away, regarding queries or problems arising. She recognised that I had dealt with them, if any, using my own initiative.

By this time Jennifer was refilling the glasses and as I took a sip of wine, I commented that one of the good things that came out of the war was the liberation of women from the kitchen sink, for those that wanted to be liberated. I added that women like Jennifer were taking on responsible jobs – before the war, that would have been unheard of. The only advice I could give Jennifer, was what a very good and dear friend had given me before the war – never ever develop an inferiority complex – advice which I had found invaluable. I drank some more wine and continued with my theme, saying that women were entering a man's world, so men have good reason to be jealous, or envious, and so may feel inferior themselves – she should feel proud of her sex and the world was definitely changing. I asserted that the main reason why we had a successful association was because I treated her as an equal.

Jennifer changed the subject, asking me if I was married. When she asked about children, I explained that we were married in 1940 and I went into the services. We had decided to wait until after the war to have children – if children had come along by accident, we would have been delighted, and accepted them, but there were none so far. Jennifer explained that she went away for three months each year, to visit her father and to escape from the worst of the English winter, and to enjoy the South African warm sunshine. Her mother was English and her mother and father had met in England, during the First World War – she was the only child of the marriage. Her mother was killed in a car accident when some fool motorist hit their car head on, during the early part of the last war. She was lucky to survive the accident – when telling me this, she pulled her hair aside to show a four-inch scar, on the left side of her face, on her cheek near the ear. She had had plastic surgery, but it was plain to see that there was still a slight disfigurement.

Jennifer had received compensation for her mother's death, and for her injuries. Breaking off to take another sip of wine, she explained that she had used the compensation, investing it by converting the Warren houses into bedsits. I commented that it was clearly a shrewd decision and then asked her if she was English by birth. Indeed she was, although her father was thinking of marrying again, a South African woman. She had met her on the last trip to South Africa.

I jokingly said that now she had so many properties in the Warren, it should be renamed Tait Square and Jennifer agreed, saying with a regretful sigh that she would like to do so in memory of her mother. Whether it was the effect of the wine, or the soft Guy Lombardo music playing in the background, I blurted out that I found her a very attractive woman, in spite of what I had just seen, paying the compliment without any ulterior motive. Jennifer thanked me for my kind remark, confessing that she had lured me there under false pretences, as she was feeling in need of company, and thought of me as we seemed to get on so well together. I was surprised that she did not have a man friend but Jennifer ruefully explained that she did have but when he saw the scar he just disappeared. She had not seen him since and there had been no one else – a comment she made with some regret.

While we had been talking, we were sitting on opposite sides of her desk. Jennifer rose from her swivel chair and I, thinking our conversation had come to an end, rose from my chair also and stood beside it. Jennifer came up to me, standing very close to me – in fact I could feel the contours of her body against me. Her jacket was still draped over her chair where she had taken it off before I had arrived, being such a warm evening. I could see she had a very trim figure. Pressing her body even closer, she asked me if I would mind if she kissed me – before I could give an answer she put her arms around my neck, kissing me full on the mouth. Her kiss was full of pent-up passion, warm and moist, sending shivers down my body. She clung on to me, eager to sense my response and I returned the kiss with the same intensity. We continued kissing and petting, eventually pulling ourselves away as we had to, before one thing led to another.

As we parted, Jennifer said she really hoped that it had not spoiled our business association. Now recovered from this sudden burst of passion, I said quite clearly that business was one thing, pleasure another, so why should it cause a problem. Reluctantly I said I had to leave as I had told my wife that I would not be too long. I said teasingly that I hoped she felt a little better, making my way to the door. She said it was not perfect but definitely a lot better.

Weeks went by – Jennifer was now in South Africa visiting her father and I in the meantime, in her absence, finished another two houses for her. I managed this work in addition to my refrigeration commitments by doing the electrical installations after the builders and carpenters had left for the day – in this way, I had found I could work much faster and without hindrance.

I had been to another auction, taking Jock along for the ride and the experience, hiring a van locally. I had a successful day bidding for more cabinets and sealed systems. All the others that I had bought were working perfectly without any problems. I had been in business for seven years and my success had enabled me to change my car for a two-year-old Vauxhall Wyvern. Apart from the prestige, it had the advantage of a much larger boot, giving extra space to carry goods for my business.

Together, Grace and I bought things for the home and swapped the original TV for one with a larger screen. We also purchased a radiogram – Grace's favourite music was ballet and she would sit for hours listening to it, Swan Lake being her favourite. I was not making a fortune, but a very comfortable living, besides building a healthy bank balance.

My old Ford Popular had served me well although it was not of much value now to me, so I asked Jock if he would like to have it, as a gift. He was well pleased as he only had two more years to go for his twenty-five years' police service.

Grace was doing very well at her job. One day when she came home, she explained to me that she had to attend a conference with her boss, for a week. She said she had tried her hardest to get out of going but her boss insisted because she was the only one that could take shorthand accurately and fast. She could not explain in detail what the conference was about, but it did concern Britain's application to join the Common Market – negotiations were at the preliminary stage. I bravely told her she did not have to worry about me, I would manage. The conference was to take place in one month's time, and when the day finally came, Grace had to go. I took her to her office building – on the way, I arranged for Grace to phone me between 6.30 and 7.30 any evening at home, if she felt like having a chat. Arriving at her office, we parted with a loving kiss, and I took her case in and left it in the care of the doorman.

I was at home making out accounts one evening – one of these was for Jennifer Tait. While I was preparing it, my mind wandered, thinking of Grace. Just then the phone rang, I picked up the handset and said, without thinking, "Hello darling", expecting it to be Grace. Instead it was Jennifer, asking me how I was. I was quite surprised as I did not expect her back for another month. She explained that she had arrived back just a few hours previously and she thought she would give me a ring to see how I was managing. She asked me if I was doing anything special that evening, clearly hoping I was not planning anything. I replied that I was only making out accounts, adding that I did not know how people could say they enjoyed doing paperwork, as it bored me to tears. I explained that Grace was away for the rest of the week, coming back on Friday evening. Jennifer suggested invitingly that, if I felt like shedding a few tears over a drink with her later on, she would be pleased. I said it would have to be after 7.30, and she asked me if I had eaten yet. I admitted that I had done nothing about food, and she told me to call round about 8 o'clock if I fancied the idea. I assured her that I would be there.

Grace had not phoned, so at 7.45pm I left for Jennifer's flat. She greeted me with a welcoming peck on the cheek and I returned the kiss. Jennifer suggested that we should go upstairs where she had a surprise for me. She led the way up the stairs, me following and missing nothing of her shapely legs.

Her bachelor flat was very modern in design, and ideal for a professional woman. It was tastefully furnished with a three-piece suite in a floral pattern fabric, with matching curtains, and a warm glow coming from the coal-effect electric fire in the hearth. Persian carpet and rugs covered the floor. The highly polished coffee table near the settee was enhanced by an elegant arrangement of flowers in a crystal cut-glass vase. There were several pictures on the wall and one on the mantelpiece of a man and woman, which I assumed was of her father and mother. I thought the room was cosy and inviting. From the radiogram there was soft music from Guy Lombardo, which appeared to be her favourite band. All that seductive atmosphere and the soft-shaded wall lights were designed to put me into a romantic mood, especially when I saw the table set for two, overlooking the vast expanse of Peckham Rye. On the table there was an ice bucket with a bottle of expensive champagne. I was beginning to think I was a lamb being led to the slaughter – the sacrificial lamb.

I had sat myself on the settee with a drink offered by Jennifer – while I was drinking it she had disappeared, returning dressed in casual clothes. She sat beside me on the settee and I asked whether the photograph was of her parents, pointing to the one on the mantelpiece. I calmly stated that I could see where she got her good looks from, using my charm to woo her. I was sitting comfortably on the settee whilst Jennifer had gone to the table to pour two more drinks from the bottle in the ice bucket, offering one to me, then sitting down beside me. She offered a toast to our association, and I asked teasingly whether she meant business or pleasure, to which she replied immediately and unwaveringly, both. She said to me that she had noticed that I had completed two more houses while she had been away – I was pleased with her reaction. I asked about her father and whether he was re-married yet. I was intrigued about Jennifer's feelings about him marrying again, but she was clear that it was up to him – she did not seem to want to talk about it.

Jennifer persuaded me it was time to eat as she was famished and expected me to be hungry as well. The meal was all ready – she had prepared a casserole, with new potatoes, and fresh minted peas, with fruit and cream to follow, and cheese and biscuits with freshly ground coffee. It sounded very good to me. During the meal, Jennifer spoke about South Africa most of the time, saying how much she enjoyed going and being there. She said that she was sure that I would like it, with all the beautiful sunshine. After a very satisfying meal, I returned to the settee, while Jennifer cleared the table, taking the dirty dishes out to the kitchen and returning almost immediately, saying her daily help could wash up in the morning.

She went to the dining table to pour two generous drinks, gave one to me, put hers on the coffee table and sat down beside me. Snuggling up to me, she confessed that she really liked me, then finished off her drink and rose telling me that she would not be a minute. As she left the room, she suggested that I should help myself to another drink and pour one out for her. I was placing her drink on the coffee table when Jennifer returned and sat next to me on the large settee, having changed into a white satin housecoat. When she stretched out to reach for her drink, the thin satin coat parted exposing her bare, graceful legs and she suggested that I should take off my jacket as it was becoming quite warm in the cosy room. She helped me slide out of my coat, leaning over me and pressing her body against me, while doing so. I was feeling the heat – of that there was no doubt – not so much from the room temperature but from the closeness of her.

Snuggling up to me as close as she could get, she asked in a seductive whisper whether I really had to go home that night, pointing out that my wife was away and it would not be much fun staying on my own. I was surprised at the sexy tone of her voice and protested that I really should leave, but asked if she meant that I should stay with her for the night, teasing her. Unhesitatingly, like a flash of lightning, she said that was exactly what she meant. She had been thinking about me all the while she was away, and purred that she had been looking forward to us meeting again. I asked her whether that was the reason she had returned early and she admitted it was so, moving closer, practically on top of me, to give me a kiss full on the mouth, the force and suddenness of which left me almost lying down on the settee, with my head resting on the arm. Jennifer said quietly that it was not too comfortable there so we should go into the bedroom, easing herself up and holding onto my hand firmly to pull me up to my feet. The effort in doing this caused the housecoat to fall open completely showing her naked body and firm shapely breasts. Jennifer led the way to the bedroom still holding my hand. When in the bedroom, she helped me to undress and slipped off her housecoat and after a passionate embrace, we both got into bed. Immediately Jennifer began caressing me, and whispering in my ear. We both soon became very aroused sexually – she was clearly hungry for sex and I did my best to oblige, much to her satisfaction. During the night, she woke me several times, when we aroused each other to peaks of sexual ecstasy and fulfilment. She really was something warm and passionate, releasing a turmoil of pent-up emotional feelings with great gusto. She was very exciting to be with and adorable to make love to – she let herself go with sheer abandonment, as though she was really enjoying her new-found sexuality. In the morning I slipped into the bathroom and whilst under the shower, Jennifer decided to join me, ready for more physical contact – I wondered what I had let myself in for. Although I was very much aware that I was cheating on my wife, I told myself that one cannot be a saint all the time, but also remembered the mental turmoil I went through with Maria. In a strange way, I greatly enjoyed this extramarital experience. We towelled each other down, taking our time, then somewhat reluctantly dressed.

After a steaming cup of coffee, we went down to the office before the office manager came to work. Jennifer pleaded with me to make another date – she was really keen to see me again. I was a little uncertain but she suggested the following Thursday when she could have a meal ready for 8 o'clock. I agreed that this would be fine, giving Jennifer a lingering kiss before I left, saying that that would have to suffice until Thursday. I slipped quietly away, with a pang of misgiving lying heavily on my heart

– I knew what was expected of me. Jennifer was sexually demanding but I really did not want to become a stud just to satisfy her new-found sexual needs. When sexually aroused, she was insatiable, and hungry for sex.

While walking to my workshop, after leaving Jennifer's, I thought deeply how I was going to resolve this dilemma I was facing in an amicable and friendly way, now that I had not shown the strength of character I had with Maria. Grace and I had gone through too much to allow this affair to jeopardise our future happiness. I did not want to refuse flatly to go along with Jennifer's sexual needs – that might have had a disastrous effect, turning Jennifer from a very loving person into a woman scorned. This problem occupied my thoughts all day long. It was not as though I had done the chasing – it had just occurred. I decided, if the opportunity arose on Thursday, to discuss the problem we both faced, in what I hoped would be a friendly way, and that she would react favourably.

On the following Thursday, I entered the office at the suggested time – Jennifer was alone. When she saw me, she greeted me with the sweetest of smiles saying that she would not be long, but just had to finish off a few pressing problems. She invited me to go up to the flat and help myself to a drink and to pour one out for her too. I climbed the stairs to the flat, entered the sitting room and walked over to the antique chiffonier sideboard, where there was a wide selection of bottled drinks. I poured out the drinks, took mine over to the window, and looked out across the expanse of Peckham Rye, remembering the time in 1940 when I was crossing the Rye on my way to see Grace the evening the German bombers started their assault on London. After four months of continuous bombing London had remained defiant.

Jennifer entered the flat, bringing me back to the present, and went straight to her bedroom and changed into casual clothes. She came over and stood by me, as I was still looking out of the window. She said she felt a lot better for a change of clothes and gave me a kiss on the cheek. I offered Jennifer her drink which she took, thanking me and snuggling up close to me, whispering in my ear that she thought we might go out for a meal. She explained that she had had a hard day and really did not feel like preparing a meal, preferring to relax and enjoy my company. She wondered whether I knew Carlo's at the bottom of Rye Lane, but although I had heard of it, I had never been inside – I had heard from one of my customers that his ravioli was particularly good. Jennifer suggested that we should go there in her car which was parked just outside. I offered to drive and Jennifer thought this was fine, if I wished to. We finished our drinks and went downstairs – on the way Jennifer handed me the car keys to her very smart deluxe four-door Humber saloon. I opened the passenger door for Jennifer to climb in and, once she was comfortably seated, I closed it, acting the perfect gentleman.

I negotiated the roads to Carlo's, parking the car in a nearby side street. On arriving at the restaurant, I opened the door for Jennifer, to be greeted by Carlo, a dapper little Italian, full of pleasantries. She gave her name to Carlo, explaining that she had phoned earlier for a reservation. Carlo was very effusive and led us to a table in a secluded corner – I wondered if she had asked for this when phoning from her office. The table was already set for two. Carlo lit the candles, and when we were seated, he offered us the menu. Before ordering, Jennifer whispered to me that she wanted the meal to be her treat so I should order what I fancied, saying this with a most seductive smile. We both ordered Carlo's special ravioli with vegetables, followed by strawberries and ice cream, biscuits and cheese, and coffee served with a fine Napoleon brandy.

During the course of eating, Jennifer was rubbing my legs with her shoeless toes, under the table. We spoke about many things – Jennifer being inquisitive, asked questions about Grace, where and when we had first met. I told her a little about my earlier life, my years in the charity home, the gang, my friends and pals before the war. I described how, in spite of my thorough search, I had completely lost trace of them, wondering if they were alive or dead, and how much I owed them for shaping my future life. While sipping our brandy, Jennifer spoke about her mother's ironical death – she had come to England to spend some time with her when she was still at university. Her mother had arrived in June 1939 for a stay of three months – when war broke out in early September, she was reluctant to travel back on the long sea voyage, in case the ship got torpedoed on the way back to South Africa. Instead, her mother was killed in England, a tale which momentarily brought back painful memories.

Glancing at her watch, Jennifer commented that we ought to leave as it was getting late. Leaving the restaurant, walking back to the car, Jennifer put her arm through mine, hugging me close and tight, so much so I could feel her breast bobbing up and down as she walked along, giving me an erotic sensation. I drove back to the flat, once again parking the car in a pull-off in front of her office. Jennifer invited me to come up to the flat to have a drink of some sort.

We made our way up to the flat – I felt like the reluctant lover, as I had an idea what was to be expected of me. Once inside the flat, Jennifer slipped into the kitchen to put the kettle on, and while waiting for it to boil, went into her bedroom to change into her white satin housecoat. She brought in the coffee, placing it down on the coffee table, just in front of the settee where I was relaxing. She sat down beside me to pour out the coffee and as she handed it to me, she asked me whether I would be staying the night as it could be our last chance to be together for a while. She snuggled up closely to me hoping for an answer of yes.

I thought carefully about my response and told her that our affair could not continue and, although I liked her tremendously, I was, after all married, and I loved my wife. Jennifer admitted this but said that when I first walked into her office to quote for the work, something clicked inside her. She had tried to suppress her feelings towards me, but I awoke all the dormant feelings she thought that she had lost. She said that she did not mind sharing me for an occasional fling. Jennifer stood up from the settee, pulling me up with her, leaving the coffee untouched, to lead me to the bedroom, saying that we should make the most of what we had. In the bedroom she allowed her housecoat to fall to the carpet and stood there naked with just an inviting, sensuous smile, showing off her long, shapely legs and beautiful body. She coaxed me to undress and together we got into bed.

Our lovemaking was lengthy, passionate and fulfilling. I teasingly asked Jennifer whether I would have a peaceful night's sleep that night and she told me to wait and see, giving me an adoring goodnight kiss and a hug. I did not get a peaceful night as Jennifer was intent on making the most of what she had. Lying there afterwards near to daybreak, I asked lovingly and softly to Jennifer, who had her head resting on my shoulder, and her leg across my body, how long we had known each other. She thought it was about three years and wondered why I had asked, puzzled what the question was going to lead to. I explained that in all that time, and especially more recently, I had seen the scar on her face and had taken no notice of it. I wondered why she felt so self-conscious about it, because if a man really liked or loved her the same way that I did, he would take no notice.

I had no difficulty in telling her that I found her a very attractive woman, who deserved something better than the occasional fling – she was a loving affectionate person besides having a beautiful body – and I knew she was marvellous company to be with. She had such a lot to offer to the right man, as well as being a shrewd and successful businesswoman – what more could a man want?

Jennifer listened quite intently without interrupting and thanked me for my vote of confidence, lifting her head to give me a kiss. I was a perfect morale booster and with a heavy sigh, she whispered that she really wished she had met me before I knew Grace. As she had told me already, she was going to South Africa shortly and asked me very seriously why I couldn't go with her, saying that we would have a wonderful future together. Jennifer continued by saying that she would offer me a partnership, as she was thinking of doing the same type of conversions in Johannesburg. She was sure that we would make a wonderful team as we had a special relationship, and understood each other. There had never been any problems all the while we had been together, whether it be work or pleasure. As an extra lure, she suggested that she could book a berth in a luxury liner so that we could be travelling together. I gave her a big hug, saying that it would be a splendid idea but pointed out that she seemed to have forgotten that I had a business to run, and more importantly, a wife who would never agree to me going anywhere without her. I had been four years away during and after the war, so we knew what separation meant. Much as I was sorely tempted by her offer, I regrettably had to tell her it was out of the question. As soon as I had said this, Jennifer became all emotional and pleaded to make love again, even if it would be for the last time together. It was perfect and sensual lovemaking that we enjoyed that night, with Jennifer purring with happiness, even if it was tinged with some sadness at our separation. In the morning before parting, Jennifer asked me if I would continue doing her work and of course, I told her that I would. Jennifer came up close to me and asked to kiss me for the last time, for old time's sake. I readily responded, teasingly agreeing only if that really was the reason. I took her in my arms and gave her a long lingering kiss, full on the mouth. As we parted she said wistfully that that kiss would have to last her a long, long, time.

Leaving Jennifer and not feeling very happy with myself, I went to my workshop, calling in at the dairy on the way. There had been one enquiry for a fridge, nothing very urgent. I left a note for Jock to say that I would be at home if I should be wanted. I had decided to go home to catch up with some sleep and I slept a lot longer than I planned. Eventually I awoke, had a wash and shave, feeling a lot better for the effort – now refreshed, I decided to finish off the paperwork and tidy the flat before Grace came home.

Grace arrived home late in the afternoon and I greeted her with a kiss and a hug, wondering why she had not called me as I would have driven to the station to pick her up – in the event, she had been offered a lift. I put the kettle on for a welcome cup of tea and told her to leave her case until she had had a cup, fetching the tray while she made herself comfortable after the journey. I asked Grace how the conference had been, keen to hear all about it. She told me that it had been a splendid week and that she was glad she went. Meeting the representatives from other countries had been quite an experience. She had been booked into a beautiful hotel, with splendid accommodation and service. In between drinking her tea, she said that she had telephoned me the previous night and I asked with some twinge of conscience what time this had been. When Grace said it was about 9.30pm, I explained that I had waited until 7.30, adding that as I loathed paperwork and had spent some time on my accounts, I went out to have a meal and a drink with a friend, trying to stick to the truth as much as possible. I asked whether she had phoned again later and I breathed a quiet sigh of relief when she said she had not tried again.

I changed the subject as quickly as I dared, asking Grace how she felt about going out for a meal. This was a welcome idea and she set off to change and freshen up first. She could leave the unpacking until later, which pleased me. I said that she could then take her time to tell me all about the conference, provided that it would not be breaking any of the rules of the Official Secrets Act.

For the next three months, while Jennifer was away, I had been busy also finishing off another house for her. When time allowed, I spent some evenings at home with Grace and relaxing. On one such evening, the phone rang – it was Jennifer Tait, always formal as usual when she telephoned, just in case she might be overheard. Before I could say a word, she pleaded that I should call round as she really wanted to show me something. I asked if the next morning would do, but she said it was rather important, so could I come straight away, hastening to add that it had nothing to do with our past relationship. I could already detect a note of excitement in her voice when she added that she would not sleep that night until she saw me. I asked her to wait a moment while I explained to Grace that it was Jennifer Tait on the phone and she wanted me to go round to see her on a very important matter. Grace accepted that it could be important and did not mind me going out in the evening, if it possibly meant more business. I told Jennifer to expect me in about five minutes – she was extremely grateful that I could do as she wished.

On the way to her flat, I was thinking all sorts of things, even trying to speculate about her urgency. I arrived and was greeted by Jennifer in a very happy frame of mind – I wondered if it was because she was with me and explained that I could only stay for a short while, because Grace and I were going out, hoping that the lie did not show. Of course I was pleased to see her, but I felt I had better keep my distance. Jennifer promised that she would not keep me long and invited me upstairs. When we had both entered the sitting room, Jennifer turned on her heels to face me and held out her left hand. On her third finger was an unmistakable one-carat engagement ring. When it finally registered with me, I exclaimed that it was wonderful news. We were now sitting down at the dining table, the ring sparkling in the light. Jennifer asked whether I remembered our last night together and I responded that I could hardly forget. She reminded me that she had called me a morale booster – she had thought a lot about what I said that night. I recalled that I had really aroused her womanly feelings that had been dormant for so long, and asked who the lucky man was, and I did mean lucky. Jennifer replied by saying that Charles was a South African diamond dealer whom she met on the ship going out. I commented that it was just as well she was on her own, because if I had been with her, it could have cramped her style. Jennifer continued by saying they had met once before, on a previous trip. This time they had bumped into each other, literally, and that broke the ice, so to speak. It just snowballed from there, with them spending the whole of the trip together. He confessed he had always admired her from a distance. I remarked that he had got good taste when he saw it and asked her how long they had been engaged. It was just before she left to return to England and he had phoned her twice on the ship's radio-phone. The first time was to wish her bon voyage – he knew all about her business interests in England and she thought that he supposed he would snap her up before anyone else did.

I was really happy for her and said she could not know how pleased the news made me, asking her if she minded if I gave her a congratulatory kiss, leaning over the table to do so. There was no passion behind the kiss – it was just as two friends would kiss. Jennifer explained how, when they first bumped into each other, she dropped several things. Charles had helped her to pick them up, apologising for being so clumsy – it was then he saw the scar on her face but as I had said, it was as though it was not there. When I asked whether a date had been set for the wedding, Jennifer said that they really had not had any time to discuss it. Charles had said that while Jennifer was in England, he would be coming to Europe himself on business, so she supposed they would talk about it then. He had an office in Johannesburg, and visited Europe quite frequently. I interrupted saying that he now had two good reasons for coming. Jennifer added that nothing had been decided about where they would live after they married, so there was quite a lot to discuss and consider. I wondered whether they would marry in England or South Africa or more romantically on board ship on their way out – that question giving her a thought, although she said that at that moment she had no idea.

When I asked her whether she had slept with him yet, she promptly replied that with Charles, she intended to be patient. If he wanted to wait until they were married, that would be fine by her, but I queried whether she could be patient that long, looking into her eyes hoping for an honest answer. Jennifer said that with me, she had to find out for herself whether she was still attractive to men. I interrupted her to ask whatever had given her the idea that she was not attractive. Although she knew that I was happily married, she had to find out, she could not help it – the feelings I aroused in her got the better of her emotions. I was relieved and told her how glad I was that it had all turned out for the best, and wished the two of them all the happiness in the world, hopefully heading into a long and happy marriage.

Jennifer invited Grace and I to have dinner with her one evening as she was very anxious to meet Grace. I was sure that it could be arranged, suggesting that a Saturday would be best as we would all be free, with no worries about work the following day. I excused myself and said I would have to be on my way as Grace would wonder at the delay – we exchanged kisses on the cheek before I departed.

On my way home, I felt relieved about the way it had all resolved itself. As soon as I arrived home, I apologised to Grace for my delay – I had been at Jennifer's much longer than I planned. Grace enquired what it was all about and I explained that it was about a dinner date to celebrate Jennifer's engagement and marriage proposal – the following Saturday had been suggested, if it would be suitable for us both. Grace agreed that the idea was fine.

There were few local restaurants to choose from – Carlo's, of course, was out of the question. Sometimes on special occasions, I had taken Grace for a meal at a Greek restaurant in Greek Street, Soho, in London's West End. I had acquired a taste for Greek food during my Army service while in Greece and although Grace was not all that keen at first, she too had come to enjoy it. In the morning, before going to work, I telephoned Jennifer's office to say that, instead of her going to a lot of trouble shopping and cooking, I had a suggestion to make. I explained that I knew of a pleasant and cosy Greek restaurant in Soho and asked whether she would prefer to go out for the evening and celebrate in style – after all, I pointed out, it was not every day one became engaged. Jennifer replied eagerly that she thought it was a splendid idea, so I suggested that I should call for her at about 7pm – Jennifer added as an afterthought that I should make it at 6pm, so that we could have an introductory drink before leaving for the restaurant. I thought that this was a good idea on her part and agreed to the suggestion, saying that we would meet on Saturday.

Jennifer and Grace had never met, having only spoken to each other on the phone when Jennifer wanted to get in touch with me, or leave a message. I suspected that they were both curious about each other and I was eager to see their reaction when meeting each other for the first time in person. As arranged, Grace and I called at Jennifer's office at around 6 o'clock on the Saturday evening. I made the introductions and the two women kissed each other on the cheek, as well as shaking hands. I said it was a pity that Jennifer's fiancé was not there as that would have made a perfect evening. She mentioned that Charles had phoned earlier, to see if she had arrived home safely. Grace smiled and said how thoughtful of him that was, and how he must love her a lot. We were asked if we would mind staying in the office as it would only be for a short while and was hardly worth the trouble of going upstairs. Jennifer poured out the drinks and handed them round – I raised my glass in a toast to Jennifer and the lucky man whom I hoped to meet one day.

Jennifer was wearing a sky-blue, calf-length cocktail dress, with a fur stole. Her only jewellery was her engagement ring. Grace was not to be outdone – both women were looking radiantly attractive. She was wearing the earrings that I had sent her from Greece – Jennifer remarked how much she liked them and I said there was a story to tell about them but not that night. We had finished our drinks and decided it was time to leave. I suggested that Grace should sit in the back of the car with Jennifer to keep her company on the way.

I negotiated the London traffic, eventually arriving at the restaurant, where I was pleased to see there were no parking restrictions, so I left the car outside. On entering the restaurant, we were warmly greeted by George Pompodulas, the owner, who showed us to a table where the ladies were helped to sit down. The restaurant was quite small, with about twelve tables, some of which were already occupied, all with clean white tablecloths, and adorned with posies of flowers and lighted candles. The place had subdued wall lighting, and a musician playing a balalaika complemented the warm, cosy atmosphere. Grace sat next to me, Jennifer opposite. I straightaway ordered a bottle of Retsina, a very popular Greek wine.

Grace complimented Jennifer on her engagement ring and she reached her hand across the table for her to take a closer look – Grace remarked that she thought it was a beautiful ring. It did in fact put Grace's small solitaire to shame – when I purchased it in 1940, there was not a great deal of choice although it was the best I could do at the time.

Grace asked whether they had set a date for the wedding and whether they would live in South Africa afterwards. Jennifer was not sure as they had really not had the chance to discuss what they would do. She expected that when Charles visited Europe shortly, they would be able to finalise their plans, but until then they could only think about their future together. Jennifer asked Grace how long we had been engaged and Grace looked at me and said that it had been for about six months although times were different then. The waiter brought the wine, and poured it out – I asked for an extra glass 'for absent friends' and raised my glass again to make a toast to the lucky man and his fiancée, hoping that they would have a long and happy marriage. Jennifer responded to the good wishes, thanking us both for our support and friendship.

The rest of the evening went quickly by, with the party greatly enjoying our meal and the pleasant flow of conversation. Both women enjoyed each other's company, so much so that Jennifer moved to sit opposite Grace. She asked Grace if I had told her that she would like us both to come as her special guests to the wedding. She responded by explaining that I had mentioned it although at that time and in the foreseeable future, the department she worked for would be extremely busy, with all the negotiations continuing to do with Britain's entry into the Common Market. She did not even discuss it with me, because of the Official Secrets Act. Suggesting that a date set for a weekend should not pose any problems, Jennifer said how much she hoped we both could be there as our presence would mean a lot. She also needed a matron of honour, and was thinking and hoping that Grace would help her out as she had no other living relatives. While Grace and Jennifer were discussing the finer points, the musician was playing a tune that I had heard many times before, when in the café at Salonica – for a brief moment my thoughts went back to Maria, wondering if she was married yet and what else had happened to her. Jennifer spotted my faraway look and I became aware of her quizzical gaze. I muttered that the music had reminded me of someone I knew in Greece, and Jennifer's womanly intuition persuaded her not to pursue the subject, guessing it was something to do with a girl. I came back to the present, hearing Grace saying to Jennifer that she would love to be her matron of honour without giving a firm answer or making any commitment for a while, as it would depend on what date was set for the wedding. They agreed to talk about it when a date had been set.

Grace decided to change the subject, asking Jennifer what she was going to do about the Warren – but at that time she did not really know. The properties had brought her a very good income and they had been a marvellous investment. She said that she was really lucky to have met me as I had been a great help – she patted my hand that was on the table. Before leaving the restaurant, I asked Jennifer to tell me about her office manager and explain why he had never taken to me. The man was like that with all other men – he had been an old friend of her mother's, so Jennifer supposed that he was keeping a fatherly interest in her welfare – she assured me that it was nothing personal. I was relieved as I had begun to believe that it was something about me that the manager disliked.

Before we left the restaurant, we each took a sip of wine from Charles' glass to wish him well in his absence, me picking up the glass for the first sip, and then handing it to Grace.

We made our way to the car for the drive back to Peckham. As I was approaching Jennifer's flat, she invited us both up for a coffee, but Grace declined the offer, saying it was getting a little late, and thanking her for the invitation. I asked Grace if I could see Jennifer to her door and, when we reached the office door, I said with some sadness that it would be the last time we would see each other, unless there was another dinner date, next time hopefully with Charles. I repeated my comment that Charles did not know how lucky he was to have such a wonderful person.

Jennifer smiled and told me that, now she had met Grace, she could understand why I turned her offer down because I loved her very much. I asked her to please keep in touch about their wedding plans, as I was quite sure that we would be able to be there. Jennifer gave me a peck on the cheek, thanking me for everything, and saying with feeling that it had been a wonderful evening. She assured me that she would pass on our regards to Charles when she next spoke to him.

CHAPTER TWENTY-THREE

When Evan next saw me, he reminded me of a previous conversation and asked me whether the following Tuesday evening would be a good time to visit his girlfriend's pub – I readily agreed as I thought that we had nothing special planned. I declined his offer to pick us up at home as I thought it was best we made our own way there. If Evan had taken us, he would have had to bring us back and, as I said with obvious meaning, I did not want to stop his or his girlfriend's enjoyment after the pub closed. Evan just grinned at the remark, with a slight blush.

We found the pub with little trouble – it was situated in one of the many back streets of the area known as Kennington in south-east London. We found Evan already there, sitting at the bar talking to a very attractive blonde, introduced to us as Evelyn – as it was her night off, she was sitting at the customers' side of the bar. Being Tuesday, there were not many drinkers in the bar. The pub consisted of two smallish bars, which would not need many customers to be completely filled. Evelyn at a guess was in her late twenties – she was of medium height with a full figure, very fashionably dressed, her blonde hair set in a permanent wave style. She was wearing a lavish display of jewellery – on most of her fingers were gold rings set with rubies and diamonds – she looked like a walking jeweller's shop. Her mother was similarly adorned, wearing as much jewellery as well as expensive-looking earrings.

Shortly after we had all had a drink, a tall well-dressed man entered the bar – Evan greeted him as 'Smithy' with a warm welcome. He then introduced him to us saying that we actually lived quite near him. Judging by Smithy's acknowledgement, I must have been a topic of conversation at some time between him and Evan, who bought the newcomer a drink – I thought he was obviously a regular customer. He said a pleasant good evening to Grace and Evelyn and joined our company, staying with us for the rest of the evening until closing time. He seemed to be on friendly terms with Evelyn. At closing time Grace and I decided not to stay, although invited to do so. Smithy, as he liked to be called, said he would be going as well, leaving the two lovebirds to their own devices. I offered Smithy a lift as it was raining and he gratefully accepted. He said that normally he would walk, chiefly for the exercise as he did not have a car. If Evan did not give him a lift when it was raining, he would order a taxi.

It was only a short distance to the Elephant and Castle, a well known south-east London landmark. After dropping him off, I made my way home to Dulwich. Over a period of time, Grace and I visited the pub many times if we fancied an evening out. Whenever we went there, Smithy was always there too, going for the exercise, as he called his trip for his regular nightcap.

The place had a quiet and peaceful pub atmosphere where people could talk to each other at a normal conversational level, without having to raise one's voice to be heard. Many of the pubs of the day either had the television blaring or loud music, making it very difficult to have a normal conversation. In Evan's girlfriend's pub, soft background music was played to create an intimate and cosy atmosphere. At closing time, I would offer Smithy a lift home but he only accepted if it was raining as he preferred to walk. He was a bachelor, aged about 60 years, tall, clean-shaven and slightly balding, his well-groomed hair greying at the temples. He was always dressed in a smart business suit. During the many discussions I had with him, I discovered Smithy was a South African by birth. When he was demobbed after the First World War, he decided to stay on in England. Sometime in his early life, he was engaged to an English girl – for some reason she broke off the engagement with no explanation. Smithy never bothered about any further permanent relationships with women – he quite lost faith in them, so remained a bachelor. He eventually set himself up in business, after his demob, in a very busy main road shop in the Elephant & Castle district, as a confectioner and tobacconist. At one time, it was two shops made into one, giving him quite a big floor space, which he used to its full advantage. His shop was an integral part of a Peabody Estate, with at least one hundred flats above his and the other shops.

Smithy's shop was in an ideal position, equal distances from the Trocadero and Trocette cinemas. When the Trocadero was built, it was said to be the largest cinema in Europe, holding at least a thousand patrons when full. It always had two feature films plus a one-hour stage show of international artistes, comedians, and variety acts, or some of the best bands of the day, presenting altogether a very enjoyable evening. People used to come from some distance as it was the best show in south-east London, all for prices ranging from one shilling and threepence (6½p) to three shillings and sixpence (17½p). For the last show on a Saturday night, one had to queue for at least an hour to be sure of a seat. The Trocette was a smaller cinema, usually showing two feature films and an hour of cartoons, comedy and newsreel, at the same price as the Trocadero. With all the cinema-goers calling in, it made Smithy's shop very busy. His shop was the only one of its kind in the vicinity – there were kiosks in the cinemas, but Smithy's shop had a vast selection of all kinds to choose from, to satisfy most cinema-goers' needs.

In those days, most sweets were displayed in shops loose in jars, so it meant weighing and bagging them. He also had a good selection of boxed chocolates, ideal for husbands treating their wives or boys their girlfriends. It was amazing how he managed to cope on his own – people did not seen to mind queuing for what they wanted, which may have been because they had not yet climbed out of the queuing habit from the war years, especially if something special was being offered.

On odd occasions when I was in the area, I would pop into Smihy's shop just for a chat. Despite the endless stream of customers, he always found the time to talk, as though it was a welcome relief from serving. I thought that sometimes he felt lonely – his mother had died earlier on, leaving him on his own. Smithy never spoke about whether he had any relatives either in England or in South Africa. He worked long hours, seven days a week, from seven in the morning to eight at night, Mondays to Fridays, and nine at night on Saturdays and Sundays, without even closing at lunch time. I often wondered how he coped, being single-handed.

When I first saw the shop, it was like a fortress with steel roller shutters up at the front windows and the entrance to the shop door which in turn was locked and barred with heavy padlocks from the outside. The only window at the back of the shop was barred and cases of minerals were stacked against it, as a further precaution against being burgled. Smithy said that his insurance company had made him do that, as he had been burgled twice before. With all those precautions one would have thought his shop was burglar-proof, but the ingenuity of a burglar's mind is unbelievable when he decides to raid a place. The Peabody Building was four storeys high, at least sixty feet from street level to the roof and all the flats were heated by coal fires. How the burglars found the right chimney goodness knows – certainly whoever descended down the chimney must have had plenty of nerve to be lowered that distance. The chimney pots had been removed. The whole business must have been a time-consuming operation, as only small amounts could be hauled up at a time. Needless to say, Smithy's shop was cleared of cigarettes and tobacco, cigars, pipe tobacco and also all the boxed chocolates. It must have been thirsty work, because the villains helped themselves to ice cream and bottled drinks. Smithy had the flat directly above the shop and during the time the burglary was continuing, he said he never heard a thing. What may have made it easy for the burglars to find the right chimney was that fact that he never used the fireplace for heating but only for burning rubbish at odd times, so it was not boarded up. The burglars must have known this. When he unlocked his fortress shop, as he thought, he had the biggest surprise of his life to see he had been burgled – he just could not believe what he saw – he was flabbergasted. The police found nothing except the removed chimney pots – they said it had the hallmarks of a certain person, but without absolute proof, there was nothing they could do. It was certainly a well-planned operation. At the time, a packet of twenty large cigarettes cost a shilling (5p).

Smithy had direct accounts with the manufacturers. To achieve this, one had to have a turnover of at least a thousand pounds a month with each supplier. In the pub one evening after this had happened, Smithy told the story of the burglary – he had to smile at the ingenuity of the burglars and even the insurance company thought it funny, and paid up with a smile.

During the warmer weather, Smithy had a very good bottled soft drink and ice cream business, especially at weekends when he sold many family-size ice cream blocks in various flavours. A good part of his present deep freeze was taken up making ice lollies for the children. Although not near a school, he found it difficult to cope with the demand.

When all three, Evan, Smithy and I were in the pub one evening, Smithy in casual conversation mentioned that his deep freeze storage was insufficient for his business. Evan suggested to Smithy that he should let me make him one, as he had seen what I made and how very good they were. I added that the advantage would be that I could make any size to order. Smithy confirmed all this with me, as he had not been aware of my interests up to that point. We agreed to meet at the shop in the early afternoon the next day to talk about it.

I called in as arranged and the outcome was that I made quite a large deep freeze for him. Delivery was arranged for one week later when it was ready to be installed and left in working order after I had showed Smithy how to use it. A week later I called with my account to find that Smithy was highly delighted with the results, handing me a cheque in settlement. Smithy bought his lolly-flavouring syrups from a well-known national company and I was able to supply him with some specially shaped lolly moulds.

I had been very busy – it was summer, with very little time for socialising or going to the pub. It was a couple of months since I had last seen Smithy. One evening at home I answered the phone – there was a man's voice on the other end of the line, saying that he hoped I did not mind him ringing at that time of the evening, but he had been told it was the best time to speak to me personally. He gave his name as Mr. Philips. I asked what I could do for him and was asked in return to call on the man, who was not an existing customer, at an address in a street just off the Borough High Street in south-east London. By a strange coincidence, I was going to my wholesaler in the morning and the address given to me was quite nearby. I explained that I would be in that area the next morning and suggested that I could be there at 11am, if that would be a convenient time to call. Mr. Philips replied that he would be pleased, so an appointment was fixed.

In the morning I called at the wholesaler's first and then travelled on to the address I had been given. I immediately thought I had made a mistake as the imposing building was the Head Office of a worldwide soft drinks company. Luckily a man was just climbing into one of the company's lorries and I asked him if there was a Mr. Philips in the company. The driver told me that Mr. Philips was their Managing Director – I was immediately curious. What would such a big company want with me? I thought the only way to find out was to go in and ask. I entered the impressive entrance, going over to the receptionist/telephone operator. I introduced myself, saying that I had an appointment with Mr. Philips. While the girl was checking, I had a quick look around, still puzzled about what was to come. I was swiftly shown into an imposing office where Mr. Philips rose from his huge, well-polished mahogany desk, meeting me half way, holding out his hand for a welcoming handshake, at the same time offering me a comfortably upholstered chair in front of his desk. He said he would come straight to the point, as though he had fitted me in between other appointments. He explained that he had heard that I had made a deep freeze for a Mr. Smith, saying this as though he was not too sure. I readily confirmed the statement, upon which Mr. Philips said that he would like me to make one for them, not quite so large, but which could make about four dozen lollies at a time. He also asked whether I would be able to supply the same type of moulds as I supplied to Smithy. I said it would be no problem and Mr. Philips gave me a written order for a deep freeze, to be delivered as soon as possible, asking when it might be delivered. I assured him that it would be in about ten days or could be sooner. Philips asked me to call him by telephone the day before I was due to deliver, giving me his business card. The deal was sealed with a handshake before I left the Managing Director's office, and the building.

On my way back to my workshop, I found myself quite near to Smithy's and decided to call in. As usual, several customers were in the shop – when he was free, he said cheerfully that it had been a long time no see. It was a busy time for him at that time of the year. I replied that

Smithy would never guess where I had just come from, and whom I just left – swiftly Smithy jokingly suggested The Queen. Showing Smithy the order I had just received, he said that my name was mentioned during their discussions. As he could see, there was no price asked for or given. Smithy explained that he dealt with the company for his lolly flavourings and when the rep had called for his monthly order, he noticed the fridge I had made for him. He had asked all sorts of questions, admiring the cabinet and Smithy supposed he must have mentioned it to his boss. He had told the rep that it was working perfectly, doing all he wanted it to do – he was more than pleased with it, and told the rep so.

I set to work and had the order finished and on test within the week – it had meant working late most evenings. It was working to satisfaction doing exactly what Mr. Philips wanted it to do, so I phoned him up as requested, making arrangements for its delivery. When it was delivered, Mr. Philips asked if he could have it on test for a week in their warehouse, reassuring me that it would be quite safe there. I showed him how to use it and he in turn assured me it would be under his personal supervision. He also asked me to phone him in a week's time, which of course, I agreed to do. I shook hands with Mr. Philips saying if there were any problems, he should give me a ring. I left the premises still rather puzzled about the whole business.

I had been caught up with other work, keeping very busy and had forgotten all about the test. Two weeks later, when I was about to phone Mr. Philips, he phoned me, and I rapidly apologised for not getting in touch, explaining I that had been very busy. Mr. Philips quite understood the situation and asked if I could call in to the office the next morning, agreeing a meeting at 11am. He explained that the deep freeze was working perfectly, doing what 'we' want. The word 'we' had me thinking – I had told Grace what had been going on between them and she was just as puzzled as I was. I had to bide my time and find out what it was all about when I saw him the next morning.

The following morning, I called on Mr. Philips as promised and he came out of his office all smiles, leading me to the warehouse where the fridge was on test. He showed me the results of the previous few days' testing and said he was pleased with the results, then suggesting that we returned to the office. I followed and when seated in the office, I was asked whether I would like a cup of coffee. While we were waiting for the coffee to arrive, Mr. Philips outlined his plans and future intentions. What the company wanted to do was supply deep freezers to their best customers who bought their lolly-making syrups. Just as the coffee arrived, Mr. Philips continued to describe how they had found from experience that the best sites were near schools adding that they covered a wide sales area. I thought that there must be hundreds of schools in the London area alone. Mr. Philips picked up a piece of paper from his desk and gave it to me – it was an official order for fifty deep freezers to the same specification as the one on test.

While I was studying this splendid order, I was frantically wondering how I would cope with fulfilling such an order, although keeping a calm face for the man opposite. Mr. Philips gave me another piece of paper which was a cheque for a thousand pounds, momentarily taking me by surprise. He explained that it would help me get started on materials. Mr. Philips had assumed that, by having the order and cheque ready, I would jump at the chance. I had to do some quick thinking, saying that I was not equipped to carry out such an order – the best I could presently complete was one a week. I was also thinking that mild steel sheeting was in short supply as most of it was going to the car makers to boost exports. I asked for a moment to think. Compressor units were no problem, or copper tubing. It meant I would have to have a bigger workshop and special machinery, including a spot welder, and sub-contract some of the work out. Each cabinet had to be hand-made with my present facilities. I asked for a couple of days to think it over and also find out about sub-contracting and, most importantly, the availability of the necessary materials. Thankfully, Mr. Philips agreed with my request so I departed leaving the order and the cheque on his desk for the time being.

That evening, I spoke to Grace about the events of the day – I felt indirectly that she would be involved and I wanted to give Grace a clear picture of my own involvement if I should take the order on. I explained to her that it would mean I might have to employ full-time sheet metal workers, provided I could acquire the materials – I could cope adequately with the refrigeration side. It might even mean dibbing down into our savings, I offered, but just to mention this to Grace was like waving a red rag at a bull. I added that I supposed that I could go to my bank for the finance, but I did not really want to get into their clutches. Grace had been in deep thought all the while I was saying this and asked me if I really thought that it would be worth all the trouble and problems it could cause. I was doing all right as I was, judging by the accounts she made out for me – I was earning a good living, with a healthy bank balance. As far as Grace knew, all the while I had been in business, I had never been in debt, or overdrawn at the bank. She worried that I might go to a lot of trouble to fulfil the order and then be stuck if there was no repeat order. What would I do then? She pointed out that large companies were not always loyal to their suppliers – I could be left high and dry. Rather up the creek without a paddle, I added.

It was the first time Grace had ever expressed her views or opinion on how I should run my business, and I welcomed her input, saying that she was right, I would turn the order down. Grace showed visible signs of relief when I said this and in the morning, I telephoned Mr. Philips asking to see him and making an appointment. I again visited the offices and was shown into Mr. Philip's room. After our handshake, I told him that after careful thought and consideration, I could not undertake the order as the best I could do would be one unit a week, but thanked the company for offering me the opportunity. Mr. Philips said he understood and asked if they could purchase the one that had been on test. I agreed and arranged to send on my account in a few days' time. With some regret I told Mr. Philips that I really wished I could make all the others for him, but at the same time felt the heavy burden lifted from my shoulders. There was also a look of sadness on Mr. Philips' face – he had felt confident that I would accept the order.

On my way back to my workshop, I called in to see Smithy to tell him about my decision. I said jokingly that now I would never know if I would be a millionaire or not. Smithy tried to console me saying perhaps it was the right thing – in his considered opinion, one had to be very large or very small to succeed in business. He did not think there was any in-between. When I saw Grace in the evening and told her I had reluctantly turned down the order, a look of relief crossed her face and she gave me a kiss to cheer me up. We tried to make light of my decision, saying that what one never had, one never missed.

A few months later, Smithy told me that the order had gone to a North Country firm and it was almost a year before they took delivery of their first fridge – he had gleaned this information from the company rep. I wistfully thought that they might as well have accepted my offer of one a week, at least they would have been selling their lolly syrups in the meantime and could have supplied quite a lot of their customers with freezers at the same rate.

CHAPTER TWENTY-FOUR

When Grace and I were first connected to the telephone, we sent one of the free 'new subscribers' cards the GPO supplied to Valerie, Grace's pre-war best friend. Like a bolt out of the blue, when Grace picked up the handset in answer to a call one evening at home, the caller was Valerie. Long time no see, was her greeting remark and Grace responded that it had to be all of five years since they last met. Although they sent each other birthday and Christmas cards, there had been no personal contact during this time. Valerie asked about me, to learn that I was doing fine with my own business, making a steady living. She then asked whether we would feel like calling over one Sunday afternoon, when the pub was closed. Grace asked her how soon she was suggesting for the get-together and the swift reply was the coming Sunday if we were free. Grace explained that I left all the weekend arrangements to her, so there would be no problem there. She accepted the invitation and said how she was looking forward to seeing them at 3pm on the Sunday.

When I arrived home that evening, Grace gave me three guesses as to who phoned earlier on and I confessed that I would not have a clue, feeling more hungry than keen about guessing at riddles. Grace happily told me that Valerie had invited us to tea the next Sunday. I thought it was a great idea, adding that I would like to see her again, it had been a long time. I remembered how I used to pull her leg about husband-hunting, and all the good times we had before the war.

After Sunday lunch, we set out to visit Valerie's pub in Putney in south-west London. On arrival, we were greeted with open arms by Valerie, who kissed us both on the cheek. George, her husband, greeted Grace with a kiss and me with a handshake, saying how good it was to see us both. He had heard so much about the two of us from Valerie, he was looking forward to this meeting. I commented to Valerie that pub life had not changed her a lot – she was still slim and just as attractive as when I saw her last – she was flattered by my words, thanking me for saying the nicest things.

Valerie, as was to be expected, was all dressed up, looking very smart and fashionably attractive – I had never seen her any other way, always smartly turned out. After the initial meeting in the empty bar, Grace and I were shown into the bar parlour, a room with easy access to the bar. It was a pleasant, comfortable-looking room, with dining table and chairs, a three-piece suite, with other homely effects, as well as wall-to-wall carpeting with a floral pattern on a green background. When we were all seated, Valerie told Grace that her mother had died recently from some diabetic complication, news which Grace found sad as she had liked her, always being treated as one of her own. Valerie was the only child, she had no close relatives. Being the only child, her mother had spoilt her. Her father was killed on active service in the First World War. Her mother had never married again, so Valerie had no half-brothers or sisters. She and her mother had a good relationship and got on well together.

George asked us both if we would like a drink, to which I responded that I would really like a cup of tea if there was one going. Valerie berated herself for being silly, saying she should have remembered how Grace liked her tea, dashing out to put the kettle on – she added jokingly that it would be her Civil Service training. Grace explained to Valerie and George without going into too much detail, how I became self-employed as a maker of deep freezers, and other refrigerated equipment, also servicing and repairing them. She described how my late boss had found himself in some sort of financial trouble, and had done a moonlight flit, enabling me to take over, since when I had been doing extremely well. Grace gave them a brief résumé of the order I had turned down, with a look of admiration for me in her eyes, making me feel a little self-conscious. I told Valerie that I could not have done any of that without Grace's trust and faith in me. George was a quiet sort of man, preferring to listen to conversation rather than make it. Valerie did most of the talking – for all the while I had known her since before the war, she was never at a loss for something to say, always cheerful and topical.

The table was set out – this would be Valerie and George's main meal for the day. Ham off the bone was already cut and served on the plates. There was a selection of boiled new potatoes, lettuce, tomatoes, beetroot and garden peas, with a choice of salad dressings. For dessert there were fresh strawberries and Devon cream, followed by a steaming cup of coffee, made with real coffee beans. It was a really lovely meal thoroughly enjoyed by all, with a great deal of pleasant chatter throughout. George and I had a brandy each and the two girls had Tia Maria. When we had finished the main meal, we moved to the settee and easy chairs, George and Valerie on the settee and Grace and I in the easy chairs, to finish our coffee and drinks.

Valerie mentioned to Grace that they were thinking of selling the pub and moving outside London as it was becoming far too crowded – although this was good for business, people were not so friendly as they used to be. When George's father had died, he took over the pub with its friendly, family atmosphere – now everyone seemed to be in a desperate hurry, without even time for casual conversation. They thought they would like to take on a country pub, where life would be a little more relaxing. They explained that, in spite of the part-time staff, they never seemed to have any time to themselves, and to be together. George said with a wistful sigh that he could not help thinking there was more to life than work. I agreed, saying we were finding that as well – where a journey used to take ten minutes it is now fifteen. I seemed to spend a good deal of my time sitting in my car in traffic jams, or waiting for the traffic lights to change. Grace was finding it the same – she had to leave home fifteen minutes earlier than previously to complete the same journey to her office, and coming home was just as bad. Even if I went to pick her up, it would not make a great deal of difference.

I asked them where they were thinking of moving to, but they had not given it a great deal of thought – at the moment it was just an idea, although the West Country or Sussex would be their first choice, explained George. He felt it should be somewhere where there was a beer garden, with a play area for the children. Valerie continued by saying that the noise from the traffic outside on weekdays was unbearable, especially in the summer time when the doors and windows were open. Sundays were not so bad, usually being reasonably peaceful and quiet.

Valerie asked Grace whether she still went to the club, as we had always kept our membership going. She explained that we went very seldom, only when we were in a nostalgic mood. It was there, she reminded Valerie because she had been there, where she and I first met.

I supposed that they did not go to the club at all and Valerie agreed, saying that they never seemed to find the time to go anywhere together those days, adding with regret in her voice that the pub took up most of their time. I also asked, as a matter of interest, where the two of them met – George was about to answer, but Valerie took over saying that they had met at the club, just as Grace and I did. When Grace and I married and went to live at Hayes, going to the club lost some of its attraction for her but it was somewhere to go weekends, being on her own. Her mother was not too keen on the idea, because of the risk of being caught in an air raid but there was really nowhere else to go. She was glad however, as otherwise she would not have met George, giving him a loving smile.

George had travelled over to Forest Hill to attend a friend's wedding – most wartime weddings were quiet affairs. He and his friends had come to the club for a celebration drink – he had approached Valerie and asked her for a dance. While Valerie was talking, she held George's hand. After the dance, as they were both unattached, he had asked her to join the party – from there on their friendship blossomed into love for each other. When George's father died, George took over the pub, and because of that they did not see each other for a long while. He knew that she went to the club most weekend evenings and as he could not get in touch with her not being on the phone, he took a chance, going over to the club one Sunday evening, leaving the pub to his part-time staff and hoping that she would be there. He was missing her as much as she was missing him and Valerie was sure that absence makes the heart grow fonder, and that was the way it affected them.

When they met at the club that evening, he proposed there and then, saying how much he missed her – she was missing him too and she accepted his proposal immediately, leaving the club straightaway to go to her mother's, to tell her the good news, and to collect a few personal belongings, after which they went straight over to Putney. Valerie looked at Grace and smiled, saying that it was all done in a hurry, like our wedding – they were married within the month. She had tried to contact Grace in Hayes, but time was short, so she had to make other arrangements although she would have loved us both to have been there. Grace said she fully understood and added that we owed them a wedding present, asking me to collect it from the car. I returned with the carefully wrapped package, giving it to Valerie with a warning to be careful unwrapping it. It was a 10" high, clear glass Webbs' floral design, engraved vase. Valerie gave both of us a kiss, thanking us and George shook hands with both of us, equally pleased with the present. Valerie exclaimed how much she liked it, saying it would look wonderful in the bar, filled with flowers.

Time was now getting short and George excused himself to prepare the bar for the evening trade, telling Valerie to stay as he would call her if he needed any assistance.

Valerie spoke about old times and how their lives had changed for the better, a sentiment that Grace thoroughly agreed with. I said to Valerie how wonderful it had been seeing her again, and of course, meeting George, adding that I hoped it would not be as long before seeing them both again. We agreed to leave as soon as the bars opened for business, setting off after kisses and handshakes all round. In the car on our way back to Dulwich,we talked mainly about our friends, really hoping to see them again soon.

CHAPTER TWENTY-FIVE

I had now been in business for ten years, and during this time I had done extremely well – at the beginning it was touch and go, but the Italian ice cream boom had helped me to become established. After the first two years, business just came my way and fell into place. In my small way of business, I had little competition. Now the bigger companies were getting their act together, with their appointed dealers covering most of the country. New companies were springing up, as they realised that there was a vast market to satisfy in the domestic refrigerator requirements of the future. Mass production was the answer with deferred terms of payment being offered to their prospective customers.

The after-the-war spending spree was now over. Money was becoming tight whereas it had been freely available when I first started in business. There was no way I could compete with the big boys, with their cheap imports from Italy of small domestic units which were now flooding the market, not only refrigerators but twin-tub washing machines and spin-dryers as well as domestic deep freezers. Over the years, many of the commercial installations were converted to semi-sealed or sealed systems, making servicing almost redundant.

I had to give my future some serious thought and many ideas came into my head. One thing was for sure – there was no way I could compete – that would be the quickest way to bankruptcy. I thought about opening a retail shop, selling electrical goods instead of making them, but that would mean employing staff. I could concentrate on electrical installations. There were several options open to me, but before deciding on anything, I would have a word with Grace first – there was no desperate hurry for a change. I knew that my days as an independent trader would come to an end. I felt that I had skimmed off the cream, making a good deal of money. I decided that I would let the big boys like Frigidaire and Prestcold fight it out between them over who was going to corner the refrigeration market.

For some time now Grace had not been her normal self – something was bothering her. She was never the type to cry on my shoulder – if she had a problem she much preferred to sort it out herself. I could not stand her moodiness any longer, asking her what the problem was. I said that I knew there was something wrong so perhaps we should talk about it so that I could help. Grace explained that her boss was due to retire shortly and the man appointed to take his place wanted to bring in his own secretary – this would leave her in limbo. Grace had been required to attend a meeting with the Establishment Appointments Board, to discuss her future within the Civil Service. First they wanted her to become an Established Civil Servant instead of being a temporary and secondly they had said that she would become extra to staff requirements for their department. They proposed making her a floating shorthand typist, filling in for people who were away sick or on holiday. This really did not appeal to her at all, saying that she had become so used to her own department, she would feel like an orphan without a home. I said I knew exactly what she meant, remembering the eight years I spent in the charity home as a youngster.

We discussed the difference between being a temporary and an established Civil Servant. Grace explained that, as a temporary, she would be entitled to a lump sum gratuity within a month of leaving the service, depending on the length of service. As an established Civil Servant she would be entitled to a pension at the age of sixty, whether in their employ or not. My advice was that she should pay the full National Insurance stamp while at work, as she was eighteen months older than me. This would entitle her to a Government pension when she was sixty in her own right, instead of waiting for me to be sixty-five. If she left before she was sixty, I would pay the full stamp as my part-time employee, or until such times as she took a new job. Grace felt a great deal better after talking this over with me, but still not sure how her future plans would work out.

I came home one evening full of frustration – the London traffic was becoming worse. I seemed to be spending more time sitting in my car than working and I had been forced to give up my lucrative work in London's West End because of parking and traffic restrictions. I had seriously been thinking of moving outside London and making a completely fresh start. The idea appealed to me, possibly solving the present problems I was faced with, but I did wonder how Grace would feel about a change.

If I had a problem, I would rather meet it head on than hope it would go away. It was with this in mind that I approached Grace, asking her how she would react to the idea of moving out of London to a place in the country. I suggested that she could find herself a part-time job. Much to my surprise, she jumped at the chance – she had always had a hankering to have a dog and this might give her the opportunity. I said that I would rather that we did not make a hasty decision, but that we should think about it for a while. Grace's immediate response was that there was no need to wait, we should just do it. I had never known Grace to make up her mind so quickly, or make rash decisions – she was not the emotional type. Taking it one step further, I said that I could always go back to doing electrical work and my knowledge of refrigeration could be an advantage. When Grace leaped so readily at the suggestion, I cautiously asked her whether she was serious about the uncertain future we might face, and the changes if we went ahead – I could not give her any guarantee how it would pan out, but my sixth sense told me that it would be a successful venture. Grace looked me straight in the eye and said that she was deadly serious.

That discussion took place around Christmas time in 1955. For the past few years at Christmas, Grace and I had always visited a licensed seaside hotel that had a ballroom – it was the only time I could get away for a break. We both thoroughly enjoyed the change, and meeting new people. Being winter, I was not overwhelmed with work and working a normal day gave me some leisure time. My manufacture of deep freezers had slowed down, but I still earned a good living doing service work and supplying the occasional service cabinets to grocers.

One day in early February, I decided as I had time to spare, I would have a look around for a property. I had nowhere in particular in mind, and found myself motoring out towards Tunbridge Wells, passing through the town and going towards Groombridge. I spent some time looking around the surrounding countryside, taking note of properties that interested me, and the dealing agents' phone numbers.

It was only an exploratory journey – the property I was looking for had to be on a bus route, and near a mainline railway station. On another occasion I found myself about seven miles the other side of Tunbridge Wells, on the Eastbourne road. The countryside in that area really took my fancy. For some unknown reason, I turned left off the Eastbourne Road into the village of Wadhurst. The route to the village was beautiful, the road just twisted and twined through undiluted countryside – it really appealed to me. It was awakening from its long winter's sleep, trees were bursting their buds and hedgerows and fields were looking fresh and green. I thought this was the place when reaching the village. I parked the car to have a more thorough look around – I had already passed the mainline railway station and had also noticed bus stops.

There was no café, so I popped into a friendly-looking pub for a drink and something to eat. The landlord could see I was a stranger, so was curious to know who I was. The conversation was casual, but at the same time he was trying to find out more about this stranger. The landlord introduced himself as Bob and I told him I was looking for a property around those parts. Bob suggested that I should go to the estate agent opposite as they might be able to help me. I stayed in the pub for a while, finding out more about the surrounding area and points of interest. There were few other customers in the pub. Bob was about 50 years of age, of medium build and clean-shaven, with thick-lensed glasses – he was slightly balding with his remaining hair slicked down with a good dressing of hair cream.

I finished my drink, said cheerio to Bob then went across the road to the estate agent – I could see they were one of national repute. I entered the office and was greeted by a very pleasant young lady, asking me what they could do for me. Before entering the office, I had spotted a very large auction sale notice, but it did not really register, as I thought it was for a farm being sold off. I explained to the young lady, who had a lovely smile, that I was looking for a property around the area, preferably a cottage, giving her some idea of what I had in mind. I asked if she had anything to offer. She crossed over to another desk and picked up what looked like a book, handing it to me, saying that perhaps I might find what I was looking for in the folder. It was a catalogue of an estate of some thirty-odd properties being auctioned off – a mixture of houses and cottages, most of which had sitting tenants. There were five cottages being offered freehold with vacant possession on completion. Studying this quickly while in the office, I noticed the auction was in a month's time, at the agent's London premises. Time was now getting short so I made arrangements with the young lady to come down on the following Saturday to view some of the property. I asked about keys so that I could inspect the premises but was told that no keys were required, as they were left unlocked – I could inspect at any time.

When I returned home, I did not say anything to Grace – I had no intention of raising her hopes, or my own for that matter. Before leaving home on the Saturday, I told Grace I might be back a little later than usual, not saying where I was going or what I had in mind, hoping that she would not mind just for once, as it could be beneficial to us both. Grace had not made any plans for that evening so she kissed me goodbye saying she would see me when I turned up and that she would delay tea until my return. The weather forecast was rain for most of the day but I was not put off by this – in fact I welcomed it, thinking to myself that it would be a good day to see if the roofs leaked.

I had been studying where to find the properties from the map on the back page of the catalogue, which had been locked in the glove compartment of the car, out of sight of Grace's peering eyes. When I arrived at the first property I wanted to inspect, I found a pair of semi-detached weather-boarded cottages. Although picturesque, with good-sized gardens, they did not appeal to me. I guessed that basically they would require too much maintenance. The third cottage was brick-built in the Sussex style of half-hung tiles – the catalogue said that it had been empty for two years. I entered through the back door by raising the cottage-type latch – the door was made of heavy tongue and grooved wood, painted a dirty brown colour. The back door led into a fair-sized scullery, and beyond this, immediately in front, through another door into the front room – they were two fair-sized rooms. In the right-hand corner of the scullery, as one entered by the back door, was the bread oven, and next to this a dirty, shallow earthenware sink with a tap over it. Outside and opposite the back door a short distance away was a brick-built woodshed, with a modern flush toilet partitioned off – the drainage was to a septic tank. Upstairs were two main bedrooms, and along a short passage were stairs leading up to the attic. This surprised me as it was really a large room. From the attic window and from the front window of the main bedroom there were superb views over undiluted countryside – on a clear day one could see the South Downs.

I looked very carefully for signs of a leaking roof but, in spite of not being in use for quite a while, there was no sign of dampness and I thought that the day's rain had been a good test. All the windows of the cottage seemed to be fairly new, all with diagonal or diamond-shaped leaded lights, adding to the attraction of the cottage. The garden was about a quarter of an acre, to the side of the cottage, and running parallel to the 'A' classified road. A little way down this road was a Post Office and general store, with a bus stop outside. The bus passed the main London–Hastings railway station, going on to Tunbridge Wells, a large provincial town seven miles away.

I thought this was it – I had already visualised what I would do to improve the property making it a really lovely home. I was certain that Grace would like it although on first sight it looked awful and at its worst, particularly in the wet of a rainy day.

On my way home I called in at the estate agent, once again being greeted by the lovely smile of the young lady. I asked if I could see the manager and she looked a little peeved at my request. The manager came out of his office and I asked the girl to stay, saying that I thought only the manager could give me the answer to what I was going to ask. I said that I was interested in a property, pointing to it in the catalogue and asked if the manager could give me some idea of the likely auction price. The manager replied that, at a guess, depending on how many might be bidding, he thought that it would be between £800 and £1000. I said that I would like to know whether, if I could arrange the purchase price with my bank, would it be possible to take out a mortgage for half the purchase price, to be repaid over a period of four years maximum. The manager could see no reason why not, saying that it could be arranged with little trouble. I wanted to be sure that I could rely on that information and I was reassured by his solemn word that it would be a private mortgage, not through a bank. I was happy with that and shook hands with the manager. Turning to the young lady, I apologised if I upset her, but she was not at all bothered, responding to me with the sweetest of smiles.

I had still not said anything to Grace although I was bursting to tell her. There was still more to do before all was finalised and I wanted to surprise her, if all went according to plan. Normally I had no secrets from her, apart from the Jennifer affair, and she was now married and living in South Africa – although we were both keeping in touch, I had no intention of allowing the affair to upset my relationship with Grace.

The day of the auction arrived. I had seen my bank manager and had arranged the necessary finance, organising a letter of credit stating that finance was readily available for the purchase price. Bidding started on the occupied properties first – all these were fairly new properties built on a small estate for the farmworkers. These were being sold at ridiculous prices, being bought by the bidders for investment purposes. Eventually the five vacant cottages came up for auction, one of which was the one I was interested in. As luck would have it, these had excited little interest – bidders at the auction only seemed to be interested in the tenanted properties. When my cottage came under the hammer, I kept my fingers crossed, hoping there would be a lack of interest. Bidding started at £650, going up in £50 bids and when the hammer finally fell, I had bought it for £850, well within my carefully worked-out budget.

Allowing time for the cheque to clear, I visited the estate agent's, where we shook hands, the manager saying that he had been expecting me who responded by congratulating the manager on being right about the price, to my good fortune. After a short conversation mainly about the auction, I gave him my address and phone number, also my solicitor's address and phone number. I then went to the cottage to make it secure and to tidy it up. Finally, I called on the builder that Bob had recommended and he agreed to draw up plans for modernising the cottage, and to submit them to the Council for approval. He would also apply for a grant which was available to owner-occupiers, for modernising old properties. By the time this was all finalised it was the beginning of May. The builder had got the plans passed, for the alterations and a new extension as well as cutting the hedge to make a drive in to a proposed new garage. The Council had also agreed to the discretionary grant for improvements to the property – all my efforts had come to fruition and I was feeling very proud of myself.

I asked Grace not to make any plans for the next Sunday and when she asked why, I said that I had a major surprise for her, adding that it was no good asking questions, she would find out on Sunday. I specifically asked Grace if we could have lunch a little earlier on that Sunday as I would like to leave about 2pm. If she had pursued the subject more vigorously, I was not too sure what sort of answers I would have given.

The cottage was about twenty-seven miles from Dulwich and the drive to Tonbridge was very pleasant. After leaving Tunbridge Wells, the countryside really opened up, quite beautiful and a pleasure to drive, particularly at that time of year. On the way, Grace knew we were not visiting and she asked several times where we were going, but I always responded that she would find out when we arrived. I advised her to just sit back and enjoy the scenery and the ride. In fact, Grace did make a comment on how the countryside looked, remembering that was why Kipling had chosen to live down that way – there was no finer place in the world than England in the springtime, I thought.

Eventually we pulled up outside the cottage and again Grace asked where we were in a puzzled and bewildered way. "Your new home!", I said proudly, inviting her to go inside. Of course the cottage looked in a bad state of repair inside although I had been assured by the builder that it was structurally sound. The builder I had engaged for the alterations and the building of the new extension, kitchen, bathroom, and separate toilet had given me a copy of the proposed plans. When Grace entered the back door and saw the general condition, I watched for her reaction, a mixture of surprise and puzzlement. I told her that I had the same feeling when I first saw it, before my imagination saw what it could look like, sometime in the future. I took out the plans provided by the builder, and laid them after unfolding, on the dirty brown sink. I outlined my plans to Grace saying that as she could see, it required a good deal of work, but nothing too expensive to make good. I described carefully that what I had in mind was to brick up the bread oven, pointing to it, to knock down the dividing wall and to put an RSJ girder across to make the two spaces into one large room. I planned to take up the uneven quarry tiled floor, that had been worn away over the years by heavy farmworkers' boots, and concrete the floor. The scullery would become our new dining room and I planned to install a new Claygate fireplace in the sitting room. Taking Grace to the back door and stretching out my hand, I said that that would be her new kitchen, bathroom, and separate toilet. I returned to the plans and pointed out where she could see how the kitchen would be a fair size, with a worktop at least ten feet long, a deep white sink and cupboards underneath.

Grace did not say a word all the while I was talking – she just listened in awe. I then took her upstairs to show her round. In the large master bedroom, I led Grace over to the window and asked her to look at the view, thinking how fantastic, waking up each morning to see such scenic beauty. I then guided her upstairs to the attic – Grace was as surprised as I had been when she saw it. I excitedly said that if I did decide to go into business as an electrical contractor the attic could be my office, where I could also fiddle around with my stamp collection, and not worry about leaving the room tidy like I had to at Dulwich.

We made our way back downstairs again and I said that the garden was a mess after two years of neglect, but there would be a drive in and a new garage, pointing to where it was planned to be. I proposed that we should travel down to the cottage at weekends from Friday evening to Sunday evening, spending our time doing the place up. There was no great hurry as it was not as if we were desperate for a place to live. As Grace could see, it had all the main services although it would mean cooking by electricity for a while, until we finally moved in. I told Grace how I had arranged a mortgage, which roughly worked out at two pounds a week for the following four years – I would pay this quarterly – and with the bank money I would get back about £400 which would help to pay for the new extension. I also told her how the builder had arranged for a Council grant to help with the cost of modernising.

Putting my arm around Grace's waist, I turned her towards me and tentatively asked her what she thought. She grinned at me and said there was only one word for it – wonderful. She was intrigued how I managed to keep it all a secret and I confessed that I had wanted to tell her many times but thought that if it did not pan out as I expected, it would only lead to disappointment for both of us, so I decided to say nothing until it was all finalised. Now it was all finished, I promised, she could at last have the dog she always wanted.

Grace admitted that she had thought I was up to something but not in her wildest dreams did she think it was to be a new home in the country, and tears of joy began to show in her soft, brown eyes. After Grace had recovered from the initial surprise, I said that I had wondered what her answer would be. Again Grace said it was simply fantastic and my question whether she really did like it drew a very reassuring "yes". She did say again that she could not see how I had managed it all and I answered that there had to be a lot of my mother in me as she too was an expert at scheming.

Just then a man appeared at the back door, saying that he had heard voices and wondered what was going on. He was a typical Sussex man, speaking with the local accent. He appeared to be about 50 years of age, and was dressed in casual clothes – he was clean-shaven, with bushy eyebrows and blue eyes and had a crop of greying hair and a weathered face, with a white forehead, indicating that he was a farmworker. He stood about 5' 9" tall. He said that his name was Charlie, and that he lived next door with his wife and youngest son. His wife had just made a pot of tea, and he asked whether we would like one, inviting us to come and join them. Grace accepted the offer saying how kind it was to be asked.

We walked next door with Charlie leading the way. When inside his cottage, he introduced us to his wife as their future next-door neighbours. Once we were all seated around the table, I introduced Grace to Charlie's wife and while we were drinking our tea, I explained that we had just bought the house next door. I described how we would only be coming down at weekends, from Friday to Sunday, until it was fully renovated, hopefully during both winter and summer – I told Charlie that I had engaged a builder to do the major work. We stayed for a while, finding out more about the area, thanked them for the tea and then went to our own cottage to lock up and make everything secure.

The two cottages, semi-detached, stood alone, the nearest neighbour some distance away. There was a farm building on the other side of the road and by one side of Charlie's cottage there was a fenced-off field belonging to the Milk Marketing Board, who tethered their bulls out in the summer months. A pathway lead to woodlands and across country – an ideal place to run a dog, I thought. On the main road was the principal entrance to the Breeding Centre, its main function being for artificial insemination, for better milk yields, and to breed better beef cattle.

On our first Saturday at the cottage, we went along to a local secondhand furniture shop in Wadhurst to buy a bed, table and chairs – just the bare essentials. We brought bedding with us, taking it back home on Sundays to keep it aired.

Usually on our way home, we would call in the pub to have a drink and chat with Bob and his wife, Sunday evening never seeming to be a busy time for the pub. Bob's wife reminded me of my Chiswick landlady, being very much alike in height and appearance. The Sunday visits became a regular occurrence, eventually all four of us becoming good friends.

One Sunday afternoon during our first summer at the cottage, Grace's twin sister and her husband paid an unexpected visit. Her sister was immediately impressed with the cottage, despite the general appearance, since no major works had been started, only some general tidying up. I had been marking out the garden for borders and rose beds, the hole in the hedge had been cut so I could park my car off the road and I had started to peg out space for the garage and driveway in readiness for hard-coring. Her twin sister's husband, Eddie, took a good look around the property, not saying anything while doing so. He was in a business partnership, as builders, with a bricklayer and a carpenter, in Lewisham in south-east London, mainly concentrating on bomb damage. After his general inspection, he asked me how much I had paid for the property. I thought he was going to say something like 'dump' but he checked himself. I told him the figure and Eddie showed surprise and seriously said I must be mad. I countered by saying that Eddie's trouble was his lack of imagination – he only looked at things in pounds, shillings and pence. I promised that I would make him eat those words in three years' time and three years later I did – we could not keep him away from the place, especially when I told him the pond at the back was full of fish – tench, carp, perch and roach. The pond was at the back of our property although it did not belong to us. During the summer Charlie and I would spend some time fishing, but only as a means of relaxing from working on the cottage. When Charlie was working in the hop fields for his boss, he would cast a fishing line in a stream that bordered the field. On a few occasions he gave Grace a couple of trout, accepting nothing in return.

Grace was enjoying her weekends, always looking forward to the next when arriving home. She was really thrilled and looked forward to the day when we could move there to live permanently. The builders had now started on the extension. They had already knocked down the dividing wall and put the girder in position. Grace just could not get over the difference it made, changing the two rooms into one very nice large room. We could now start on the room, burning off the dirty brown paint, and preparing the walls ready for paper-hanging. I boxed in the girder.

I had four years to go on my existing lease on my workshop, with the option of a further seven years. I advertised the workshop in a national property newspaper and a company from Newcastle in north-east England bought it to use for a London depot. Jock had now retired from the Police Force, after twenty-five years' service and had found himself a steady nine-to-five job in security. My idea was gradually to wind down my business in Dulwich – I felt I had skimmed off the cream, and it was no longer a viable proposition to stay in the refrigeration business. I had contracts for servicing, deciding that I could carry on doing these from home, until our move to the country.

At weekends down at the cottage, I had been making tentative approaches to local people about electrical contracting – most seemed to think that there was plenty of scope as there was only one electrician in the village and the general opinion was that he was expensive. When the time approached to move to the cottage, I notified all my customers that I was moving out of the area, thanking them for their support and custom. I felt that I did not want to leave them in the lurch, but give them time to find someone else. I went with Grace to have a farewell drink with Evan and Smithy. I thanked Evan and his brother for all the assistance they had given when I first started in business – I also found time to have a farewell drink with Ben and Yorky.

Grace had handed in her resignation notice – she had not been happy working there as a 'roving' shorthand typist. She had always kept in touch with her old boss, sending Christmas cards and the occasional letter. He responded by saying how much he was enjoying his retirement and wishing her all the best in her new life and venture.

The day came when we moved to our new home to live there permanently. It had taken three years of weekend steady grind to get it as we wanted, but we had enjoyed every minute. For three winters we had travelled down to the cottage. Whenever we arrived, we found there was a nice warm fire to greet them in the sitting room. I had not asked Charlie to do this, but he had thought that it would be a nice, neighbourly gesture. He refused to accept any money for doing this, but would accept an ounce of his favourite tobacco. I had built a coal bunker at the back of the new extension, so the coal was dumped in there.

One of the women at Grace's old office had a two-year-old pedigree Labrador dog which had grown too big for their small house – when it wagged its tail, one of her children would get knocked down. She said she had tried her hardest to find a new home for it, without success – the only option left was to have it put down. When Grace heard of this, she pleaded with her colleague not to put it down but to please hang on to it a little while longer. She said she would take it when we moved into our new home in the near future – happily, the woman agreed to Grace's plea. Arrangements were made to bring the dog the following Saturday after we had moved in as we wanted to have the cottage straight before doing so.

When I was tearing out the old larder from under the stairs in what was then the scullery, it opened up a nice big recess. I said to Grace that it would do for the dog's bed – I arranged to put an old car bench seat in there so the dog should be comfortable. I had built a garage large enough to take the car, allowing plenty of space for electrical stores, should I decide to go into business as an electrical contractor. When the builder was building the extension, I said that I would be doing the electrical work, to which the man asked whether I was an electrician. I replied that I was indeed a fully qualified electrician. I asked him about the prospects of starting an electrical business in the area and the builder thought that there were many people waiting for new supply lines to be erected. That was work that was scheduled to be done, but the war interfered. This gave me food for thought.

The telephone had been transferred from Dulwich and connected to a local automatic exchange free of charge. We were now able to make calls without losing patience.

During the first week after moving, we worked hard, arranging the furniture, laying the carpets, hanging curtains and all the other chores necessary when moving house. By the weekend, we had everything shipshape and ready for the dog. The young couple brought the dog as promised. We did not know what to expect although, being a two-year-old he was likely to be very lively. When we saw the dog, I could see why the young couple had had problems. He had a beautiful black shiny coat – at a later date, one of the neighbours nicknamed him 'Cherry Blossom'. He had been well looked after, and looked in the peak of condition – he had a good sniff around and I suspected that he wanted to get his bearings. The couple stayed for a meal. Afterwards they gave Grace the dog's vaccination certificate, and the spare tins of dog food – just as well they did for Grace had forgotten to buy dog food when she had gone shopping. They also brought the dog's basket. They said that they were truly sorry to part with the dog but they had little choice – it either meant parting with it or moving into a larger house. However, they were pleased that they had found a home for him, particularly as there seemed to be plenty of space there. He should feel at home and comfortable, I told them, pointing out where I had placed his bed. Grace asked what the dog's name was – the couple had called him Satan because he was so mischievous when a puppy but I changed this to Mick at a later date. After an hour's stay, the young couple said they would have to be on their way as they had left their children with their grandmother, promising to collect them by 6pm. When they rose to leave, the dog took no notice, as if he knew this was his new home. He did not stir from his new bed, ignoring the basket. It did look small for such a large dog when he stretched out on his new bed. Now Grace's life was complete – for a while the dog received more attention than I did.

Mick settled down much more quickly than we expected – he soon found himself a lady friend, a local farmer's bitch golden Labrador by the name of 'Lager'. Over a period of time they produced three litters of pups, some brown, some black, but none dual-coloured. The farmer was highly delighted. He had some connection with the police and as soon as the pups were old enough, he took them to be trained as police dogs. At first, I was a little worried, because when Mick decided to pay a visit to his lady friend, it meant he had to cross a field where there were sheep. Fortunately, Mick had a one-track mind – he was only interested in Lager, completely ignoring the sheep. Sometimes she would pay Mick a visit when she was out with her master, and when working in the fields, she was always allowed to ride on the tractor, I supposed for company. When taking Mick out across the fields for his exercise, I sometimes met the farmer and stopped for a chat. He told me about Mick's first visit to his farmyard when he had a narrow escape from being shot. Being a strange dog on his own in the district, the farmer did not take too kindly to him – it was only his dog name tag that saved him. The farmer explained to me that the sheep did not belong to him. He rented the field out to another local farmer – he had a perfect right to shoot any dog or dogs worrying sheep, and ask questions after. The farmer's reassuring comment was that I should not worry now that he knew the dog – he would be perfectly safe, for which I was most grateful. If anything like that had happened to him, Grace would be heartbroken – in fact, the farmer had met her when she had been out with Mick.

It was not long before all the local people got to know Mick, when Grace was out walking him. He was a wonderfully good-natured dog – he seemed to adore children. He would never pick a fight with another dog, although, if forced into a scuffle, he was quite capable of looking after himself. Grace came to know a lot of local people through Mick – he had such a beautiful black coat that attracted comments from passers-by

In the stores one day, when calling over to do a bit of shopping and use the Post Office, the owner's wife started to talk to Grace, asking her if she had settled in yet. She mentioned that if she was looking for a part-time job, there could be one available at the Insemination Centre – the person doing the job at the time was leaving to have a baby. She suggested that she should go over to see the manager, giving Grace his name. Grace mentioned this to me and I said why not, as it was only a five-minute walk from the cottage. It could be handy for her and the dog, was my advice. Grace already knew some of the inseminators, as their office was just the other side of Charlie's pathway. Grace went along to make an appointment with the manager. Instead, he invited her into the laboratory and explained to Grace the type of work involved, being secretary to him and the Veterinary Officer as well as doing the PAYE for the weekly paid staff. The hours would be 8.30am to 3pm with an hour off for lunch. He asked whether Grace would be interested and she said that she definitely would be. Straightaway he suggested that Grace should start the following Monday, to give her time to get used to doing the PAYE tables so that, when Mrs. Williams left, she could take over without any problems. When she asked about references, the manager observed that he did not think that that would be necessary as she seemed to be over-qualified. As an afterthought, he added that she would be working a five-day week and said he would look out for her on the next Monday. Grace could not believe her luck – she was walking on air. She could not get back home fast enough to tell me her good fortune. She told me not to worry about Mick as she would take him out in the mornings. Grace also took him out at lunchtime, and again at 3.30pm for a long walk. At weekends, we both took him out, exploring the countryside winter and summer – all three were enjoying our new-found freedom.

I had decided to set myself up in business as an electrical contractor. I put an advertisement in the local Church Magazine and visited local builders, leaving a business card. One day when I was going to a customer's house, I passed a large new building site. Calling in to see the site foreman, I asked if I could have the opportunity to quote for the electrical installations. The proposed properties were a mixture of three-bedroom bungalows, three-bedroom houses, and three-bedroom chalet bungalows, all together on a site which would consist of twenty-two detached dwellings, all brick-built with separate garages. This would be a nice contract to get, I thought. When I asked for the opportunity to quote, the site foreman told me they already had an electrician. In reply I said that there was no harm in sending in a quote anyway and the foreman said he supposed not, giving me the specifications for each property. Shaking hands with the foreman, I thanked him, then left his office.

I prepared the quote and took it back to the site foreman, by now becoming quite pally.

About a month later, I could see that the first two bungalows were nearly ready for carcass wiring. This was about the beginning of December. As I had not heard from them, I thought it would be a good idea to call in and see the foreman. Shaking hands when greeting each other, I quite casually, almost jokingly, said that I did not know whether I had to buy him a bottle of whiskey for Christmas. The foreman rapidly replied that I should make it two bottles. Two days later, by post, I received confirmation of the order of acceptance, to carry out the work. The same day two bottles of the best brand of whiskey were taken to the office. The foreman had explained that the other bottle was for the Clerk of Works, who was in charge of contracts at their Head Office. The foreman told me I had two days to carcass wire the first bungalow. To have it ready in time for the plasterers, it meant I had to work late in the evening by the light of a Tilley lamp.

Chapter Twenty-Six

Grace and I, and not forgetting Mick, had now settled in very well, giving us time to explore the local countryside by car. One particular trip we both liked was a visit to Hastings by the back roads, travelling by way of Burwash and passing Batemans, the one-time home of Rudyard Kipling, and then along the South Downs to Battle – a really fantastic ride. On the occasional summer Sunday evening, all three of us would go along to visit a local beauty spot, known as the Bedgebury Pinetum. Here was a vast selection of conifer trees of species from all over the world, planted and cultivated by the Forestry Commission in several acres of well kept ground. Each tree was tagged with its Latin name and country of origin. Dogs were allowed to run freely, so Mick was in his element with so many trees to choose from, although all the trees were protected by a wire mesh.

Grace was now in her fiftieth year. It was while walking around the Pinetum that she once said she would like to learn to drive the car. She observed that it seemed so easy the way I did it – it would make her less dependent on me when she wanted to go anywhere. The manager at the Centre had asked her if she could drive as it would help him out a lot if she was mobile. I asked her if she really wanted to learn and she assured me that she had been thinking about it for a long time. As she was really serious about it, I promised that I would acquire a provisional licence form in the morning – she could fill it in and send it to Lewes County Hall with a cheque for the fee. Within a week it came back duly authorised – Grace was really pleased with herself but I jokingly said that was the easy part, not wishing to dampen her enthusiasm.

One evening I decided to take Grace out on her first practice drive, patiently explaining the controls of the car and their purpose. I explained that at first she would have to think what to do, but after a while it would come automatically. I drove to a long straight road, little used by other motorists, and pulled up, switching off the engine. I instructed Grace to sit in the driver's seat, having to swap round. When she was seated, I advised her to make herself comfortable, adjusting the seat and the driving mirror to her liking. I showed her how to start the engine, making sure that the gear lever was in neutral. The car had three forward gears and a reverse gear – most of the lesson consisted of stopping and starting the car and becoming used to the gears and controls. A couple of times Grace stalled the engine when starting off or stopping and I told her not to worry about it as all learners did that – on odd occasions, even experienced drivers – I was trying to boost her confidence. After several lessons on this quiet road, Grace was rapidly gaining confidence and experience with her driving. On the last visit, I suggested that she could drive back home if she felt up to it, but at no more than 30mph – it was a distance of about three miles. Going back towards the village was slightly downhill. Being 7.30pm, there were not many cars parked on either side of the road, although normally there would be, making it easy to drive through the village – this Grace managed without any problems. I had given Grace good warning to turn left at Wards Lane – she knew exactly where this was, as she walked the dog down this almost traffic-free lane. Some distance from the lane, she was advised to put the indicator on to turn left, and to change down into second gear to make sure that she completed a good slow turn. Just as Grace was going to turn left, another car came up the lane to turn right into the main road. To avoid a collision, Grace swerved too much to the left, running the car up a steep bank, the car coming to a standstill at a 45° angle, stalling the engine. It looked as though any sudden movement would make the car roll over onto its side. The other driver saw what had happened and left his car where it was, coming over to offer assistance – he was a little shaken himself at having such a narrow escape.

The passenger front door was firmly wedged against a staved type of fencing, the driver's door could only be opened a couple of inches before fouling the road. The other driver asked whether he should go to the garage in the village for assistance but I did not think that would be necessary. With the door firmly wedged, the only way out was through the sunshine roof but, before attempting this, I gave the other man the key to the boot of the car telling him that inside he would find a saw, and asking him to find a stout tree branch to wedge under the driver's door handle. I hoped this would steady the car while I attempted to climb out. Grace seemed to be well composed while all this was going on.

With the door now firmly wedged, I eased myself out very gingerly, trying not to rock the car too much. When out, I dropped down between the rear door and the fence, making my way towards the road. While I was clambering out, Grace had started to cry, the only time I had ever seen her do that. After assessing the awkward angle the car was leaning, the other man and I decided to pull the car back onto level ground. Grace was a little more composed now. Going up to the driver's door, I asked Grace to release the handbrake, but keep her foot on the foot brake, also to make sure that the car was in neutral gear. I was trying to be as calm as possible, saying to Grace that, as we pulled the car back on the road, if it should roll over, she must not panic, as we could lift her out through the roof. With luck and good fortune, the car was eased back onto the level road surface. All three of us were visibly relieved, and I opened the door for Grace to get out. When emerging from the car, she was clearly trying to be as cheerful as possible, commenting that now she knew how miners must feel when trapped. I helped her out, still a little shaken by the experience.

The other driver offered to go for assistance to the local garage. I had a good look around the car, lifting the bonnet, but surprisingly discovered that all seemed to be in order. I started the engine with no problem – there did not seem to be any obvious damage that one could see. I explained to the other driver that we only lived just down the main road, and asked him how he was. Fortunately he was unharmed and felt fine, climbing into his car to drive away. I shook his hand warmly and thanked him sincerely for his assistance, without which it might have been a different story.

I did not want to drive down the very long lane, where there was no way of turning the car round, so I decided to reverse back onto the main road, only a short distance away. Not knowing how the steering was going to respond, I asked Grace to see me safely back – she was by now fully recovered and composed. As soon as I tried to steer the car I realised that something was wrong – although it responded, it was stiff and heavy, requiring a lot of effort to steer properly. Once back on to the main road, fortunately never a busy road, Grace climbed into the passenger seat. For safety's sake, I drove very slowly the short distance to our cottage. Not risking driving into the entrance to the garage, I left the car on the lay-by near Charlie's cottage. This gave me the chance for a closer inspection to assess the damage. For the short distance I had driven the car, the nearside tyre was quite warm, suggesting that the tracking was out of alignment. I thought it best to leave the car on the lay-by for the night and go indoors.

As soon as we entered the cottage, we were greeted by Mick in his usual boisterous welcome – I could see why the young couple had had problems with him, his welcome was always the same, most times with his lead in his mouth, as much as to say "about time too". While Grace was making a pot of tea, I took Mick across the fields for his last run for the day.

Back indoors, we were enjoying our tea when Grace said how sorry she was for what had happened. I tried to cheer her up by saying that it was just bad luck – thinking how many times we had walked that lane, and never seen another vehicle. It could have been a lot worse if she had not had the presence of mind to steer the car sharply to the left. If she had not steered that way, she almost certainly would have hit the other car just where the driver was sitting – her reflex action was good. The outcome of a collision like that could be anyone's guess. The other driver was partly at fault as he was well over the middle of the lane – I thought that, judging by the angle of his car over the centre of the lane, he was obviously going to turn right towards the village, which had certainly cut down Grace's turning space. If she had been going a little slower, she might have negotiated the turn without any problem. I reassured her that she should not worry about it as the car could be repaired. I said that the important thing was whether she wanted to carry on driving. She pondered for a few seconds and hesitantly replied that she would like to continue. I suggested that the following week I would look through the local paper to try and find us a smaller car – I believed that mine was too powerful for her to learn in. A smaller car would be easier for her to manage as a beginner – she could have her own vehicle to learn on. Grace agreed that I was right and she was pleased at my suggestion. I said that in the meantime, she should study and learn the Highway Code.

In the morning, I phoned the Ford agents the other side of the village to make arrangements for my car to go in for repair, asking if they had a car they could lend me while mine was under their care, explaining that I needed a car for my business to get around to my clients. The garage man told me that there would be no problem with that, so I told him to expect me in thirty minutes. I managed to drive the car to the garage but by the time I got there, the nearside tyre was almost in shreds. I explained the circumstances and told them to renew all the tracking if need be and fit two new front tyres. I knew the two brothers who ran the garage, having done some electrical work for them, so I asked them to give me a ring when the car was ready for collection.

On the following Friday, provincial newspapers were available and I had the local paper delivered with our regular daily national paper – Grace loved to do the crossword puzzles, most times managing to solve the hardest of them. Scanning through the local paper under cars for sale, I noticed that there was a 10 horsepower Ford Prefect for sale at Brenchley, a local village. I made a phone call to arrange to view the car the following day at 2.30pm –Grace and I found the address quite easily, from the instructions the car owner had given us. The all-black, four-door saloon was in very good condition inside and out and had obviously been well cared for. After a general inspection, I asked if I could take the car for a trial run, which the owner readily agreed to. I left Grace there, talking to the owner's wife. While out on the test run, I asked if I could drive the car back to the owner's house and when we had returned, I suggested that Grace should sit in the car to get the feel of it, asking her whether she liked it. I explained to the owner that the car was for my wife to learn to drive, mine being too big and powerful for her to handle with safety. I asked Grace what she thought about the car and she replied that it would really suit her just fine, saying this with her eyes full of sparkle. After a little haggling, mostly over the price, Grace began to show a little impatience, thinking she was going to lose it as the discussion dragged on. Eventually a price was agreed and I offered ten pounds as a deposit, saying the balance would be paid in cash. Arrangements were made to collect the car the following Monday evening. I took the particulars of the car for insurance purposes. It was already taxed – that was what most of the haggling was about, as the owner wanted to keep the tax, I wanted it as a part of the sale. In the end this was agreed to. The owner gave me a receipt for the deposit, we shook hands on the deal and Grace and I left.

On the way home, I raised the problem with Grace, about how we were going to get the car back home. We had always kept our Sunday visits to Bob's pub for a drink and a chat, these days more of a social call. While talking in the pub, the conversation drifted to my problem with getting the other car back home. Bob said it was no problem as he could run me over to Brenchley. Rather than me picking up Bob, he offered to collect me as he said it would do his car good to have a run. Grace thanked Bob for his kind offer and he assured her that he was glad to be of assistance. We duly travelled to Brenchley and the drive back greatly pleased me. The Ford handled very well, the steering was light and positive, the brakes good, and the engine smooth. I thought that Grace should be pleased and happy with it, as it was much easier for her to handle. When back home, I parked it on a spare piece of ground by the garage and Bob parked his car, wondering whether I wanted a hand. Grace came over to have a chat to Bob, at the time being really pleased to admire the car. After a while, Bob returned to his car to drive home, expecting to see us some time later.

During the next week, I inspected the car thoroughly, replacing any parts I thought should be replaced – I wanted to make sure Grace would not have any problems with the car while out driving it. While I was working on the car, Mick settled himself on the front passenger seat, but it was always a problem to get him out and most times we had to bribe him with a morsel of food to entice him out of the car – it usually seemed to do the trick.

It was usual practice for me to have my electrical materials delivered and put in my garage at home. One day when I was in urgent need of materials to finish off a job, I waited for the delivery man who arrived on most days between 1.00 and 2.00pm. When the driver arrived, he noticed the Prefect with the 'L' plates and asked me who was learning to drive. I explained that it was my wife who was learning although I could not always find time to take her out as often as she would like. Grace had met the driver several times, as her lunch break coincided with his usual delivery time, and sometimes he had enjoyed the welcome cup of tea Grace offered him. I also had met him before – he seemed a trustworthy sort of man, in his late forties, small in build, but always cheerful. I knew him as Fred.

Fred said what a lovely car it was to learn to drive in, adding that, if it would help out, he could spare Wednesday evenings, and also as long as Grace wanted on a Saturday, to give her some extra lessons. I asked Fred where he lived and he said that it was at Tunbridge Wells, with the bus from the village almost passing his door. I thanked him sincerely for his offer of help and promised that I would have a word with my wife to see what she thought and let him know. Later that evening, I mentioned to Grace that I had had a conversation with Fred and I asked her how she felt about him taking her out for driving lessons on Wednesday evenings and for as long as she wanted on Saturdays. I added that I thought it would be a great help as she knew she could not always rely on me. Grace said she thought it was a good idea, so arrangements were made with Fred to come over the following Wednesday – it was summer time with the lighter evenings.

The following Wednesday evening, Grace went out for her first real driving lesson – it was basically a one hour's practice session to familiarise herself with the car. After each lesson, I would take Fred home to Tunbridge Wells and, on the way back, would call in to Bob's pub for a drink and a casual chat. On Saturday afternoons, when the traffic was at its heaviest in Tunbridge Wells, Fred would take Grace through the town centre, to get her used to driving in traffic – she soon became much more confident and experienced with each visit. Then Fred would direct her to a quieter part of the town to practise three-point turns and parking the car in tight places. During the course of each lesson, as a way of relaxing, he would find a quiet place to park the car and would ask her questions on the Highway Code, preparing her for her driving test. Grace became a very competent and confident driver under Fred's tuition. She knew the Highway Code backwards and Fred could no longer catch her out on his trick questions. Grace spoke very highly of Fred's patience and understanding, and I admitted that her progress was fantastic, much better than if I had been teaching her, I confessed to Fred.

After returning home from Tunbidge Wells one Saturday, the three of us, Grace, and Fred and I were enjoying a welcome cup of tea and discussing the best way forward for Grace to progress. Fred suggested, and we all agreed, that she should now book six lessons with a professional driving school. Then she should apply for a driving test. He arranged to just come over on Saturdays for further practice, as the nights were drawing in. I thanked Fred for all he had done but Fred continually refused to take payment in cash or kind for his time, saying how much he had enjoyed helping out.

I asked Grace how she felt about taking her test. She asked Fred whether he thought that she was ready and he reassured her that she was as ready as she would ever be. Between them it was finally agreed that Grace was ready to take her driving test as soon as possible. After lunch one Sunday, as it was such a nice day, they decided that they should go for a spin in her car, for an hour or so. I secretly thought I would make my own assessment of Grace's driving abilities, to see if she was up to driving test standard. I suggested that we went to Hastings and she should do the driving – she could think of me as the Test Examiner. Grace wondered about Mick, but I thought it best while she was learning that he was not in the car – we were well aware of what a fidget he was. We agreed to leave the dog at home and Grace chose her own route to Hastings.

Grace chose to go down to the main London to Hastings road rather than across country by the back roads. I very quickly saw that she could handle the car expertly, carrying out all the manoeuvres skilfully and keeping to a steady 55mph. When we reached Hastings, she made her way to the seafront for a breath of sea air. We took a very pleasant stroll along the front, then returned to the car to go back home. On the way back, I asked her to turn off the main road to go home by way of Burwash, a much more scenic drive than the main road. We arrived home safely and without incident.

I left the car on the lay-by, promising to put it away later. I suggested that, after our meal we could go to the Pinetum, in my car as there would be more room for Mick, who was getting impatient – he knew it was his time for going out. I took him across the fields for a short walk, just to stretch his legs. When back indoors, I had to admit to Grace the reason for the afternoon's drive – I was assessing her driving skills, to see if she was ready for her test. She said she had thought it was something like that. When I asked her if my presence had made her nervous, she said it had made no difference – I hoped that she remained so when the real examiner was sitting next to her. I continued by saying that I would make arrangements with a Driving School in the morning, checking with Grace what time would suit her best. It was agreed that late afternoons would be preferable.

I telephoned the Driving School and it was arranged for an instructor to come on Mondays and Fridays at 4pm. I asked if my wife could drive her own car, to be told that it would depend on the instructor. For the first lesson it would have to be the instructor's car, to make an assessment – that was standard procedure as his car was fitted with dual controls. The instructor came on Friday at 4pm as arranged. Before they left for the lesson, I told Grace not to be nervous, as she was doing so well. I pointed out that it would be a strange car, but basically the same, and she would quickly adapt, as though she was driving her own car. The controls would be slightly different but the instructor would show her before driving off. I wished her good luck, giving her a kiss, and promised to take Mick out – the exercise would do me and the dog good.

When they returned, the instructor told Grace she could use her own car for the remaining lessons – this really boosted her confidence. Before leaving, the instructor said he would submit an application for her test when he arrived back at his office. The day came when Grace had to go to the Tunbridge Wells Driving Test Centre with her instructor. I stayed at home keeping my fingers crossed, waiting for her return. Grace failed the test so another application was made for a re-test as soon as possible.

The date for the second test arrived and she duly reported to the Test Centre, with her instructor. To her dismay she failed again, having the same examiner as on her first test. Out of frustration, she asked politely why she failed but he told her that he was not allowed to give reasons. Grace asked how she was to correct her faults if she was not told, but was given the ungracious and curt reply that that was her problem. Grace returned home almost in tears, saying to me that she was certain, in fact positive, that she did everything right – she could not understand why, nor could her instructor. When the third test date arrived, I had a word with the instructor before Grace set out, asking him what examiner Grace had on her previous tests. He told me that that particular examiner had a reputation for failing women – his idea was to keep them off the road as long as possible. I told the instructor to make sure that she had another examiner this time – if she was given the same examiner, she should make the excuse that she did not feel well. I could then change to another test centre. In the event, Grace had different examiner and passed – the examiner made a point of congratulating her on her driving skills. Excited, she returned home to tell me the good news that she had passed.

I recalled that I had promised her another car when she passed her test as a celebration present. The Prefect had done well, but was six years old. I took Grace to a local car dealer on the main Hastings Road where Grace saw the car she wanted – it was a two-door, two-year-old Ford Cortina Mk I in a pastel shade of primrose. It appeared to be in excellent condition, with low mileage on the speedometer clock, so I started my usual procedure of a thorough inspection, having put it on the garage hoist for an underneath examination. We both drove the car to make sure it was the one Grace wanted, returning well pleased to the dealer's garage. I started to haggle, chiefly over the part exchange allowance for the Prefect. I tried to convince the dealer that it was in perfect order, and offered him the chance to take it out on the road to try it out for himself, saying that since I had owned it, it had been a good reliable car. The man declined my suggestion. Grace had fallen in love with the Cortina, and began to fear she was going to lose it, because the dealer and I could not agree. In frustration, she said to me that the dealer was meeting me half way, so why not settle for that. Grace thought that saying this had brought the discussion to a close but I had not given up yet, saying to the dealer that if he put two new tyres on the front, they had a deal. The dealer agreed without hesitation. Grace then knew that she was the owner of the car she wanted and was all smiles. The dealer and I shook hands on the deal and I asked when I could collect the car. It was fixed for any time after midday the following day and the dealer promised to give it a complete service as well as fit the new tyres.

During the drive back home, I told Grace that she would not have lost the car – I spotted her look of admiration, how much she liked the car. Even if the dealer had not agreed to put the new tyres on, I would have bought it. My philosophy was that one had to take dealers to the brink, to test them out to see what they would agree to. I thought that Grace had a really nice car and I hoped she would have many miles of enjoyable driving. Grace thanked me and gave me a kiss of approval.

As Fred persisted in not taking money for Grace's driving tuition, I instead insisted he accepted an 18-carat gold wristwatch as a token of gratitude and appreciation – he was as pleased as me that Grace had passed her test.

CHAPTER TWENTY-SEVEN

One evening, a few months after we had settled into our cottage, I received a phone call from the builder who had done the alterations. The builder asked me if I would be interested in doing some electrical work for him, explaining that he had a large conversion job to do at one of the local farms. I was happy to say yes. The man did not require an estimate as I could complete the work on a time and materials basis. He described the premises as an old oast house being converted into a residence. We arranged to meet the next morning to go over the plans and electrical specification, and I suggested that I would be there around 10am. I had by now finished the estate work I had taken on and had little other work on hand except just simple jobs for the people moving in, so I could give my undivided attention and time to this new project. I had been given the address where to go.

The farmer had bought the 300-acre farm at about the same time as I bought the cottage at the auction. I was told by the builder that the owner of the farm was a retired, high-ranking officer of the Royal Navy. Besides the oast house, there were a number of farm outbuildings, also a farmhouse. One day while I was working at the farm, the farmer began to chat to me – he seemed a friendly and affable type of person. One would never have guessed that he had held a high position – he introduced himself to me as Commander Molyneaux. He outlined his plans for the farm. His intention was to have a prize-winning herd of Jersey cows with the help of his son who would manage the farm. His son at that time was attending an Agricultural College, for an extensive course on farm management.

The oast house when finished would be the Commander's home and the farmhouse would be his son and daughter-in-law's home. At the moment they were all mucking in together in the farmhouse. The Commander went on to say that he was a widower – his wife was a Wren during the war, but was killed by enemy action. I expressed my sorrow, not really knowing what to say. I thought I would change the subject, saying that I had studied the plans for the oast house with the builder and how surprising it was what could be done with those old places. I thought that the Commander would have an extremely nice residence when finished.

When motoring around the countryside, I had noticed that all the dairy farmers in the area placed their full milk churns at the roadside on a wooden stand by their farm entrances. These were roughly at the tailboard height of a lorry, so when they were on their rounds, all the milk collecting contractors had to do was to roll the churns onto the lorry. Some of these full churns could stay in the summer sun for a long while, before being collected – this system had been going on for years, not moving with modern times at all. These observations gave me an idea. While we were talking one day, I mentioned to the Commander the very long time the churns stayed in the summer sun before being collected. I added that surely the milk must be affected by being left in that way. I thought that there had to be a better way in that day and age, with the advances in technology. The Commander asked me what I was suggesting and I responded by saying that, when the cows were milked, the milk should go straight into a refrigerated vat or container. Then it could be collected by specially made bulk tankers. The tankers would not have to be refrigerated, if the milk was cold when collected, although it would be better if they were. The whole idea would be more hygienic and less hard work. The Commander made no immediate comment on my suggestion but, judging by the expression on his face as he walked away, it certainly gave him something to ponder over.

Some time later I answered the phone at home – it was Commander Molyneaux. He apologised about the short notice but asked me if I could call at the farm between 12 and 12.30 that very day. I readily agreed as I was only working locally and could make the appointment with little disruption to my planned schedule. I arrived at the farm as requested to be greeted by the Commander with a welcome handshake and a warm thank-you for coming at such short notice. The Commander introduced me to a Mr. Thompson, from the milk collection agency. We shook hands and the Commander asked me to repeat to Mr. Thompson what I had told him about refrigerated milk storage and bulk tanker collection. Whilst I repeated what I had said, Mr. Thompson was making notes. The only real problem I could see, I explained, was not so much the milk going directly into refrigerated vats instead of churns, but it would be the collection by means of special tankers.

When I had finished talking, there was quite a pause while Mr. Thompson finished making his notes. Without any hint, he then asked me how I would like to come and work for them, as their technical adviser, at their factory in Wales – he believed that my idea had great possibilities and added that it would be a chance to put theory into practice. The mere word 'factory' put me right off the idea but I politely thanked Mr. Thompson for his offer. I then explained that, since I moved into the area, I had started an electrical contracting business and was doing extremely well. In any case, I doubted whether my wife would agree – she had made new friends and enjoyed living there. I continued by saying that regrettably, under the circumstances, I had no choice but to turn his tempting offer down. Mr. Thompson was not going to give up that easily and asked whether he could change my mind by offering me a good salary, plus free accommodation while settling in.

Commander Molyneaux was present all the while Mr. Thompson and I were talking, wondering what the outcome might be, knowing that I had a lot more work to do for him. As though I was reading the Commander's thoughts, I said to Mr. Thompson that I was very sorry to have to turn his offer down but I had commitments there, the Commander being one of them. I continued by offering to install the refrigerated vats if that would be helpful, should he go ahead with the idea. Mr. Thompson was making more notes and I reassured him by saying that I had extensive knowledge of refrigeration, being my main source of income before moving down to Sussex.

When I arrived home that evening, I mentioned to Grace the job offer which I had turned down. I explained my refusal of the job by saying that we were nicely settled there, making new friends and enjoying our new way of life. We owned our cottage which was very nicely situated, and we had no regrets about moving from London. I added that it was a bold decision we made at the time but, as it had turned out, a wise one. I asked Grace what she thought about it all – she responded without hesitation that it was something that she had wanted to do for a long time – it was absolutely right.

Chapter Twenty-Eight

The year was now 1968 and I was 52 years of age. Since moving down to Wadhurst to live in our cottage, I had had seven good years of electrical contracting. I was lucky enough to get the contract for a small private housing estate and electrical work for Commander Molyneaux in his farmhouse and outbuildings and also an oast house he was having converted for his private residence.

I was beginning to think I was getting a bit too old for climbing ladders and working in roof spaces and I was seriously thinking about giving it up – not that I wanted to because I made a very comfortable good living and had a healthy bank balance.

One evening, after our meal, sitting comfortably in our sitting room with Mick, our dog, lying fully stretched out on the settee with his head resting on Grace's lap in doggie contentment, I thought it would be the best time to discuss with Grace the thoughts I had in mind. I said to her "there is something I want to talk to you about". She sensed that this was not the normal everyday conversation between husband and wife: "what about?" she asked with curiosity shining in her lovely brown eyes.

"Our future" I replied.

"What about our future" she asked incredulously, wondering what I was going to say.

"If anything happened to me" I explained "you would have very little income on which to live – so what I am suggesting is that I am seriously thinking about giving up the electrical contracting work – not because it hasn't given us a good living: it has, as you will know by doing all my paperwork. As you know, I have been working over at Mayfield, the next village, and I've heard a whisper that there is a sub-Post Office and general store about a mile outside of the village up for sale. How do you feel about becoming a post master's wife?"

"Not a bad idea" Grace replied.

"Would you like me to look into it, then?"

"Yes, may as well."

When I was next over in Mayfield, two days' later, I popped in to have a chat with the present owner of the store. The sub-Post Office was situated about a mile outside of Mayfield village, at a place called East Hill. About halfway down on the left hand side there was a turning off leading to a huge Council estate. When I entered the sub-Post Office, I noticed that the shelves were mostly empty of stock to sell.

I walked up to the counter and spoke to the man standing behind it, asking if he was the owner.

"Yes," he said.

Just to reassure him that I was not wasting his time, I said that I heard he had the business up for sale, at the same time passing him my business card. I mentioned that I was thinking of giving up electrical work and was looking for a business to buy. "Can we talk business?" I asked.

"Of course," he replied.

"Is the business in the hands of an agent?"

"Yes," he said.

"In that case, if you would give me their name and telephone number, I will contact them, if that is all right with you. When I get the details from the agent, I will give you a call and make an appointment to come over and finalise."

I received the details from the agent and from what I had seen inside the shop, I thought that he was asking rather too much money so I telephoned the owner and asked to make an appointment to come and speak with him. A date and time was agreed and I went over to see him. The stumbling block was the price he was asking for the business. I asked if I could see his books showing the shop's takings: I knew the Post Office salary, £400 per year. He told me his books were with the auditors, which I took with a pinch of salt! I then asked what were his weekly takings and this he was very vague about, therefore, I decided to take the bull by the horns and said "I will make you an offer and as far as I am concerned, you either take it or leave it". To my surprise, he accepted it! I then asked for his solicitor's name and telephone number and said "can we shake hands on the deal?" I then gave him my solicitor's details in Wadhurst. I purposely dragged out my time in the shop to see how many customers came in – only two who bought stamps from the Post Office.

The shop itself was a nice size but in my opinion, the space could have been better used for display purposes. It seemed to me that the owner was just living off his Post Office salary. Before leaving, I did say that if I was not appointed as Post Master I was afraid that the deal would not go through; but I personally could see no reason why it would not.

When I arrived home, I explained to Grace the living accommodation, which was in excellent condition, consisting of a nice large lounge and kitchen and upstairs two large bedrooms, bathroom and a separate toilet: there were also outbuildings, a small garden, a garage and a big back yard.

"That sounds good to me" said Grace.

"Would you like me to press on with it?"

"Yes, if that is what you want."

I continued by saying "There is no need for you to give up your part-time job and no need to sell our cottage: I can find the necessary money for the purchase."

The deal was successfully concluded and we moved in on 22nd February 1969. I had no illusions about the task I was confronted with but with the right management I was certain in my own mind that this could give us a good living.

Chapter Twenty-Nine

The first week I took over I had a lady call who introduced herself as Mrs. Williams who used to "do" for the previous owner – would I be interested?

"Oh, what hours and days did you work?"

She told me from 9–12 two days a week – Mondays and Fridays.

"What were you paid?"

She told me and I said "Do you think you could do Wednesdays as well?"

"Yes, that can be arranged," she replied and continued, "if you wish I could also make a lunch for you".

"That's very kind of you, Mrs. Williams." We shook hands. "I'll see you on Monday," I said.

During our conversations, she became quite a source of information about the village in general and its people.

I had been in the shop about a month when a very smart-looking young lady walked in. She came up to the counter, which I was standing behind, and introduced herself as the niece of the previous owner. "I have called to collect some outstanding debts owing to my uncle, which I understand you have collected for him."

"That's right," I replied, "have you any letter or authorization to collect this money?"

"No," she replied.

"In that case, Madam, I am sorry – I DO have the money but unless I get some authorization from your uncle, I am holding on to it."

At that time, Mrs. Williams happened to be passing the entrance to the shop and she saw the person *she* recognised as the previous owner's mistress. Mrs. Williams told me, after the young lady had left, that the previous owner had told her that when his "friend" was short of money she came in and took some from the till – if there was no money in the shop till, she would then go over to the Post Office till and take money from there! Whether this was with the owner's consent or not she could not say but come the end of the week, when he made up the Post Office books, he always had to put up money to cover the deficit and this, I imagine, was the reason why he wanted to sell the business!

During this same week, a man came into the shop with cow dung all over his Wellingtons! He introduced himself as 'Mr. Farmer'.

"How can I help?" I said. He told me that he had two young children and a daughter of 17, whose name was Jill. "My two young children will come into the shop for sweets; let them have whatever they want and also anything that Jill may purchase: book it down to me and I will come in at the end of each month and settle up with you."

At the end of the month, he duly came in to pay his bill.

"Can we barter?" he asked.

Surprised, I asked, "What have you got in mind?"

"In my van I have half a sheep" (he knew to the penny how much he had to pay me).

"Is it legal?" I asked.

"Yes," he replied. "I am allowed to slaughter one animal per month for my own use. He went outside and brought back the half sheep. We shook hands and he went on his way.

My problem now was – what was I going to do with half a sheep? I had the idea of putting it in the bath as I did not want blood dripping all over the place! When Grace came home and saw the half sheep in the bath she nearly had a fit!

"What's that doing there?" she said.

"I bartered with Mr. Farmer," I told her. Fortunately, we had sufficient refrigeration when I had cut the sheep up that same evening.

When Mrs. Winter came in, as she always did on a Monday, for her pension and to give me her order for delivery on Friday, I asked her if she could do with a leg of lamb, knowing that she had a big family. "It's all legitimate and it will be much cheaper than if you bought it from a butcher."

"Yes, please," she said. "Will you deliver it on Friday with the rest of my order?"

"Yes," I agreed.

When Mrs. Winter came in the following Monday, I asked, "How was the lamb?"

"Beautiful," she replied, "it just melted in one's mouth."

This became the pattern of Mr. Farmer paying his bill: it alternated between lamb and pork and each time, Mrs. Winter purchased a leg.

When Jill came into the shop next, I asked, "Can you do me a favour, please, Jill?"

"Of course," she said, "what is it?"

"Would you please tell your Dad, when he comes into the shop again – would he please wash his Wellingtons first as I had to go around and wash away the smell. Please point out to him that it IS a food shop." Mr. Farmer got the message and the next time he came in he did apologise.

I knew that one has to speculate to accumulate so my first task was to fill all the empty spaces on the shelves. In the centre of the shop there was a home-made dexion angle stand, which looked a bit of an eyesore and took up a lot of space for what good it was.

I realised that there was nowhere in the shop during the warmer weather for the display of fats and bacon so I contacted a shop fitters and a refrigeration company, the shop fitters to make me a three-tier open display unit with a flat top for the purpose of installing a six-foot open refrigerated display to sell fats and bacon, with a two-foot worktop for weighing and wrapping the bacon. This got rid of the eyesore of the dexion angle display and also when it was all installed it gave a marvellous display of goods and proved to be money well spent. The bottom shelf was devoted to detergents and household goods; the middle shelf to tinned fruit, tinned meat, soups and other tinned goods; the top shelf was for bread, delivered by Lyons three times a week – Mondays, Wednesdays and Fridays – and cakes once a week. At the time, Lyons made a delicious coffee gateau and it was very popular with two spinster sisters, who always had one gateau with their Friday delivery order: they never seemed to tire of it. There was a good selection of biscuits, which were on a special stand attached to the front of the counter. The favourite in those days were Jaffa Cakes.

CHAPTER THIRTY

Grace loved the living accommodation and she was quite happy with the way things were going. I had managed to run the shop single-handedly for the past two years, the shop was now doing extremely well and I now needed help. Discussing this with Grace, we decided to employ a part-timer and Grace agreed to give up her part-time job to help me in the shop.

Our part-time worker was Mrs. Butcher and she was a gem. I had to explain to her not to get the two tills mixed up: if she had to go to the Post Office till for change to please make sure that the correct money was put back.

I needed space for the display of various types of dry cell batteries to power transistor and personal radios, which were now becoming very popular. The only place I could see to put the display rack was on the glass divide between the shop counter and the Post Office counter. Before doing so, I telephoned the Post Master in Tunbridge Wells and asked him as the Post Office was now taking up a lot of my time, would there be any extra pay attached. His reply was "if you are getting busier, then you must be taking business away from another Post Office".

"No extra pay then?" I said.

"I don't think so but I will look into it."

I had no compunction about putting this rack up and hiding the Post Office! It was a good move on my part because the income from selling the batteries was a good earner. I never did get any extra pay from the Post Office. What made my Post Office a lot busier was that people were transferring the collection of their pensions to my Post Office, now that there was a good selection of stock in the store, rather than walk up a steep hill to the main Post Office.

CHAPTER THIRTY-ONE

As Grace was now helping in the shop, I asked her if she would kindly take over the toiletries section: she was more likely to know a woman's needs, therefore, if she gave me a list by Sunday of what she wanted I could collect the goods on Monday at the Cash and Carry.

I also got in touch with the local carpenter to make me a vegetable stand to be placed in the shop's bay window. This proved to be a very successful move; in fact, with all the improvements that I had made there was now no more available space to be used.

Judging by our weekly takings, which were improving week by week, I was quite happy with our situation.

In about a year's time, Grace was coming up for 60 years of age and she expressed a wish that she would like to retire. "Will you like to live in the cottage?" I asked.

"I don't know," she replied, "I have heard that Norfolk is an up and coming county and I wouldn't mind moving up to there."

"I tell you what, do you think that you and Mrs. Butcher could manage the shop on your own for a couple of days whilst I go up to Norfolk and have a nose around to see what properties are available?" I suggested. "Say, next Monday and Tuesday?"

"Yes, that should be OK."

I motored as far as Diss, on the borders of Norfolk and Suffolk, staying at the Park Hotel which I booked into for two nights. There was nothing suitable available in Diss, so I went on to a town called Wymondham, 10 miles south of Norwich on the main road – the A11. There I popped in to two or three estate agents and one gave me several properties to view. Most of these were in the same road but there was one all on its own – about four miles outside of Wymondham. I stopped for a bite of lunch and talking to the café owner, I asked him about sports facilities in the town. He told me that Wymondham Dell Bowls Club had a six-rink indoor and a one-rink outdoor bowling green. I went along there and fortunately the secretary was there and I asked if we could have a chat. "Of course" he said.

"I may be moving into Wymondham in the near future – what are the chances of me joining your Bowls Club?"

"No problem," he said.

In the afternoon, I went along to see the property in Milestone Lane. I pulled up outside: the left hand side of the semi-detached cottages was beautifully finished, it had obviously been renovated but the cottage on the other side was in a very poor state but had something like a third of an acre of ground. Whilst I was mooching around, a lady appeared and said "Can I help you? I am the lady who lives next door. My name is Mrs. Perfect."

"Yes, please," I said. "I am interested in this property."

"My husband is usually home around 4 o'clock. In the meantime, I'll show you around *our* place so that you can see how we have improved our property."

When I was inside their cottage, I was amazed at how well it had all been done. Mrs. Perfect told me that the kitchen and bathroom were additions and with the alterations there were now three upstairs bedrooms. Just then, I heard a heavy lorry driving up; at this time there was no garage but plenty of space to park a lorry off the road. Mrs. Perfect and I were sitting at the kitchen table and she introduced us "This is my husband,

Sid." Turning to her husband she said "This gentleman is interested in buying the next door property". She poured her husband a cup of tea and the three of us sat around the table and discussed business. Mr. Perfect explained to me that the two cottages were left to him and his wife by an aunt.

"As you can see," he said, "we have had this place renovated to live in."

"Yes, I said, "and whoever has done it has made a very good job of it."

At that time local councils were instructed by the Government of the day to give grants to renovate old properties. "Who did the alterations for you?" I asked.

"My son-in-law – he is a builder. Would you like to go and visit him?" Mr. Perfect asked. He telephoned ahead and then took me over to visit.

The builder explained to me that with the first property he had got a £3,000 grant, including the cost for central heating. "You may well get that for the other property – would you like me to enquire into it?"

"Yes, please," I said.

Mr. Perfect then took me back to his cottage, where we discussed the purchase price. Before going into Mrs. Perfect's place, I had had a good look around the cottage next door and although it was quite dilapidated, having been empty for a good couple of years, the building itself was in good condition. What really made my mind up was that Milestone Lane was the perfect place to run a dog!

Whilst Mrs. Perfect was making another cup of tea, I asked her husband what he wanted for the property. He gave me a price, which I thought was too much. I told him that this would be a cash transaction; there would be no question of a mortgage but a straight cash deal. It was obvious that they wanted to sell the property so I thought that I had a little leeway. "I tell you what I'll do," I said, "I'll make you a cash offer on the basis of our discussion."

A price was finally agreed, a little above my first offer. "Can we shake hands on it?" I asked.

"Yes, of course."

"Can I have the name of your solicitor? I will give you mine."

It was obvious that we could not live in the property as it was, certainly not while the builders were going about their work, therefore, it was arranged between the builder and myself to buy a caravan for Grace and me to live in whilst the work was in progress.

I then got in my car and drove back to Mayfield.

When everything was finalised, I put my business up for sale and after four good years of trading, our average takings were about £350 per week.

CHAPTER THIRTY-TWO

Moving to Norfolk was the best thing we ever did. When the cottage was finished, Grace, although she had liked the Wadhurst cottage, really adored this one. It took me some two years to get the garden into order but that was a labour of love.

It was at Wymondham Dell that my bowls career really took off. In the eleven years that we lived in Norfolk, I received several hundred pounds in sponsorship, won the County Triples and, in doing so, got to the Finals of the Nationals, where I received a Runners-up Silver Medal. Also, the same year, I won the SAGA National Over-60s Singles Title: for this I got a £200 voucher for a holiday. I had skipped for Norfolk County in the Middleton Cup – a National competition, also the Liberty Trophy Indoor National Competition. I was now the proud possessor of three County Bowls Badges – Sussex, Kent and Norfolk.

In 1983, Grace was suddenly taken ill and she died on the 22nd August of that year. It took me a while to make up my mind and I decided to move south again. I bought a one-bedroom flat on a new estate in a place called Longfield on a mainline to Victoria, London. There I continued with my bowling with some success.

In 1991, at the age of 75, I won the Champion of Champions Singles Title with cataract trouble – this I thought would now be the end of my successful bowling career but fate decided otherwise.

Chapter Thirty-Three

A couple of years' later, I was out in Australia for my usual three-month visit and I heard from my friend, David, that he had arranged with the hospital for me to have a cataract operation on my right eye. As there was plenty of time, I wrote back to him and said that I would be coming back home for the operation. The operation was not a success and when the consultant examined me afterwards he found that I was now blind in my right eye. I was registered as a Blind Person.

In about 1997 I went to Eastbourne and booked in at the Palm Court Hotel which was run by the Blind Association. One evening at dinner time, a man sat next to me and introduced himself and his wife, who sat opposite. His name was Peter. "Are you an ex-serviceman?" he asked.

"Yes," I replied.

"Are you a St. Dunstaner?"

"No."

"Would you like to be?" he asked giving me some idea of the services that St. Dunstan's offered to ex-servicemen. He gave me a slip of paper, giving me the address and telephone number for St. Dunstan's Head Office in London.

When I was back at home, I photocopied my Discharge Papers and send a copy to St. Dunstan's in London. I received a letter from them asking me to report to their London office where I was examined by their own eye specialist: I was then told that I was now a St. Dunstaner and accordingly given all the relevant information. A part of the information was that they had premises at a place called Ovingdean, near Brighton.

At my first visit there I was really amazed at what St. Dunstan's offered their members, apart from residential care: a full-size heated indoor swimming pool; workshops where members could make picture frames and household items; they also offered to teach computer skills. For indoor and outdoor occupations there was archery, riffle shooting and – what amazed me more than anything else – there was a full-size one-rink indoor bowls green, which I was told held two tournaments a year, at Easter and around the end of October for two weeks! I was given the name of the person who organised this and she was extremely helpful so I promptly booked myself in for the next tournament. The organiser's name was Joan Osborn. Her husband, at the age of 83, was a bionic ex-serviceman!

Bob Osborn, Joan's husband, took part in the Normandy landings, aged 20. The first part of his duties was successful and, standing by his tank, having a smoke whilst waiting for further orders, a German shell suddenly came over and blew an arm and a leg off! The paramedics must have been on the scene very quickly because he was swiftly flown back to England to a hospital in Basingstoke, where the medical staff gave him not much chance of survival. He was unconscious for three days and medical personnel were amazed at his recovery. He was in hospital until such time as he could be removed to Stoke Mandeville, where he was fitted out with a false arm and leg.

Joan, at the time, was on the nursing staff. Joan and Bob were both born and bred in Wales. Bob was always ready for a joke and a laugh and because of their love of music they got on famously together. When Bob was discharged from Stoke Mandeville they got married. Bob was sent to St. Dunstan's at Ovingdean for rehabilitation and to learn a trade.

Joan had now been organising the Bowls Tournaments for some twenty years, giving ex-servicemen and women with eyesight disability lots of pleasure and she was well appreciated by the participants. It will be a sad loss when she finally gives up this job, which she has run so successfully.

T H E   E N D

Printed in the United Kingdom by
Lightning Source UK Ltd., Milton Keynes
137847UK00001B/336/P